STELLA MARIA SARAH MILES FRANKLIN

(1879-1954) was born into a pioneering family settled in the mountain valleys of the Australian Alps in New South Wales. She lived on her father's station, 'Brindabella', growing up with her six younger brothers and sisters, until reduced circumstances forced her family to move down from the mountains. Miles Franklin wrote *My Brilliant Career* when she was only sixteen. Publication in 1901 brought her instant fame and a notoriety so unwelcome that she forbad its republication until ten years after her death. She moved to Sydney in 1904 where she worked as a domestic servant for a year, writing for the *Bulletin* under the pseudonym of Mary Anne and preparing *My Career Goes Bung*, the sequel to *My Brilliant Career*. This book was rejected by publishers as too outspoken and it was not published until 1946. Miles Franklin then went to America where for the next ten years she worked for the Women's Trade Union League, managing its national office in Chicago and editing its magazine, *Life and Labour*. During these years she wrote only one book, *Some Everyday Folk and Dawn* (1909).

With the outbreak of the First World War she went to London, at first working in slum nurseries and then in 1917 joining the Scottish Women's Hospital Unit which was stationed at Salonika in the Balkans. After the war she returned to London where she worked as a political secretary for the National Housing Council in Bloomsbury. In 1933 she returned to Australia where she was to spend the rest of her life. Under her own writing name she published three more books: *Old Blastus of Bandicoot* (1931), *Bring the Monkey* (1933) and her famous *All That Swagger* (1936). She also wrote an acclaimed series of Australian pastoral novels under the pseudonym 'Brent of Bin Bin': *Up the Country* (1928), *Ten Creeks Run* (1930), *Back to Bool Bool* (1931), *Cockatoos* (1945), *Prelude to Waking* (1950) and *Gentlemen at Gyang Gyang* (1956). Her autobiography, *Childhood at Brindabella*, was published posthumously in 1963.

Virago also publishes *My Brilliant Career* and *My Career Goes Bung*.

VIRAGO
MODERN
CLASSIC

NUMBER

211

SOME
EVERYDAY FOLK
AND DAWN

MILES FRANKLIN

WITH A NEW INTRODUCTION BY
JILL ROE

Dear Roz,
Take Care
Have Fun,
I'll see you
soon,
Love
meniel
xx
Happy
Birthday 89

Published by VIRAGO PRESS Limited 1986
41 William IV Street, London WC2N 4DB

First published in Great Britain by William Blackwood & Sons

British Library Cataloguing in Publication Data
Franklin, Miles
Some everyday folk and Dawn.——(Virago modern
classics)
I. Title
823[F]   PR9619.3.F68
ISBN 0-86068-500-4

Printed in Great Britain by
Anchor Brendon, Tiptree, Essex

GLOSSARY OF COLLOQUIALISMS AND SLANG TERMS.

AUSTRALIAN.	AMERICAN EQUIVALENTS.	ENGLISH INTERPRETATION.
Billy	A tin pail	A camp-kettle.
Blokes	Guys	Chaps—fellows.
Bosker	Dandy or "dandy fine"	Something meeting with unqualified approval.
Galoot	A rube	A yokel — a heavy country fellow.
Larrikin		A hoodlum.
Moke		A common knockabout horse.
Narked	Sore	Vexed—to have lost the temper.
Gin	Squaw	An aboriginal woman.
Quod		Jail.
Sollicker	Somewhat equivalent to "corker"	Something excessive.
Toff	A "sport" or "swell guy"	A well-dressed individual—sometimes of the upper ten.
Two "bob"	Fifty cents	Two shillings.
To graft	To "dig in"	To work hard and steadily.
To scoot	To vamoose or skidoo	To leave hastily and unceremoniously.
To smoodge	To be a "sucker"	To curry favour at the expense of independence.
"Gives me the pip"	"Makes me tired"	Bores.
"On a string" "Pulling his leg" }		Trifling with him.
Kookaburra	A giant kingfisher with grey plumage and a merry, mocking, inconceivably human laugh—a killer of snakes, and a great favourite with Australians.	

INTRODUCTION

Miles Franklin completed *Some Everyday Folk and Dawn* in early 1905, four years after the publication of *My Brilliant Career*, the splendidly rebellious novel which made her name. Like several other novels written after *My Brilliant Career*, it was promptly rejected by Australian publishers as 'small beer'. Publication was delayed, though briefly compared with *My Career Goes Bung*, a sequel to *My Brilliant Career*, written in 1902 but not published until 1946. Fortunately for Franklin, *Some Everyday Folk and Dawn* contained issues relevant to the increasingly frustrated and militant suffrage campaign in Britain, and early in 1909 she signed a contract with Blackwoods, who anticipated good colonial sales. So *Some Everyday Folk* appeared later that year, under the same imprint as *My Brilliant Career*.

By that time Miles Franklin was thirty years old and living in Chicago. Apparently she took the typescript with her when she left Sydney in April 1906 in search of the fame and fortune which eluded her in Australia, despite her best efforts at a career, literary or otherwise (including a fact-finding foray into domestic service in 1903–04 and hope of the stage in 1905). Once settled in Chicago, where she was employed in the office of the National Women's Trade Union League, she returned to it. It is pleasing to think of Franklin, whose education extended no further than elementary schooling in rural New South Wales, correcting

the proofs while attending summer school at the University
of Wisconsin (Madison) in mid-1909. She reassured herself
that the rather awkward title was thought 'cute' by new-
found friends. And, as the dedication to English male suffra-
gists and the brief glossary translating Australian slang into
American and British equivalents suggest, her ambitions
now extended in every direction.

Some Everyday Folk and Dawn, Miles Franklin's second
published novel, was received amiably. But it was not
quite what people expected and sales were modest. It soon
fell into obscurity, owing partly, perhaps, to lack of interest
in its insistent feminism. Franklin encouraged Blackwoods
to advertise it as political — "As the 'suffragette' tactics in
London are not abating, I think that to advertise the story
along those lines would bear fruit" — but, according to
clippings transcribed in the Franklin papers, reviewers
overlooked the issue of women in politics — admittedly
rather old-hat in Australia by 1909 — stressing instead
cultural nationalism in praising Franklin as "the first
native writer untinged by alien notions" and "the un-
impeachable local colour" which had served to sell so
many colonial products on the international market in the
past. Perhaps it was tactful to overlook the novel's many
flaws, but the general verdict was inspiriting: "a truthful
and realistic picture of everyday country life", said the
Australasian.

Whereas *My Brilliant Career* has been through numer-
ous editions, *Some Everyday Folk and Dawn* has not pre-
viously been reprinted. The limited critical commentary
to date has been content to notice a couple of lively
characters, the faded topicality of the suffrage issue and
fierce reflections on the double standard of morality,
though, given a pervasive neglect of context, it is doubtful
whether all those who have commented have perused the
entire text. Recently it has been contended that the novel
has been consistently underrated, but only in order to
advance cantankerous and anti-feminist judgements about

the author, accused of 'funk' and flight from reality.

Such unsympathetic and ahistorical approaches have compounded the problems of a twenty-five-year-old understandably anxious to see her name in print again, and further obscured what is interesting and significant in the novel. Probably the absence of rigorous editing has told against it too; time taken to tighten a text of over a hundred thousand words would have been time well spent. But good editors are rare and authors impatient. Franklin had waited long enough, and what she had to say seemed relevant.

She has two main things to say, and says them in typically forthright style. The first is that marriage is a material question and should be treated as such. The second is that women are citizens in their own right, and should take their responsibilities seriously. Both points relate to the position of women and debate about it in Australia in the early twentieth century, and reflect Franklin's increased feminist awareness and commitment.

The novel draws directly from Franklin's experiences and observations of Australian life at the turn of the century. It is set where it was written, in the New South Wales town of Penrith, some fifty kilometres west of the state capital, Sydney, and now part of the metropolitan area, where the Franklin family lived from 1903 to 1915 and Miles Franklin spent part of 1904. Old Penrith — transcribed as Noonoon, a palindrome we are informed — is faithfully portrayed as an established centre of European settlement in Australia, something of a backwater by 1900, but mellow, fruitful, respectable. It provides the setting for "some everyday folk" and Dawn, the best type of Australian girl of the period.

Something of Sybylla Melvyn survives in Dawn. The wild colonial girl declares, "I wouldn't care if a man were the Prince of Wales and Lord Muck in one, if he couldn't do things without muddling, I'd throw water on him" (p. 25). She is high-spirited and keen on women's rights.

Dawn's matrimonial chances and grass-roots politics at an historic moment constitute the novel's two principal themes.

In this, Franklin's first attempt at a romantic novel, romance is never serious. Like many feminists before and after, she is preoccupied with marriage. Matchmaking carries the tale along even amidst electioneering. Against the commonsense view that women should be realistic is juxtaposed the anonymous narrator's more sophisticated perception that "swell girls" like Dawn are disadvantaged in the marriage stakes; and, contrary to the idea that it is always a mistake to marry outside one's religion or class, the narrator determines to improve Dawn's chances, "to place her in more equal competition with the winners". Here, the very modern and now rather jaundiced Miles improves upon the expertise of her predecessors, the colonial women novelists like Ada Cambridge who so gently and authoritatively explored the problem of marital choice under the confused social circumstances of colonial society by exposing the marriage market itself.

The marriage market was in poor shape at the turn of the century, a point recovered by recent historical research on the delayed impact of the Great Depression in the 1890s which diminished the marriage chances of women in Franklin's generation. Dawn's idea of escaping to the stage was popular at a time when Eleonora Duse and singers like Dame Nellie Melba made all seem easy; but that redoubtable woman of the people, her guardian Grandma Clay, believes that the stage is "terrible lowerin'" of women, and the narrator has reason for scepticism. An experienced female culture addresses Dawn's real problem in a refreshingly down-to-earth manner. An authentic but unimpressive gallery of local youths illustrates the truth expressed by Mrs Bray: Dawn's prospects are particularly poor since "It's like a year the pumpkins is scarce, you can sell little things you'd hardly throw to the pigs another" (p. 198).

Can a "suitable knight" be found in Noonoon? That

sounds quaint. But the nuances of caste and class are the
matchmaker's stock-in-trade; and the narrator's self-
imposed task (which produces some strange crypto-lesbian
scenes) may be read as a sex-loyal attempt to recast the
marriage bargain, a theme increasingly familiar to
Edwardian readers. As well, Franklin is true to the times.
Mark Girouard has shown in *The Return to Camelot* (1981)
that by the early twentieth century the chivalric code had
been thoroughly democratised. Not only did men espouse
it with enthusiasm, but it was a godsend to women as a
means of measuring male behaviour in secularised societies,
particularly new societies, where mid-Victorian notions of
"the gentleman" proved elusive, and both demography
and economics made the marriage market disorderly.

For those who think the time has come to document
changes in masculinity, Franklin provides evidence. In
Australia the bush heroes she knew best were being super-
seded by the more mundane types of bourgeois society,
what Grandma Clay calls "worthless crawlers" and "pauper
nobodies". Franklin's bitterness may seem premature, but
her derisory portrait of Mr Pornsch is at one with the
heavy-handed satire of "Mr Fat" currently enlivening the
radical nationalist weekly, the *Bulletin*. The argument
appears to be that ordinary women should make terms
according to the canons of respectability and temperance
(and a stake in the country), while girls in comfortable
circumstances should look to chivalry — and eugenics. It
is entirely in tune with the advanced liberalism of the day
that brawn is preferable to brain:

> Some men have brain and muscle, but this is a combi-
> nation as rare as beauty and high intellect in women,
> and almost as startling in its power for good or evil; but
> apart from the combination, the wholesome athlete is
> generally the more lovable. (p. 93)

Genetic engineering seems to be catching up with these
once-bold sentiments.

Even so, "One might think better of marriage" (ch. 27). After the success of *My Brilliant Career*, Franklin was taken up by feminist élites: in Sydney the Rose Scott circle, and in Melbourne, which she visited in 1904, the Goldstein group. Unhappy personal experience with men like the famous Australian poet "Banjo" Paterson heightened her feminist consciousness. More widely, women were subject to contradictory pressures, some of which are noted, for example the NSW Commission into the Decline of the Birth Rate in 1904, an infamous inquiry deploring recourse to family limitation, which Australian women espoused early and effectively. How offensive then that Grandma Clay's impromptu midwifery — an incident based on Franklin's mother's efforts which are still recalled at Penrith today — should be thoughtlessly mocked by men as "rabbit-ketchin'".

The implication is that women themselves must act for both protection and self-advancement. Recounting the marital experience of the women of Noonoon leads the writer into the broader theme of women's rights, where marriage and the suffrage are linked and the prospects for women as citizens canvassed. Mrs Bray's advice is, "get something in your own hands, as a married woman is helpless to earn her livin'; and once you have any children you're right at the mercy of a man, and if he ain't pleased with you in every way you're in a pretty fix, because the law upholds men in every way." "We ain't got the vote none too soon," she adds vigorously (p. 318).

In 1904 universal adult franchise was achieved in New South Wales, the oldest of the Australian colonies. In these colonies, notable for their democratic achievements, adult males were enfranchised in the 1850s. Neighbouring New Zealand, which often led the way in subsequent "state experiments", had extended the franchise to women in 1893, and two Australian colonies followed suit, South Australia in 1894 and Western Australia in 1899. Although women were not enfranchised in all six Australian states

until 1908, they became eligible to vote in the newly
federated Commonwealth of Australia in 1902 and did so
for the first time in the election of December 1903, when
Franklin's friend Vida Goldstein polled impressively as a
women's candidate for the Senate. The enfranchisement
of women in Franklin's native New South Wales also came
in 1902; and when women voted there for the first time in
August 1904, they more than doubled both the electorate
and the poll (though they were not entitled to stand). As
Franklin put it,

> . . . the fledgling nation, bravely in the van of progress,
> had invested its women with the tangible hall-mark of
> full being or citizenship, by giving them a right to a
> voice in the laws by which they were governed; and
> now, watched by the older countries whose women were
> still in bondage, the women of this Australian State were
> about to take part in a political election. Not for the first
> time either, — let them curtsey to the liberality of their
> countrymen! (p. 100)

By 1904 much of the melodrama had drained out of
"votes for women" in the Antipodes. As early as 1902 the
Fabian, William Pember Reeves, concluded moderately
that while women voters "have entirely falsified the vatici-
nations of the prophets of calamity, they have also, for the
present, given their more ardent champions some cause to
tone down their transports" (*State Experiments in Australia
and New Zealand*, I, p. 142). The capitalist press had
already decided that women voted in much the same way
as men, and devoted its efforts to persuading women
voters that "The true test of politics is in the home. The
touchstone is the purse" (*Sydney Morning Herald*, 3 August
1904). However, the mobilisation of women voters had
only just begun, and the time was ripe for realistic writing
about women and politics. At Penrith during the 1904
campaign, observing the "electresses" at first hand, aware
that their presence gave parochial issues a "decided fillip"

and insights into "woman in evolution", Franklin seized
her chance, the historic moment of adult franchise. The
vitality which carried Sybylla Melvyn through comes out
in Franklin's portrayal of popular politics at Noonoon.

Cynicism about paid politicians is a tradition in Australia
dating from the 1890s; but, contemplating the parliamen-
tary crawlers and roarers fawning afresh on the new
female vote, she has some real successes which will be of
special interest to cultural historians and political scien-
tists. The electoral theme prompts Franklin's liveliest and
most observant prose. She is entirely at home with the
subject, wide awake in her commentary and as vigorous as
the "honest industrious producers" of Noonoon who enter
so exuberantly into the spirit of things. Her ear for the
vernacular is impeccable, as in the heckler's "Don't
smoodge, old cockroach, let the other blokes blaze away as
we (the tax-payers) are paying dearly for this spouting"
(p. 184), or when Mrs Bray floors the opposition with
"there's always one thing as strikes me in the Bible, an'
that is w'en God was going to send His son down in human
form, He considered a woman fit to be His mother, but
there wasn't a man livin' fit to be His father" (p. 138).

In this context Franklin is probably a better commen-
tator on the position of women in Australia at the time than
most. In the 1970s, the idea that Australian women have
been "the doormats of the western world" gained ground.
An influential pioneering history of women in Australia
has encapsulated women's experiences in two stereotypes,
Damned Whores and God's Police. Where a female culture
is noticed, it is romanticised or deplored, in isolation from
the community and in opposition to male-dominated society.
By contrast, Franklin presents a progressive, self-
respecting and even prosperous female culture which is
well aware of the strengths and weaknesses of newly
attained political status, participant in, rather than victim
of, social forces. The lively and often amusing account of
women claiming their democratic rights shows the women

of Noonoon as part of a common and predominantly
liberal political culture; they realise of the vote that "It
ain't what things actually are, it's all they stand for"
(p. 258). Furthermore, they are already citizens with an
economic stake in the country, even if men usually take
the credit. "The foundation of the poultry industry"
(ch. 18) may seem a mundane subject, but Franklin gets
it right. Likewise, Carrie may be a servant but she is self-
supporting and not to be put upon; and when she marries
she does so on her own terms, as Grandma Clay once had.
The female culture of Noonoon is not only plausible but
impressive, and it should be taken into account. These are
ordinary women in the van of progress.

Not that the novelist is simple-minded about obstacles
both external and internal to their progress. Rather, she
appreciates what is distinctive about her countrywomen
and is moderately hopeful for their future as citizens of a
liberal democracy. Amidst confusions of class and the
pressures of a still dependent culture, she explores in a
lighthearted way the moral and material ground on which
they stand, and upholds it with nativist enthusiasm.
Listening to the women of Noonoon making the best of the
bad job which is marriage, the narrator concludes that the
challenge lies ahead, since they were

> unanimous in their evidence against the married state
> under present conditions, and the thoughtful student of
> life on listening to the testimony of these women of the
> respectable useful class, supposed to be comfortably and
> happily married, will know that notwithstanding the
> great epoch of female enfranchisement the workers for
> the cause of women have yet no time to rest. (p. 316)

Later in life, Miles Franklin thought hopefully about an
Australian film industry. She would have been a good
script writer. Mostly, her account of the local election
campaign is astonishingly accurate, still recognisable from
the pages of the *Nepean Times* of 1904. It was a keen

contest; the issue was ostensibly parliamentary deadlock; there were only two candidates, and although the Labor interest was strong it was still sectional at Penrith; the local candidate did have the advantage; the city slicker was endorsed by the NSW Temperance Alliance and he did attract a strong share of the new women's vote; the losing side did drag their man through the streets; and they did present him with compensatory plate. As well, numerous "experienced ranters" did visit; and all sources agree that "Mrs Gas Ranter" was the best speaker of all. Naturally, Franklin emphasises the meetings to educate women voters, as organised by Ada Grosvenor (a reflection of Vida Goldstein) along the lines recommended by Rose Scott and carried out by the Women's Political Education League, a non-party organisation; and, though she makes little of it, women's auxiliary party organisations were active. Best of all are the word pictures of overflowing meetings, well attended by the new women citizens who sat modestly up front.

Some Everyday Folk and Dawn certainly offered food for thought for the English male suffragists to whom it was dedicated. Voting was not compulsory in Australia until 1924 and Franklin makes the most of the facts that Australian women were well able to handle its rather complex prerequisites ("electors' rights" were then required in New South Wales), that they turned out in similar numbers to men, and that they filled in their ballots properly (in fact the informal vote was very small). It would be difficult to avoid the conclusion that this "state experiment" was a success, and likely to be constructive. As Rose Scott put it during the Federal election campaign in 1903, if only women voted according to conscience not party, they would, "even upon our first election day, have done something to elevate public opinion, something to purify our political life, something to exalt our nation" (*Sydney Morning Herald*, 16 December 1903).

However, there was more at stake in the election than

Franklin chose to acknowledge. In the novel the issues are presented as either perennial or parochial, as with the deadlock over rising public expenditure, so that the focal question is the women's vote. The reality was rather different, as Franklin must surely have known, even if it was not fully reflected in the rather peculiar semi-rural electorate of "Noonoon". The underlying issue was containment of Labor: the outgoing progressive administration was thought captive to Labor, a "preliminary to the great riot of Socialism *in excelsis*", according to the *Sydney Morning Herald* (27 July 1904). In advanced Australia the labour movement was already perilously close to ascendancy, and by 1910 Labor governments were in power both in New South Wales and at Commonwealth level. For anti-Labor forces, the only significant question about the new women voters was whether they would aid and abet Labor.

Franklin portrays hopeful women supporting clean politics against male vested interests; but the truth was that the terms of political participation were changing at the very moment of women's inclusion. In the election of 1904 the progressives were driven from office and a conservative government constructed. Despite an improved Labor performance, the Sydney press applauded the outcome, seeing in the first exercise of universal adult suffrage "a happy augury" because "on the first occasion of its use in New South Wales the way was made straight for the establishment of good government". The press and the politicians successfully wooed the female voter, and the emerging political parties were already organising her in a manner quite contrary to the hopes of the liberal feminist minority. It was a straw in the wind that during the 1904 campaign Sydney women political activists ignored Vida Goldstein's plea that women should resist voting on party lines. A year later the Political Labor League conference refused Rose Scott a hearing. Meanwhile the Women's Liberal League, a conservative organisation founded by

the very successful Mrs Molyneux Parkes in 1902, was
flourishing in New South Wales. The hope that a separate
women's vote might be organised "above party" was still-
born. How the narrator votes is one of the telling points in
the novel.

To test fiction against fact is often wearisome. But *Some
Everyday Folk and Dawn* invites the test, and a good part of
its interest and value is documentary. It may be that
women were more active in Australian politics at the turn
of the century than they are today simply because com-
pulsory voting has removed (or rather obscured) the need
to mobilise women voters. As well, the novelty has gone,
and the issues of citizenship have shifted from the political
to the economic field. But the dilemmas of liberal femin-
ism remain. If anything they are heightened by women's
increasing social mobility. Franklin perceived some but
not all of the pitfalls of independence. It is indicative of
her own astuteness and an advanced bourgeois society that
subsequent to *My Brilliant Career* she struggled to focus
the contradictions of gender and class which had emerged
in "the great epoch of female enfranchisement", and that
she did so without demeaning the participants. If she
remained blinkered on the great question of class, now
affecting both marriage and politics, she was not exceptional.

At one point in the novel Franklin remarks that prod-
igies must grow up: "In the career of a prodigy there
invariably comes a time when it is compelled to relinquish
being very clever for a child, and has to enter the business
of life in competition with adults" (p. 179). The novel
shows that in literature, as in life, the transition was
awkward for Miles Franklin, but that she had enough
confidence in "woman in evolution" and in her own people
to remain uncowed. Basically, the novel is an authentic
reflection of a distinctively Australian feminism.

Unhappily for Miles Franklin, *Some Everyday Folk and
Dawn* did not win her a new audience. This was the last
novel to appear under her own name until the 1930s.

Seemingly absorbed by reformist politics in America and Britain for the next twenty years, she continued to write, even feverishly. But very little of her output achieved publication and all of it was launched under pseudonyms – like the Chicago novel *The Net of Circumstance*, published by Mills and Boon in 1915, which sank without trace partly because of the extraordinary pseudonym "Mr and Mrs Ogniblat L'Artsau". Only after the success of her "Brent of Bin Bin" pastoral saga, written in London in the 1920s, did she gather the courage to publish again in her own name. She finally returned home in 1933. For all those years her reputation rested on two works, *My Brilliant Career* and *Some Everyday Folk and Dawn*. By that time, liberal feminism itself had sunk into obscurity.

Jill Roe
Sydney, 1986

Some Everyday Folk and Dawn.

———•———

ONE.

CLAY'S.

THE summer sun streamed meltingly down on the asphalted siding of the country railway station and occasioned the usual grumbling from the passengers alighting from the afternoon express.

There were only three who effect this narrative—a huge, red-faced, barrel-like figure that might have served to erect as a monument to the over-feeding in vogue in this era; a tall, spare, old fellow with a grizzled beard, who looked as though he had never known a succession of square feeds; and myself, whose physique does not concern this narrative.

Having surrendered our tickets and come through a down-hill passage to the dusty, dirty, stony, open space where vehicles awaited travellers, the usual corner "pub."—in this instance a particularly dilapidated one—and three tin kangaroos fixed as weather-cocks on a dwelling

over the way, and turning hither and thither in the hot
gusts of wind, were the first objects to arrest my atten-
tion in the town of Noonoon, near the river Noonoon,
whereaway it does not particularly matter. The next
were the men competing for our favour in the matter of
vehicular conveyance.

The big man, by reason of his high complexion,
abnormal waist measurement, expensive clothes, and
domineering manner, which proclaimed him really a lord
of creation, naturally commanded the first and most
obsequious attention, and giving his address as "Clay's,"
engaged the nearest man, who then turned to me.

"Where might you be going?"

"To Jimmeny's Hotel."

"Right O! I can just drop you on the way to Clay's,"
said he; and the big swell grunted up to a box seat, while
I took a position in the body of the vehicle commanding
a clear view of the grossness of the highly coloured neck
rolling over his collar.

The journey through the town unearthed the fact that
it resembled many of its compeers. The oven-hot iron
roofs were coated with red dust; a few lackadaisical larri-
kins upheld occasional corner posts; dogs conducted
municipal meetings here and there; the ugliness of the
horses tied to the street posts, where they baked in the
sun while their riders guzzled in the prolific "pubs.,"
bespoke a farming rather than a grazing district; and the
streets had the distinction of being the most deplorably
dirty and untended I have seen.

The same could be said of a cook, or some such indi-
vidual of whom I caught a glimpse when landed at a
corner hotel, where I sat inside the door of a parlour
awaiting the appearance of the landlady or the publican,

while for diversion I watched the third arrival wending his way from the station on foot and shouting something concerning melons to a man in a dray in the middle of the roadway.

Evidently it was the land of melons and other fruits and vegetables.

Over at the railway, loaded waggons, drays, and carts were backed against a line of trucks drawn up to convey such produce to the city and other parts of the country, while strings of vehicles similarly burdened were thundering up the street. Some carts were piled with cases of peaches, grapes, tomatoes, and rock-melons—the rich aromatic scent of the last mentioned strongly asserting their presence as they passed. On some waggons the water-melons were packed in straw and had the grower's initials chipped in the rind, others were not so distinguished, and at intervals the roughness of the thoroughfare bumped one off. If the fall did not break it quite in two, a stray loafer pulled it so and tore out a little of the sweet and luscious heart, leaving the remainder to the ants and fowls. The latter were running about on friendly terms with the dogs, which they equalled in variety and number. Droves of small boys haunted the railway premises at that time of the year and eagerly assisted the farmers to truck their melons in return for one, and came away with their spoils under their arms. Never before had I seen so many melons or so large. Some weighed sixty and eighty pounds or more, while those from sixteen to twenty-five pounds, in all varieties, —Cuban Queens, Dixies, Halbert's Honey, and Cannon Balls,—were procurable at one shilling the dozen, and nearly as much produce as sent away wasted in the fields for want of a market.

An hour after arrival, having refused the offer of re-
freshments, which in such places are not always refreshing,
I betook myself to a comparatively cool back verandah to
further investigate my temporary surroundings.

A yellow-haired girl with rings on her fingers sprawled
in a hammock reading a much-thumbed circulating-
library novel and eating peaches. This was the landlord's
daughter, and a very superior young lady indeed from her
own point of view.

I learnt that at present there would only be one other
boarder besides myself. He came up for the week-
end, and had just gone down to Clay's to see some one
there. If he could get a berth at Clay's he would not
come back; but the only hope of being taken in there
during the summer weather was to bespeak room a long
way ahead, as there was a great run on the place. It was
built right beside the river, and they kept boats for hire,
which attracted a number of desirable young men from
the city to engage in week-end fishing, picnicing, swim-
ming, &c.; and the young gentlemen attracted young
ladies, who found it difficult to be taken in at all, because
old Mrs Clay allowed her granddaughter, Dawn, to boss
the place, and *she* favoured men-boarders.

The tone of Yellow-hair suggested that perhaps the
men-boarders favoured Dawn; at all events, it was an
attractive name and aroused interested inquiry from
me.

"Oh yes, some thought her a beauty! There were great
arguments as to whether she or Dora Cowper—another
great big fat thing in a hay and corn store over the way
—was the belle of Noonoon;" but for her part, Yellow-hair
thought her too coarse and vulgar and high-coloured
(Miss Jimmeny was sallow and thin), and she was always

making herself seen and known everywhere. One would think she owned Noonoon!

"There she is now," exclaimed the girl, pointing out another who was driving a fat pony in a yellow sulky. "Talk of the devil."

"Perhaps it is an angel in this case," I responded, for though she was thickly veiled she suggested youth and a style that pleased the eye.

Whether she and the boats were sufficient to make Clay's an attractive place of residence I did not know, but already was painfully aware of conditions that would make Jimmeny's Hotel an uncomfortable location. I retired to my room to escape some of them — the foul language of the tipplers under the front verandah, and the winds from two streets that also met there in a whirlwind of dust and refuse.

There was nothing for me to do but kill time, and no way of killing it but by simple endurance. I had been ordered to some country resort for the good of my health. But do not fear, reader; this is not to be a compilation of ills and pulses, for no one more than the unfortunate victim of such is so painfully aware of their lack of interest to the community at large. There are, I admit, some invalids who find a certain amount of entertainment in inflicting a list of their aches upon people, blissfully unconscious of how wearisome they can be, but my temperament is of the sensitive order, knowing its length too well to similarly transgress.

How I had struck upon Noonoon I don't know or care, except that it was within easy access of the metropolis, and I have no predilection for being isolated from the crowded haunts of my fellows. I had descended upon Jimmeny's Hotel because in an advertisement sheet it

was put down as the leading house of accommodation in
Noonoon. Now I had come to hear of Clay's and Dawn,
and determined to shift myself there as soon as possible.
This did not seem imminent, for presently the "bloated
aristocrat" came back to Jimmeny's pub. for the evening
meal, as he had been unable to get so much as a shake-
down at Clay's. This so aroused my desire to be a
boarder at Clay's that I straightway wrote a letter to its
châtelaine inquiring what style of accommodation she pro-
vided, and could she accommodate me; and strolling up the
broken street, while a few larrikins at corners, by way of
entertaining themselves and me, made remarks upon my
appearance, I dropped it in the post-office, but had to
endure a week's inattention at Jimmeny's, and no end
of yarns from outside folk I encountered as to how
Mrs Jimmeny robbed the "swipes" who took their
poison at her bar, before I was honoured by a reply
from Mrs Clay.

"The accommodation provided by me for people is clean
and wholesome and the best as suits me. If it don't suit
them there are other places near that makes more efforts
to gather custom than I do. I can't take you in at present
as I'm too full for my taste as it is.—Yours respectfully,
                                          "MARTHA CLAY."

This interesting rebuff inspired me to further effort,
and sitting on the back verandah, under a giant fig-tree
shedding its delicious and wholesome fruit also to the
fowls and ants, I wrote:—

"DEAR MADAM,—Would you kindly apprise me when
it would be convenient to accommodate me, as I'm

anxious to be near the river, where I could indulge in boating?"

To this I received reply:—

"There isn't any chance of me accommodating you till the cool weather, and then I don't take boarders at all. I like to have them all in the summer, and then have a little peace to ourselves in the winter without strangers, for the best of them have their noses poked everywhere they are not wanted. If you want to go near the river there are heaps of houses where there isn't no such rush of people as at my place."

This firmly determined me to reside at Mrs Clay's, a desired member of the household, or perish in the attempt. Alack! I had plenty time to spend in such a trifle, for I was but a derelict, broken in fierce struggle and hopelessly cast aside into smooth waters, safe from the stormy currents now too strong for my timbers. That I had means to lie at anchor in some genial boarding-house, instead of being dependent upon charity, was undoubtedly food for thankfulness, and when one has burned their coal-heap to ashes they are grateful for an occasional charcoal among the cinders.

No other place near the river but Clay's would do me, though the valley had much to recommend it at that season, when grapes, peaches, and other fruits were literally being thrown away on every hand. So I repacked my trunk, and the 'busman who had brought me took me once more along the execrable streets, past the corner pub., near the railway station, and, it being late afternoon, the railway employés, as they came off duty, were streaming towards it for the purpose of "wetting their whistle" after their eight-houred day's work.

Leaving the misguided fellows thus worse than ignorantly refreshing themselves, and the tin kangaroos showing that the breeze was from the east, I travelled farther west to a summer resort in the cool altitude, there to await from Mrs Martha Clay a recall to the vale of melons. That I would get one I was sure, and so little was there in my life that even this prospect lent a zest to the mail each day.

I had neither relatives nor friends. Fate had apportioned me none of the former, and fierce, absorbing endeavour had left little time for cultivating the latter, while pride made me hide from all acquaintances who had known me standing amid the plaudits of the crowd—strong and successful; and fiercely desiring to be left to myself, I shrank with sensitive horror from the sympathy that is only careless pity.

TWO.

AT CLAY'S.

THE long hot days gave place to cooler and shorter, and there was none left of the beautiful fruit — peaches, apricots, figs, plums, nectarines, grapes, and melons — which, for want of a market, had rotted ankle-deep in some parts of the fertile old valley of Noonoon ere I received a communication from Mrs Clay.

"If you think it worth your while you can investigate my place now. All the summer weather folk has gone. I would only take one or two nice people now that would live with us in our own plain way and who would be company for the family, so I could not undertake to give you a separate parlour and table and carry on that way, but if you like to call and see me, please yourself."

Accordingly, I lost no time in once more patronising the town 'busman, and being his only patron that day, he rattled me past the tin kangaroo weather-cocks, the battered corner pub. and its colleague a few doors on, and entering the principal street where Jimmeny's Hotel filled the view, turned to the right across fertile flats held in tenure by patient Chinese gardeners.

Being a region of quick growth, it was of correspondingly rapid decay, and the season of summer fruits had been entirely superseded by autumn flowers. The vale of melons was now a valley of chrysanthemums, and with a little specialisation in this branch of horticulture could easily have out-chrysanthemumed Japan. Without any care or cultivation they filled the little gardens on every side; children of all sizes were to be seen with bunches of them; while discarded blossoms lay in the streets, after the fashion of the superabundant melons and orchard fruits during their season.

About a mile from the station we halted before a ramshackle old two-storey house that was covered by roses and hidden among orange and fig trees. The approach led through an irregular plantation of cedar and pepper trees, pomegranates and other shrubs, and masses of chrysanthemums and cosmos that flourished in every available space.

The friendly 'busman directed me to a gable sheltered by a yellow jasmine-tree, where I tapped on the door with my knuckle. Footsteps approached on the inside, and after some thumping and kicking on its panels it was burst open by a nimble old lady in immaculate gown, with carefully adjusted collar, and wavy hair combed back in a tidy knot and with still a dark shade in it.

"Them blessed white ants!" she exclaimed. "They've very near got the place eat down, so that you have to make a fool of yourself opening the door, and that blessed feller I sent for hasn't come to do 'em up yet; but some people!" She finished so exasperatedly that I felt impelled to state my name and business without delay, and with a prim "Indeed," she led the way across a narrow linoleumed hall, so beeswaxed that one had to stump along carefully erect.

She invited me to a chair in a stiff room and began—

"I've only got another young lady in the place now, and if you come you'll have to eat with the family."

I considered this an attraction.

"And there'll be no fussing over you and pampering you, for I'm not reduced to keeping boarders out of necessity. They ain't all I've got to depend on," she said with a fiery glance from her choleric blue-grey eyes.

"Certainly not; I'm sure of that by your style, Mrs Clay."

"But of course I like to make a little; this Federal Tariff has rose the price of living considerable," she said, softening somewhat as we now sat down on the formidable and well-dusted seats.

"But I believe you are somethink of a invalid."

"Unfortunately, yes."

"Well, this isn't no private hospital, and never pretended to be. Sick people is a lot of trouble potterin' and fussin' around with. I couldn't, for the sake of my granddaughter, give her a lot of extra work that wouldn't mean nothink."

This might have sounded hard, but with some people their very austerity bespeaks a tenderness of heart. They affect it as a shield or guard against a softness that leaves them the too easy prey of a self-seeking community, and such I adjudged Mrs Clay. Her stiffness, like that of the echidna, was a spiky covering protecting the most gentle and estimable of dispositions.

"My ill-health is the sort to worry no one but myself. I need no dieting or waiting upon. It is merely a heart trouble, and should it happen to finish me in your house,

I will leave ample compensation, and will pay my board and lodging weekly in advance."

" I ain't a money-grubber," she hastened to assure me ; " I was only explaining to you."

" I'm only explaining too," I said with a smile ; and having arrived at this understanding of mutual straight-going, she intimated that I could inspect a room I might have.

In addition to a couple of detached buildings composed of rooms which during the summer were given to boarders, there were a few apartments in the main residence which were also delivered to this business, and I was conducted to where three in an uneven gable faced west and fronted the river.

" This is my granddaughter Dawn's, and this one is empty, and this one is took by a young party for the winter," said the old dame.

I selected the middle room, as it gave promise of being companionable with those on either hand occupied, and its window commanded an attractive view. A tangled old garden opened on a steep descent to the quiet river, edged with willows and garnished by a great row of red and blue boats rocking almost imperceptibly in the even flow, while a huge placard advertised their business—

BEST BOATS ON THE RIVER TO BE HIRED HERE.
MRS MARTHA CLAY.

To the right was an imposing bridge, and on the other side of the water, right at the foot of the great range which in the early days had remained so long impassable, lay the quiet old settlement of Kangaroo.

" If you think that room will do, you are welcome to

it," continued Mrs Clay. "Seventeen-and-six a-week without washing—a pound with."

I agreed to the "with washing" terms, so the affable jehu hauled in what luggage I had brought, and at last I was installed at Clay's.

The only thing wanting to complete the incident was the advent of Dawn, but she was nowhere to be seen. As it was only eleven in the morning I sat in my room and waited for her and a cup of tea, but neither were forthcoming. In her own words, Mrs Clay "was never give to running after people an' lickin' their boots." Eventually, having grown weary of waiting for Dawn and luncheon and other things, I went out on a tour of inspection. First find was a tall dashing girl of twenty-four or thereabouts, dusting the big heavily encumbered "parler" into which my room opened.

"Good morning!" heartily said she.

"Good morning! Are you Dawn?" inquired I.

"Dawn! No. But you might well ask, for it's nothing but Dawn and her doings and sayings and good looks here! You'd think there was no other girl in Noonoon. She won't take it as any compliment to be taken for me."

"Well, she must be something superlative if it would not be a compliment to be taken for you."

"Oh me! I'm only Carry the lady-help—general slavey like, earning my living, only that I eat with the family and not in the kitchen. In the summer they hire a cook and others, but in the winter there are only me and Dawn and the old woman," said this frank and communicative individual in the frank and communicative manner characteristic of the Clay household.

Proceeding from this encounter, I went out the back way past more gardens and irregular enclosures, where

under widespreading cedar-trees I found a boy at the
hobbledehoy age chopping wood in a desultory fashion,
as though to get rid of time, rather than to enlarge the
stack of short sticks, were the most imperative object.
Driving his axe in tight and holding on to it as a sort
of balance, he leant back, effected a passage in his nostrils,
and after having regarded me with a leisurely and straight-
forward squint, observed—

" I reckon you're the new boarder ? "

" I reckon so.   I reckon you belong to this place."

" Yes, Mrs Clay, she's my grandma."

" Is that your grandfather ? " I inquired, pointing to
the old man who had travelled with me on the day of
my first visit to the town, and now supporting an out-
house door-post, while a young man with whom he talked
leant against the tailboard of a cart advertising that he
was the first-class butcher of Kangaroo, and had several
other unsurpassable virtues in the meat trade.

" No, he ain't me grandfather, thank goodness he's only
me uncle; that's plenty for me."

" Aren't you fond of him ? "

" I ain't *dying* of love for him, I promise you. Old
Crawler ! He reckons he's the boss, but sometimes I get
home on him in a way that a sort of illustrates to his
intelligence that he ain't. Ask Dawn. She's the one'll
give you the straight tip regarding him."

" Where is Dawn ? "

" Oh, Dawn's in the kitchen. She an' Carry does the
cookin' week about w'en the house ain't full. Grandma
makes 'em do that; it saves rows about it not bein' fair.
You won't ketch sight of Dawn till dinner. She'll want
to get herself up a bit, you bein' new; she always does
for a fresh person, but she soon gets tired of it."

"And you, are you going to get yourself up because I'm new?"

"Not much; boys ain't that way so much as the wimmin," he said, and the grin we exchanged was the germ of a friendship that ripened as our acquaintance progressed. I intended to settle down to the enjoyment afforded by my sense of humour. I had preserved it intact as a private personal accomplishment. On the stage, having steered clear of comedy and confined myself to tragedy, it had never been cheapened and made nauseous by sham and machine representations indigenous to the hated footlights, and was an untapped preserve to be drawn upon now.

So I was not to see Dawn till the midday dinner; she was to appear last, like the star at a concert.

A star she verily was when eventually she came before me carrying a well-baked roast on an old-fashioned dish. Her lovely face was scarlet from hurry and the fire, her bright hair gleamed in coquettish rolls, and a loose sleeve displayed a round and dimpled forearm—a fitting continuance of the taper fingers grasping the chief dish of the wholesome and liberal menu she had prepared.

Old Uncle Jake took the carver's place, but Grandma Clay sat at his left elbow and instructed him what to do. He handed the helpings to her, and she supplemented each with some of all the vegetables, irrespective of the wishes of the consumers, to whom they were handed in a business-like method. The puddings were distributed on the same principle, grandma even putting milk and sugar on the plates as for children; and further, she talked in a choleric way, as though the children were in bad grace owing to some misdemeanour, but that was merely one of

her mannerisms, as that of others is to smile and be sweet
while they inwardly fume.

Excepting this, the unimpressive old smudges hung
above the mantel, and probably standing for some family
progenitors, gazed out of their caricatured eyes on an
uneventful meal. Conversation was choppy and of the
personal order, not interesting to a stranger to those
mentioned. I made a few duty remarks to Uncle Jake,
which he received with suspicion, so I left him in peace
to suck his teeth and look like a sleepy lizard, while I
counted the queer and inartistic old vases crowded in
plumb and corresponding pairs on the shelf over the fire-
place.

Miss Flipp, the other boarder, was in every respect a
contrast to me, being small, young, and dressed with
elaboration in a flimsy style which, off the stage, I have
always scorned. Her wrists were laden with bangles, her
fingers with rings, and her golden hair piled high in the
most exaggerated of the exaggerated pompadour styles in
vogue. Her appetite was indifferent; the expression of
her eyes bespoke either ill-health or dissipation, and she
was very abstracted, or as Mrs Clay put it—

"She acts like she had somethink on her mind. Maybe
she's love-sick for some one she can't ketch, and she's
been sent up here to forget."

This was after Miss Flipp had retreated to her room,
and Carry continued the subject as she cleared the table.

"She *says* she's an orphan reared by a rich uncle; she's
always blowing about him and how fond he is of her.
She's just recovered from an operation and has come up
here to get strong. That's why she does nothing, so she
says, only poke about and read novels and make herself
new hats and blouses; but *I* think she'd be lazy without

any operation. She'd want another to put some go in her."

"She'd require inoculating with a little of yours," said I, watching with what enviable vigour the girl's work sped before her as though afraid. I also retired to my room for a rest, intending to come out and pave the way for friendship with Dawn by-and-by, for I quickly perceived she was not the character to go out of her way to make the first overture.

Some time after, when strolling around in an unwonted fashion, I was pleased to again encounter my friend Andrew. Evidently he had been set to clean out the fowl-houses, for a wheelbarrow half full of manure stood at the door of a wire-netted shed, and in the middle of this task he had sought diversion by shooting rats from among the straw in a big old barn, where a great heap of unused hay made them a harbour. In this warm valley, carpeted in the irrepressible couch-grass, there was no lack of fodder that season, and even the lanes and byways would have served as fattening paddocks. Andrew leant upon his gun, and having delivered himself of certain statistics in rat mortality, and exhibiting some specimens by the tail, he began a conversation.

"Say, what did you think of Miss Thing-amebob, Miss Flipp I mean?"

"I didn't bother thinking anything at all about her."

Andrew looked interrogatively at me and broke into a grin.

"Well, I reckon she's the silliest goat I ever came across. She came out to me and asked did I think she looked pretty, as her uncle is coming up to-night, and if she looks nice he'll give her a present or something. I reckon she'd have to look not such a mad-headed rabbit before I'd give her anything but some advice to bag her head. And he must be a different uncle to Uncle Jake ; I reckon he wouldn't give you nothing if you had on two heads at once. Here's Larry Witcom coming back from his rounds, and he promised me a bit of meat for Whiskey ! Here, Whiskey ! Whiskey !" he roared, and a small canine pet that had been hunting rats desisted from the fray and ran with his master. I also walked with him—this without exception, even in slum scenes on the stage, being the dirtiest escort I ever had had. His face was grimed, his shirt like an engine-rag, and his trousers dusty, while from a hole in the seat thereof fluttered a flag of garment —such an ingratiatingly wholesome blunderbuss of a boy !

"Here, you Larry," he yelled, "you promised me ! Come on, Whiskey ! Why, ain't he a bosker !" he enthusiastically exclaimed, as the hideously unprepossessing little mongrel stood on his hind legs and yelped in excited begging.

"Hullo, Andrew ! Don't bust ! Who's that you had with you ?—(I had turned a corner)—a new boarder, I suppose ? Rather an old piece !"

"Yes," said Andrew. "Her hair is a little white, but she ain't sour and stuck up."

"A chance for you to hang your hat up, Jake," said Larry.

"No, thanks ! I'm cautious of them old maids. If you say a pleasant word to 'em they can't be shook off, and might have you up for breach of promise like with Tom Dunstan."

"I suppose there is a danger, you being so fascinating," chuckled the butcher as I went inside, with a premonition that should it come to taking sides in the Clay household, if avoidable I would not be on Uncle Jake's.

"Who is Uncle Jake?" said Carry in response to my inquiry, as she prepared four o'clock tea; "he's Uncle Jake, that's what he is, and enough for me too, that he is. The old swab wants hanging up by the beard."

"Yes, but what place does he hold in the house?"

"Place! that of walking round poking his nose in everywhere and growling about things that don't concern him. Mrs Clay keeps him—gives him fifteen shillings a-week—because he's her brother, and you'd think he owned everything. If you want to know what he is, he's a terribly bad example to Andrew. *He's* the greatest clumsy, lumbering, dirty lump (oh, you should see his clothes, what they are like to wash, and the only way to keep him clean would be to stuff him in a glass case!), but for all that he's a very fair kid. You can't expect much of boys, you know, and have to be thankful for any good points at all. O Lord!" she here exclaimed, looking out a window, where along a path through the orchard she descried approaching a fine buxom dame in a fashionably cut dress, "here's Mrs Bray in full sail. I suppose she saw the 'busman leaving you here to-day, and her curiosity couldn't stand any longer without coming on a tour of inspection."

"Who is Mrs Bray?"

"She won't let you overlook who she is, and what she owns, and what she ' *done*,' you'll soon hear it. She's the most inquisitive blow-hard I ever came across."

Dawn now appeared and invited me to afternoon tea, which was a friendly and hospitable meal spread on a big table on a back verandah, so enclosed by creepers and pot-plants and little awnings leading in various directions

as to be in reality more of a vestibule. Mrs Bray hove
into near view and took up a seat beside a bank of lovely
maiden-hair fern.

"How are you living?" she asked Grandma Clay as she
complacently shook hands. " Nice cool weather now and
not so many beastly mosquitoes."

"By Jove! Did you know about the 'skeeters' here?"
inquired Andrew of me. " They're big enough to ride
bikes and weigh a pound. You wait till you hear 'em
singing Sankey's hymns to-night."

"If I were you I'd hold my tongue and not draw
attention to my dirtiness," said Dawn. " It's a wonder a
garden doesn't sprout upon you."

I was then introduced to Mrs Bray, who acknowledged
me genially, and seemed so flourishing, and was so com-
placent regarding the fact, that it did one good to look
at her.

After addressing a few remarks to me she had to move,
for the trimming of her hat caught in the cage of a
parakeet, and she took another seat in the shelter of a
tree-fern near Uncle Jake.

" You have some lovely pet birds," I remarked by way
of making myself agreeable to Grandma Clay.

"The infernal old nuisances!" she said irascibly, "I
wish they'd die. Andrew calls them his, but they'd
starve only for me. I'm always saying I'll have no more
pets, and still they're brought here. Some day when he
has a home of his own and people plague him, he'll know
what it is."

On the other side of the verandah above Uncle Jake
stretched a passion vine, where a thick row of belated
fruit hung like pretty pale-green eggs, and evil entering
Andrew's mind, he remarked to me—

"Wouldn't it be just bosker if one of them fell on his
old nut," and going out he returned with a pair of orange
clippers.

"Where's Carry got to?" asked grandma.

"I saw her out there doing a mash with Larry Witcom,"
said Andrew.

"Now, do you think there'll be anything in that?"
interestedly asked Mrs Bray. "I suppose she'd be glad
to ketch anything for a home of her own."

"Well, it's to be hoped the home she'd catch with him
would be better than some of the meat we've caught from
him lately—it was as tough as old boots," put in Dawn.

At this point Andrew succeeded in disturbing Uncle
Jake—succeeded beyond expectation. Uncle Jake had
just sucked his fuzzy 'possum-grey moustache in the
noisy manner peculiar to him, and was raising his tea
again, when he was struck by the passion fruit, causing
him to let fall the cup.

"Just like you! On the clean boards! Carry will
be pleased. I'm glad it's not my week in the house," said
Dawn. What Uncle Jake said is unfit for insertion in
a record so respectable as this is intended to be, and
grandma seemed to grow too agitated for verbal utter-
ance, but her facial expression was very fiery indeed as
Andrew and Uncle Jake withdrew and settled their little
score in a manner unknown to the company.

"Well, it's an ill wind that don't blow nobody no good,
and though there's a cup broke, it's got us rid of the men,
and there's never no talking in comfort where they are,"
remarked Mrs Bray, who had a facility for constructing
sentences containing several negatives. Two, we learn in
syntax, have the effect of an affirmative, but there being
no reference to a repletion, only that her utterances were

unmistakably plain, Mrs Bray might have reduced one to wondering the purport of her remarks.

"Did you hear the latest?" she said, laughing boisterously. "You don't know the people yet," she continued, turning to me, "half of 'em want scalding."

Here she burst into a full flood of gossip regarding the misconduct of the leading residents; but honest and straightforward though her communications were, I cannot include them here, for this is a story for respectable folk, and a transcript of the straight talk of the most respectable folk would be altogether out of the question. I must confine myself to the statement that Mrs Bray had found few beyond reproach, and "the latest," as she termed it, concerned one Dr Tinker, whose wife — known colloquially as the old Tinkeress — had recently administered a public horsewhipping to a young lady whom the doctor had too ardently admired. Mrs Bray had only just unearthed the facts that day, and was overwhelmingly interested in them.

"I tell you what ought to be done with some people," said grandma when Mrs Bray halted for breath. "There's no respectability like there used to be in my young days. In Gool-gool—that's where I was rared— the people used to take up anythink that wasn't straight. There was a woman there. She and her husband lived happy and respectable, with no notion of anythink wrong, till a feller — a blessed feller," grandma waxed fierce, "that was only sellin' things and making a living out of honest folk, come to town an' turned her head. I won't say but he was a fine-lookin' man, had a grand flowin' beard," grandma spread her hands out on her chest.

"Must have been lovely with a *beard*, especially if it was like Uncle Jake's!" interposed Dawn.

"How dare you, miss! Beards is a natural adornment gave to man by God, and it's a unnatural notion to carve them off——"

"Some of them do want adorning, I'll admit," said Dawn.

"He was a good-lookin' man," persisted grandma.

"Must have been with a *beard!*" scornfully contended the irrepressible Dawn.

"She must be smitten on some of these clean-faced articles," said Mrs Bray with a laugh, which effected the collapse of Dawn.

"Hold your tongue, miss! surely I can speak in me own house!" continued grandma. "And he could sing and play, and that sort of thing. At any rate, this woman was terribly gone on him, and her husband was heartbroke, and they always lived so happy till then that the people of the town took it up. They went to the sergeant and told him what they was goin' to do, and he was in such sympathy with 'em that he got business that took him to the other end of the town for that night."

"That'll tell you now!" exclaimed Mrs Bray with interest.

"And they went and collared him," proceeded the narrator.

"That'll tell you now, the faggot!" exclaimed Mrs Bray again.

"So they took him and put him on a horse, naked except his trousers, about twenty of 'em did it, and rode on either side with tar-pots; and every time he'd turn his head any way to jaw about what he'd do, they'd swab him in the mouth with it; and they had bags of feathers, and nearly smothered him with 'em, till with the black tar stickin' on every way, and all in his great beard, he would be mistook for Nebuchadnezzar. When they got him out of the town he was let go, an' they said if he showed hisself in it again worse than that would happen him. That's what the men of my day did with a bad egg," concluded the old lady, firm in the belief of the superior virtue of her generation.

"What price beards in a case like that?" came from Dawn.

"That clean-faced feller of yours would have the advantage then," said Mrs Bray. "And now I'll tell you the point of that story. It was just the men stickin' up for themselves. If that had been a woman harmed by her husband going away with some barmaid, or other of them hussies men are so fond of, there wouldn't have been nothing done to avenge her. *Her* heart could have broke, and if she said anything about it people would have sat on her, but when one of the poor darling men is hurt it's a different thing."

Mrs Bray had yet more to tell, and after another hearty laugh divulged a secret that should have pleased a Government lately reduced to appointing a commission to inquire into a falling birth-rate.

"This," said grandma in explanation, "is a girl who used to be milliner in Trashe's store in Noonoon—one of them give-herself-airs things, like all these county-jumpin' fools! W'en you go to buy a thing off of them they look as if you wasn't fit to tie their shoe-laces, and they ain't got a stitch to their back, only a few pence a-week from eternal standin' on their feet, till they're all give way, and only fit for the hospital. I won't say but this one was a sprightly enough young body and carried her head high. And there was a feller came to town, was stayin' there at Jimmeny's pub. for a time, an' walkin' round as if Noonoon wasn't a big enough place for the likes of him to own. He talked mighty big about meat export trade, an' that was the end of his glory. He married this girl that was trimmin' hats, an' she thought she was doin' a stroke to ketch such a bug, an' now she lives in that little place built bang on the road as you go into town. Larry says he often takes her some meat, he's afraid she'll starve; an' you know, though he'll take you down in some ways, he's terrible good-natured in others, and that is the way with most of us; we have our good an' bad points. But the poor thing! is that what she has come to? I ain't had a family of me own not to be able to sympathise with her."

"Well, she don't deserve no sympathy, she upholds him in his pride," said Mrs Bray.

"Pride! His pride," snorted grandma, "it's of the skunk order. He'd make use of every one because he thinks he's an English swell, and then wouldn't speak to them if he met them out no more than they were dogs. I don't think there's a single thing he could do to save his life. If there's a bit of wood to be chopped, she's got to do it, an' yet he'd think a decent honest workin' man, who was able to keep his wife and family comfortable, wasn't made of as good flesh and blood as him. That ain't what I call pride."

"There's one thing, if I ever fell in love with a man he'd have to be a man and not a crawler," said Dawn. "Some girls think if they get a bit of a swell he's something; but I wouldn't care if a man were the Prince of Wales and Lord Muck in one, if he couldn't do things without muddling, I'd throw water on him."

"What about young Eweword, are you goin' to throw water on *him*?" laughed Mrs Bray.

"Ask Carry, she knows more about him than I do."

"Dawn finds it handy to put her lovers on to me," said Carry, who was washing away the spilt tea and airing some uncomplimentary opinions of Andrew and Uncle Jake between whiles.

"Why don't you come and see me, Carry?" continued Mrs Bray.

"I can't be bothered, I've got my living to earn and have no time for visiting," said that uncompromising young woman.

"Anything new on here, Dawn?" asked Mrs Bray, turning to her.

"No, only Miss Flipp's uncle is coming up by this afternoon's train and we're dying to see him, there's been so much blow about him. Andrew is going to get out a tub to hold the tips."

"Well, I'll be going now to get Bray his tea or there'll be a jawin' and sulkin' match between us. That's the way with men,—if you're not always buckin' around gammoning you think 'em somebody, they get like a bear with a scalded head. Well, come over and see me some day," she said hospitably to me. "Walk along a bit with me now and see the way."

To this I agreed, and going to get a parasol heard the incautious woman remark behind me—

"Seems to be an old maid—a gaunt-lookin' old party—ain't got no complexion. I wonder was she ever going to be married. Don't look as if many would be breakin' their necks after her, does she?"

Mrs Bray posed as a champion of her sex, but could not open her mouth without belittling them. However, I was too well seasoned in human nature to be disconcerted, and walked by her side enjoying her immensely, she was so delightfully, transparently patronising. There are many grades of patronage : that from people who ought to know better, and which is always bitterly resented by any one of spirit; while that of the big splodging ignoramus who doesn't know any better, to any one possessed of a sense of humour, is indescribably amusing. Mrs Bray's was of this order, and would have been galling only to the snob whose chief characteristic is a lack of common-sense— lack of common-sense being synonymous with snobbery.

" You'll get on very well with old grandma," she re- marked, " she ain't such a bad old sort when you know her; she must have a bit of property too. Of course, I find her a bit narrer-minded, but that's to be expected, seeing I've lived a lot in the city before I come here, and she's only been up the country; but that Carry's the caution. The hussy! I only asked her over out of kind- ness, being a woman with a good home as I have, and did you hear her ? Them hussies without homes ain't got no call to give themselves airs,—bits of things workin' for their livin'."

" I'm afraid I'm in the same category, as I have no home," I said by way of turning her wrath.

" Oh, well, yes, but you're different; you don't have to *work* for your livin'."

" Have you any daughters ? " I asked.

" I had one, but she soon married. Like me, she was snapped up soon as she was old enough." Mrs Bray laughed delightedly.

Here was a broad-minded democrat who considered a woman lowered in becoming a useful working member of society, instead of remaining a toy or luxury kept by her father or some other man, and who, while loudly bawling for the emancipation of women from the yoke of men, nevertheless considered the only distinction a woman could achieve was through their favourable notice—an attitude of mind produced by moral and social codes so effectively calculated to foster immoral and untenable inconsistency !

THREE.

BECOMING ACQUAINTED WITH GRANDMA CLAY.

WHEN I returned the 'busman was driving away after having brought Miss Flipp's uncle, and Andrew was assisting to fill a spring-cart with pumpkins. This vehicle had arrived under guidance of a tall, fair young man with perfect teeth and a pleasant smile, which kept them well before the public, seeing they were not concealed by any hirsute ambuscade, regarding the adorning qualities of which Dawn and her grandmother were divided. The former came out to inform Andrew that the pony had to be harnessed, as Mrs Clay had promised Miss Flipp she could drive her uncle back to catch the train.

"I hope the old thing won't smash up the sulky," said Andrew. "He's the old bloke that come down here in the summer in a check suit, an' I told him you was all out an' we was full up."

"A few of him would soon fill up. He! he! ha! ha!" laughed the fair young man. "He looks as if he were always full up! He! he! ha! ha! ha!"

"Well, he's the purplest plum I ever saw," said Dawn. "He's a complete hog. He has one of these old noses, all blue, like the big plums that grew down near the pig-sty.

I think he was grown near the pig-sty, too, by the style of him. It must have taken a good many cases of the best wine to get a nose just to that colour. Like a meerschaum pipe, it takes a power of colouring to get 'em to the right tinge. And his eyes hang out like this," said the girl, audaciously stretching her pretty long-lashed lids in a way that would have been horrible on a less beautiful or less successfully saucy girl, but which in this case was irresistibly amusing. The fair young man was convulsed.

"His figure is like as if he had swallowed our great washing-copper whole and then padded round it with hay bags, and he has a great vulgar stand with one foot here and the other over there by the wheelbarrow."

"He must be a acrobat or be made of wonderful elastic, if he could stretch that far!" remarked Andrew.

"Yes, and he gets up a gold-rimmed eyeglass and sticks it on his old eye like this, and so I up with my finger and thumb this way in a ring and looked at him," said Dawn, with a moue and the protrusion of a healthy pink tongue which for dare-devil impertinence beat anything I had seen off the stage, and I succumbed to laughter in chorus with the young man.

By some intangible indications Andrew and I felt impelled to leave, he proceeding to harness the horse and I accompanying him.

"Just look here, 'Giddy-giddy Gout with his shirt-tail out,'" exclaimed the lad, breaking into one of the poetic quotations of which he was rarely guilty. "Now, I didn't know me pants was tore. I must have looked a goat!"

I offered to put a stitch in the breach, so he brought needle and thread.

"Now don't you sew me on to me pants. Dawn done that once, thought it was a great lark, an' I jolly well couldn't get out; so I busted up the whole show, and grandma joined in the huspy-puspy, and there's been no more larks like that. Thanks, I must do a get and put the pony in. Did you notice that bloke fillin' up the cart with pumpkins? He's gone on Dawn!"

"He shows good taste."

"Do you reckon Dawn's fit to knock 'em in the eye?"

"Rather!"

"That's bein' a stranger! When you are used to a person every day an' they belong to you, you don't think so much of 'em, and at the same time think more, if you can understand. What I mean is this. When I'm busy fightin' with Dawn, and she's blowing me up for not doing things and tellin' grandma on me, I can't see what the blokes can see in her; but then if I caught any one saying she wasn't good for anything, if he was a bloke I felt fit to wallop, I'd give him a nice sollicker under the ear, an' I wouldn't bother about any other girl. Do you see?"

"Yes; I'll hold up the shafts for you."

"Thanks. Well, that's 'Dora' Eweword that's doin' a kill with Dawn now."

"Dora is a funny name for a man."

"It ain't his name. He's called it for a lark because he was after a girl up in town named Dora Cowper. She serves in a hay and corn store at the corner. Things were gettin' on pretty strong, and he used to be taking her out all hours of the night and day. Some reckon she's better-lookin' than Dawn, and her mother put it around that Eweword would make a brilliant match for her, and that shooed him off at once. I reckon if I was a girl and wanted to ketch a man I'd hold me mag about it, as I know two or three now has been turned off the same way."

"Perhaps Dora Cowper didn't lose much."

"Well, he has a bosker farm, you see. He keeps a power of pigs and fattens 'em. Then he went after one

or two more girls, and now he comes here. Buying these
pumpkins is only a dodge to get a chip in with Dawn.
He has plenty lucerne for his pigs, but we have so
many pumpkins rotting we are glad to get rid of them
at two bob a load, and I suppose that is cheap to get a
yarn with Dawn. He ain't preposed to Dawn yet, but
I'm sure he's goin' to, because I asked him if he was
goin' to marry Dora Cowper, an' he said no. Dawn is
only pullin' his leg for him—she's got all the blokes on
a string. You should see her with those that comes up
in the summer. It's worth bein' alive in the summer.
We had melons here in millions. We used to open a
big Dixie or Cuban Queen and just only claw out the
middle. We used to fill the water-cask with 'em to cool,
an' every time Dawn came out to dive in her dipper,
wouldn't she rouse! Me an' Uncle Jake used to race to
see who could eat the most, but he beat. He's a sollicker
to stuff when he gets anything he likes. It's a wonder
we didn't bust. The oranges will soon be ripe, that's good
luck: I can eat eighty a - day easy. Here comes old
Bolliver!"

A huge figure as described by Dawn came out of the
house in company with Miss Flipp, and I recognised Mr
Pornsch, the heavy swell who had travelled in the 'bus
with me on the day of my first arrival in Noonoon.

With repulsive clumsiness he climbed into the vehicle,
and then said roughly, almost brutally, to his niece—

"Get in! get in!" and scarcely gave her time to be
seated ere he hit the pony and nearly screwed its jaw
off getting out of the yard.

"Cock - a - doodle - do! Ain't it nice to have a sweet
temper," loudly remarked Andrew, as he stood aside.
"He just is a purple plum. He's the kind of old cove

I'd like to get real narked and then scoot. Wouldn't he splutter and think himself Lord Muck, and that every one oughter be licking his boots!"

Dawn and "Dora" Eweword were still hanging over a garden fence as Andrew went after his cows and I betook myself to the house. Uncle Jake was in conference with his sister, and gave evidence of fearing I should pursue him, so I mercifully betook myself to my own apartment. Miss Flipp presently returned, and saying she had had tea up town with her uncle and would not want any more, shut herself in her room, from whence I soon detected the sound of impassioned sobbing. My first impulse was to ask her what was the matter, but my second, born of a wide experience of grief, led me to hold my tongue and tell no one what I had heard; but to escape from the sound of that pitiable weeping I went out in the garden, where I was joined by Mrs Clay.

"Did you see that young feller out there this afternoon? Fine stamp of a young man, don't you think?" remarked she.

"He should be able for a good day's work."

"Yes; he's none of your tobacco-spitting, wizened-up little runts like you'll see hangin' on to the corner-posts in Noonoon."

"Seems to admire your granddaughter?"

"An' he's not the first by a long way that has done that, though she was only nineteen this month."

"I can quite believe it. She is a lovely girl."

"An' more than that, a good one. I've never had one moment's uneasiness with Dawn; she took after me that way. I could let her go out in the world anywhere with no fear of her goin' astray. She's got a fine way with men, friendly and full of life, but let 'em attempt to come

an inch farther than she wants, and then see! Some-
times I'm inclined to wish she's be a little more genteeler;
but then I look around an' see some of them sleek things,
an' it's always them as are no good, an' I'm glad then
she's what she is.   There's some girls here in town,"—
the old lady grew choleric,—"you'd think butter wouldn't
melt in their mouths, an' they try to sit on Dawn.   It's
because they're jealous of her, that's what it is.   I
wouldn't own 'em! They'd run a man into debt and be
a curse to him; but there's Dawn, the man that gets her,
he'll have a woman that will be of use to him and not
just a ornament."

"He'll have an ornament too."

"Perhaps so. I've spent a lot of money on her educa-
tion. She's been taught painting and dancing. I had
her down at the Ladies' College in Sydney for two years
finishing, an' she's had more chances of being a lady than
most. Some of these things in town here turn up their
noses at her an' say, 'She's only old Mrs Clay's grand-
daughter, who keeps a accommodation house,' but I pay
me bills and ain't ashamed to walk up town an' look 'em
all in the face."

"But it's generally those who owe the most who have
the most lordly mien."

"You're right. I could point you out some of them
up town as hasn't a shirt to their back, an' they look as
they owned everythink—the brazenest things!" The old
dame's indignation waxed startling in its intensity.

"But I was going to tell you about young Eweword.
I've set me heart on him for Dawn. He's somethink
worth lookin' at an' worth havin' too. He knows how to
farm and make it pay, an' owns one of the best pieces
of land about Noonoon—all his own. Dawn don't seem

to take to him as she ought. He was after a girl here in town, a Dora Cowper, an' so she says she ain't goin' to take any leavin's; but he ain't any leavin's, she can be sure of that, for if he'd wanted Dora Cowper they'd have snapped him up, an' I think as long as a young feller don't go making too much of a fool of a girl, a little flirtation's only natural. This has been the mischief with Dawn. There's a lot of people here in the summer from the city, and they're all taken with her, and for everlasting telling her she's wasting her talents here, that she ought to be on the stage. It's a wonder people can't mind their own concerns!" (The old dame grew choleric again.) "It makes her think what I can give her ain't good enough. It's all very fine in a good comfortable home of her own, with love and protection around her, to think people mean that sort of thing, an' that w'en she walked out in the world they would be anxious to worship her. Just let her go out an' try, an' she'd find it all moonshine; but w'en I tell her, she only thinks I'm a old pig, an' only she's that stubborn I know she'd never come back. (I would be the same myself w'en young, so can't blame her.) I'd let her have a taste of hardship to bring her to her bearin's. But while I'm alive she'll never have my consent to be a actress. W'en I was young they was looked upon as the lowest hussies. I'd like to hear what my mother would say if I had wanted to be one—paintin' meself up an' kickin' up me heels and showin' meself before men in the loudest manner!"

I concluded not to divulge my profession while at Clay's, and to boot, I held much the same point of view.

"She thinks she'd like to marry some fine feller and be a toff; an' she's got this danger that's always the draw-

back of a girl bein' pretty, so many fellers come after
them at the start they get finnicky an' think they can
marry any one, an' leave it too late, an' in the end they
marry some rubbishing feller an' don't came out half so
well as the plain ones that was content with a fair thing
w'en they had the chance of it. Just the same with a boy;
it's a bad thing for them to be able to do everythink,
they are so terribly smart they end up by doin' nothink,
an' the ploddin' feller they grinned at for bein' a booby,
because he stuck to the one thing, comes out on top."

"Just so; want of concentration plucks one every
time."

"That's wot I want to save Dawn from. It's all right
while I live, an' I don't want her to be chuckin' herself
at the head of any Tom or Dick, but I won't live for ever,
an' marriage is like everythink else, you want to have
your eye on a good thing an' not humbug too much.
W'en I'm gone"—the austere old face softened—"I
wouldn't like to think of her I've spent so much money
on, an' rared with me own hand, as I did her an' her
mother before her, growin' old an' sour an' lonely, or
bein' a slave to some worthless crawler." The old voice
grew perilously soft, and saved itself from a break by
a swift crescendo.

"As I say, I suppose she's waitin' for some great
impossible feller to come along, like we do w'en we're
young; but these upper ten is the worst matches a girl
can make, an' besides there's too many trying to ketch
them in their own rank. I've had lots of 'em here, an'
to see these swell girls the way they try to ketch some
one would make you ill. Don't you think so?"

"Well, my sympathies are always with the swell girl
in the matrimonial market," I replied. "She has a far

harder time than those of the working classes. You see, so many of the well-to-do eligibles prefer working girls— actresses, chorus-singers, and barmaids, which, in addition to marriage in their own class, gives these girls a chance of stepping up; whereas the swell girls cannot marry grooms and footmen and raise them to their rank as their brothers can their housemaids and ballet-girls. To be a success the society girl must marry a man of sufficient means to keep her as an expensive toy, and this description of bachelor being scarce in any case, little wonder she has to hunt hard and tries to protect her preserves from poachers. Think of it that way."

"There is a lot in that, and that's why I like to see Dawn have young Eweword, who's a man I'd be happy to leave her to; but I daren't say a word, she's mighty touchy an' would flash up that she'd leave if I want to get rid of her. But while I've got breath in me body there's one thing I will set me foot on, an' that's these good-for-nothing skunks like bankers' sons an' them sort of high an' mighty pauper nobodies; they're fearful matches for any one. I know too much about the swells an' the old families of the colony, I'm thankful I ain't one of them. My father came out here a long time ago, an' I was born out here. He was a sergeant in the police. I am near seventy-six, an' can remember plain for seventy years back in the days w'en there was plenty convicts, an' me father, seein' his position, was put to see the floggin' of them. Me and another little girl that's dead now used to climb up a tree an' look over the wall like children would. We was stationed in Goulburn then, an' I'll never forget the scenes to me dyin' day. The men used to be stripped to the waist and tied on a triangle and walloped till they was cut to pieces, till they screamed

like little children for mercy, and poor old wretches that
had roamed the world for sixty years used to screech
Mother! Mother! like little children.   It was heart-
renderin'! An' what used they be flogged for, do you
think?—for the piggishness of the swells mostly. I'll
tell you. There was a old feller lived out at Kaligiwa—
that's more than twenty miles the other side of Goulburn,
an' there's Parry's Lagoon there called after him till this
day. He was a old Lord Muck if ever there was one, an'
by reason of that got a land grant an' men assigned, an'
he ought to have been give to them to kick—would have
been the right thing; an' then he had a lot of skunks of
sons,—took after their father, of course, an' hadn't much
chance of bein' anythink else,—an' w'en they used to ride
to town they used to have a man tied to the stirrup just
to hold it."

"What was that for?"

"What was it for?" she raged. "It was because they
was those skunks of swells that think other people is only
made as floor wipes for 'em! An' this feller used to have
to run all the way to town, and if he hadn't strength to
run all the way he'd be dragged, an' if he give any lip the
Parrys 'u'd report 'em; an' me father says he's often seen
'em flogged till their backs were like ploughed, an' then
have to run the twenty miles home. Me father used to
come in every day and fling hisself down an' cry and sob
as if his heart would break, an' say he'd rather starve
than stay in the police. Now, the Parrys got up an' one
of them had a 'Sir' sent out to his name, and you'll see
'em writ about as one of the few *old* families; and I hold
that Dawn come from better stock than them, and has
more to be proud of in her grandfather—he had some
heart in him. An' Lord! there's Miss Flipp's uncle, one

look at him ought to be sufficient warnin' to any girl.
The likes of him is common among the swells—too much
stuffin' an' drinkin' an' debochary. Nice thing if Dawn
married a swell an' he developed into a old pig like that.
I can tell you another great family of swells, the Goburnes
—entertained the Royalties w'en they was out here, an'
are such bugs one of 'em married the Governor's daughter.
They got up about the same way. In the old days w'en
things were carelesser an' land wasn't much, the old cock
of all had the surveyor that was gone on his daughter
measurin' the land, an' got him to slice in great pieces by
false measurement, an' worked the lives out of convicts—
as big a brute as the Parrys.   That's the breed of the
swells, an' I have a horror of them. The people as I
consider ought to be the swells in this country is them
that came out first, the free emigrants, and honestly
worked up the colony with their own hands, an' their
children done the same for four or five generations—
them's the only proper Australian aristocracy we've got.
That's why I have sich a contempt for this Rooney-Moly-
neux, Mrs Bray was tellin' of ; only times is different
he'd be the same, he's got the sort of pride that thinks his
wife is a black gin because she was only a milliner."

Out past the placard advertising Mrs Clay's boats
gleamed the highroad, and from where we walked could
be seen a now unused old stone milepeg, carved in Roman
lettering, its legend differing somewhat from that in
modern figures painted on the miniature wooden post by
which it had been deposed. It was one of many relics of
the dead and gone convicts who had done giant pioneer
labour in this broad bright land in the days when
Grandma Clay's mother had been young.   Fine old
grandma, daughter of a fine old dad who had wept for the

cruelty endured by the men who had worked in chain-
gangs and were flogged under his superintendence, and
thinking thus I turned to the old dame who had ceased
talking and said—

"And what of your father, did he get away from seeing
the convicts flogged?"

"Yes; me mother thought he was goin' mad. He used
to sob in his sleep an' call out and squirm that he couldn't
bear to see them flogged, an' leap up in bed in a sweat.
So he gave up the police an' we went a long way farther
back to Gool-Gool on the Yarrangung, a tributary of the
Murrumbidgee. The train in them days was only a little
way out of Sydney, an' me father got a job of drivin'
Cobb & Co.'s coaches from Gool-Gool to Yarrandogi, an'
me an' me mother an' sisters an' Jake there used to live
in a little tent at the first stage out of Gool-Gool, an' take
care of the horses. I was fond of them horses, and used
to sneak out to harness them on to the swingle-bar w'en
I was no higher than the table. It's a wonder I didn't
get me brains knocked out. I was lots smarter than
Jake there with the horses, though it ain't supposed to be
girl's work. But it came nacheral to me, an' I think in
that case it's right. That's why I never was one to narrer
girls down an' say you mustn't do ·this and that because
you're a girl. I've always found, in spite of their talk,
the best and gamest mothers is the ones that grew out of
the tomboy girls. Well, it come that me father, being a
steady man an' very kind and well liked, he got on sur-
prisin', an' soon the tent give place to a bark hut. That's
the way people worked up in my days, an' what they had
was their own. They didn't want to start in mansions
an' eat off of silver at the expense of others like in these
times! After that we moved a long way down an' took

up a position on the Murra-Murra run beside the Sydney road, where the coaches passed in the night; an' me mother made hot coffee for the passengers, an' we drove a roarin' trade, had to git girls in to help, an' put up a large accommodation house, and respectable people always made to us" (the old head went high and the eyes flashed) "because we was clean, temperance people, there never was no D.T.'s or sly grog where we had the rule. An' that's why I always like to have a few people in the house to this day. I'm used to their company like, an' feel there's nothing goin' on or doing without them. Well, I grew up in time. I can't say it meself, but them as knew me then could tell you I wasn't disfigured in any way or a cripple, an' had no lack of admirers. Me an' me two sisters had 'em by the score waitin' till we grew old enough to be married. I can tell you there was some smart fellers among 'em. Those were the times! Me sisters made what is called swell matches, an' not bein' used to bein' cooped up, their lives was failures. I was the only one married in me own circle, and my life was a pattern to the others. I was the oldest an' waited last, an' me mother was that disappointed in me that I had to run away, an' I have me reasons for fearin' Dawn is on for a swell. I seen me sisters' lives. I call them unwholesome marriages when girls marries these fellers, an' their narrer-minded people sits on her an' is that depraved they turn him agen her!" Mrs Clay was vehement.

"When Dawn's mother grew up she was Dawn's image, an' we was keepin' a accommodation house too, that is Jim Clay an' me, and Dawn's mother was reckoned the prettiest and best girl in them parts, an' had lovers from far and near; but there came a feller up from Sydney to stay, nothin' to blow about neither, but he was dreadfully gone on me daughter. He seemed all right, but I was agen him—being a swell,—till me daughter threatened she'd run away with him if I didn't let her have him peaceful, an' rememberin' me own youth, I let her have him in spite of me misgivin's. She went home with him, an' it appears he was like these crawlin' fellers —couldn't do nothink, only what their parents give them; an' w'en they found he'd married a fine, good, wholesome girl, instead of one of their own style—one of the Parrys for instance—they cut him off with a shilling, an' poor thing she nearly starved, an' took to work to keep him, an' he always growlin' at her like the coward he was, that only for her he'd have been well off. A mess-alliance his people called it, but the mess wasn't from poor Mary's side. Well, w'en it come that she was to be a mother, his people took her in and told her, if you please, that if it was a boy they'd take it theirselves and educate it fit for their family, but if it was a girl they wouldn't. The poor thing, not bein' able for anythink an' too proud to come home, stood their insults as long as she could, an' at last she sneaked out at night and set off to walk to me. It is pitiable to think of."

The poor old voice trembled.

" She had more'n a hundred miles to travel an' it took her days, but some folk was good, an' one cold night about three hours before daylight she startled me by comin' into my room. I remember it like yesterday. ' Mother,' she says, ' I'm ill; I'm goin' to die; you won't let them take my child, will you ? ' I thought her wanderin', an' she was so gentle it frightened me; for we was always saucy ladies, I can tell you—every one of us, an' you can see Dawn is the same now. But that's only a way; w'en I'm ill she's as tender as anythink. It's grandma wouldn't

this do you good, and that do you good? An' her little
hands is very clever an' nice about my old bones w'en
they ache. Well, her mother was took bad an' me an'
her father done our best, an' her baby came into the
world—a poor miserable little winjin' thing, an' its
mother turnin' over said, 'What's that light, mother,
comin' in, is it the Dawn?' an' lookin' up I see it was the
Dawn; an' she never spoke again, but went off simple an'
sudden just then, an' that's how Dawn come to get her
name. I never thought she'd live to be called by it
though. Little winjin' thing! I had to feed her on the
bottle an' everythink disagreed with her. We had to
keep a old cow especial. I remember her as clear as
yesterday—a big old cow with a dew-lap an' a crumpled
horn; we called her Ladybird because she was spots all
over. As for *them* getting Dawn! They had the cheek
to write an' say if it was a boy they'd take it. They had
the cheek after what happened—that's swells for you
again! I writ them one letter in return that I reckon
ought to last them to their dying day. I told them it
wasn't any matter to them what *my* child was; that they
had *murdered* one already, let that be sufficient for them;
that they'd get no more unless over my dead body; an'
that all I regretted was that the child had any of their
cowardly blood in it, that it almost discouraged me about
its rarin'. An' Dawn don't know her name, an' won't
unless she's married. Her father married again, an' I'm
glad to say never had another child, an' I believe hankers
for Dawn, an' he will hanker for my part; an' I've got
Dawn tootered up agen him too. Now you can see the
blow it would be to me if she took up with a swell—
there's no happiness marryin' out of yer own religion or
class. Mine was what I'd call a love match now. Jim

Clay *was* a lover! I've seen him come in with a team of five all buckin', an' it snowin' an' never anythink but a laugh out of him. He'd ride miles an' miles to see me. The crawlers about these parts nowadays toddle about on bikes or sit like great-grandfathers in sulkies, an' if it was to sprinkle they'd think half a mile too far to go to see their sweetheart. I think the heart of the world must be dyin' out."

"You'll tell me about Jim Clay, won't you?" I said; " for I am an Australian—one of those you consider entitled to be termed a real aristocrat. My people for several generations have practically worked in the building of the State, though I must admit they belonged to the leisured class at home."

"Well, that ain't nothink agen 'em when they don't make it nothink agen 'em, if you understand. If a swell can prove hisself as good an' useful a man as another, he deserves the credit, an' comes out ahead too, because he has the education, an' sometimes that is useful. I'll tell you about me young days. Lately me mind seems to be goin' back more an' more to old times."

"Grandma! Grandma!" called Dawn's rich young voice, "come to tea. Andrew and Carry want to go up town after."

As I turned and looked at this glowing vision I laughed to think of her as a "little winjin' thing," and was grateful to the good offices of old Ladybird with the dew-lap and a crumpled horn.

"You needn't be in such a hurry all of a suddent," said grandma crossly. "It's a different tune w'en *you're* hangin' over the fence talkin' somewhere. There's no hurry roundin' me in to tea *then!*"

We lingered awhile watching the afterglow above the

great range dividing the coast land from the vast stretches
of the interior, and which was no longer an impassable
barrier to the people of the State.   Now the train toiled
over a stile-like way connecting east and west, and
Noonoon and Kangaroo, divided by a mile and the river,
nestled immediately at the foot of the zigzag climb.

They lay asleep against the ranges in a slow-going
world of their own, their little houses gleaming white in
the fading light.

There was a flush on the old woman's face as she turned
houseward—also an afterglow. 'Twas a fitting nook for
her present days, the decline of those splendidly vigorous
years behind !   What satisfaction to look back on stren-
uous, fruitful years, and be able to afford rest during the
last stages !

I, too, had rest ; but it was only the ignominious idle-
ness of a young boat with a broken propeller yarded
among honourably worn-out craft to await a foundering.

FOUR.

DAWN'S AMBITION.

AFTER tea grandma took to reading the 'Noonoon Advertiser'—a four-sheet weekly publication containing local advertisements, weather remarks, and a little kindly gossip about townspeople. This was her usual Saturday night entertainment. Carry and Andrew went to town to participate in the unfailing diversion of a large percentage of the population. This was tramping up and down the main street in a stream till the business places closed, from which exercise they apparently derived an enjoyment not visible to my naked eye. Uncle Jake and Miss Flipp not being in evidence, Dawn and I were the only two unoccupied, and noticing that she was prettily dressed, I resorted to a point of common interest in promoting friendliness between members of our sex and invited her to look at a kimono I had bought for a dressing-gown.

This had the desired effect. A look of pleasure passed over the face that charmed me so, and she arose willingly.

"I'm glad it is my week to stay in and make the bedtime coffee," she said as we examined the gorgeous kimono, a garment of dark-flowered silk; and Dawn, having all the fetichly and long-engendered feminine love of self-decoration, was delighted with it.

"Put it on," I suggested, and the girl complied with alacrity. She did not make a very natural Jap, being more on the robust than *petite* scale, but she was a very beautiful girl. With my impassioned love of beauty I could not help exclaiming about hers, and the foolish platitude, "You ought to be on the stage," inadvertently escaped me, seeing this is the highest market for beauty in these days when even personal emotions can be made to have commercial value.

"Do you think so too?" she said eagerly, betraying what lay near her heart. "Do you know anything about the stage? You don't think all actresses bad women like grandma does, do you?"

"Scarcely! Some of the most sweet and lovable women I've ever seen are earning their living on the boards. I'm intimately acquainted with several actresses, and will show you their photographs some day."

"Oh, I'd love to be on the stage!" exclaimed the girl.

"Tell me why and how you first came to have such a wish."

"Well, it's this way," said Dawn, pulling my kimono close about her beautifully rounded throat and curling her pink feet on a wallaby-skin at the bedside as she sat down upon them. "I heard grandma telling you something about me this afternoon, and I suppose you think I'm a terrible girl."

"A beautiful one," I said, revelling in the curling lips and rounded cheek and chin.

"Don't make fun of me," said Dawn huffily, blushing like noon.

"Good gracious, now *you* are making fun of me. I'm

only stating a patent fact. Mirrors and men must have
told you a thousand times that you are pretty."

" Oh, them ! They say it to every one. Look here—
there's the ugliest little runts of girls in Noonoon, and
they're always telling their conquests and that this man
and that man say they're pretty, when a blind cat could
see that they are ugly, and the men must be just stringing
them to try and take them down. So when they say it to
me I always make up my mind I'd have more gumption
than to take notice, for I can't see any beauty in myself.
I'm too fat and strong-looking ; all the beauties are thin
and delicate-looking in the face—not a bit like me. I
know I'm not cross-eyed or got one ear off, but that's
about all."

I had been wont to think the only place unconscious
beauties abounded was in high-flown, unreal novels ; but
here was one in real life, and that the exceedingly un-
varnished existence of Noonoon. Not that I would have
thought any the less of her had she been conscious of her
physical loveliness, for beauty is such a glorious, powerful,
intoxicating gift that had I been blessed with it I'm sure
I would have admired myself all day, and the wonder to
me regarding beautiful men and women is not that they
are so conceited, but, on the contrary, that they are so
little vain.

" I want to tell you why I want to be on the stage. I
couldn't tell how I hate Noonoon. It's all very well for
grandma to settle down now and want me to be the same,
but when she was young (you get her to tell you some of
the yarns, they're tiptop) she wasn't as quiet as I am by a
long way. Just fancy marrying some galoot about here
and settling down to wash pots and pack tomatoes and
live in the dust among the mosquitoes, *always !* I'd

rather die. I'll tell you the whole thing while I'm about it. You won't mind, as I'm sure you have had trouble too, as your white hair doesn't look to be age."

Comparison of her midget irritation with those that had put broad white streaks in my hair was amusing, but the rosy heart of a girl magnifies that which it doesn't contract.

"Grandma wants me to marry. Did you see that fellow who was after pumpkins ?—he ought to make one of his head, the great thing! Grandma has a fancy for me having him, but I wouldn't marry him if he were the only man in Noonoon. Do you know, they actually call him Dora because he was breaking his neck after a girl of that name. He used to be making red-hot love to her. Young Andrew there saw him up the lane by Bray's with his arm round her waist, mugging her for dear life, and then he'd come over here and want to kiss me! If he had seen me up a lane hugging the baker, I wonder would he want me then!" Dawn's tone approached tears, for thus are sensitive maiden hearts outraged by an inconsistent double standard of propriety and its consequences, great and small.

"Grandma says that's nothing if it's not worse, for that's the way of men, but I'd rather have some one who hadn't done it so plainly right under my nose ; people wouldn't be able to poke it at me then. I've got him warded off proposing, and while I guard against that it's all right. Now, this is why I'd like to be on the stage. I'd love to have been born rich and have lovely dresses, and I'm sure I could hold receptions and go to balls, and the stage would be next best to reality."

"But why not marry some one who could give you these things ?"

"Where would I find him? You may bet that's the
sort of man I'd like to marry if I did marry at all," and
the dullest observer could have seen she was heart-whole
and fancy free. Certainly there would be a difficulty in
procuring that brand of eligible. There was but a limited
supply of him on the market, and that was generally con-
fiscated to the use of imported actresses, and, could society
journals be relied upon, it was the same in England; so
Dawn showed good instinct in wanting to bring herself
into more equal competition with the winners.

"Can you sing?"

"I've never been trained," she said, but at my request
went to the piano in the next room and gave vent to a
strong, clear mezzo. It was a good voice—undoubtedly
so. There are many such to be heard all over Australia—
girls singing at country concerts without instruction, or
the ignorant instruction more injurious than helpful.
These voices are marred to the practised ear by the style
of production, which in a year or two leaves them cracked
and awful. This widespread lack of voice preservation is
the result of a want of public musical training. With all
the training in Paris, Dawn would never have been a
Dolores or Calvé, but with other ability she had sufficient
voice to make a success in comic opera or in concerts as
second fiddle to a star soprano.

"You must sing again for me," I said, "and I'll discover
whether you have any ability." For the way to wean any
one from a desire is not by condemnation of it.

"Don't you say anything to grandma about me and the
stage or she'd very nearly turn you out of the house. You
just ask her what she thinks of it some time, and it will
give you an idea; but I hate Noonoon, and would run
away, only grandma goes on so terribly about hussies that

go to the bad, and she's very old, and you know how you feel that a curse might follow you when people go on that way," said the girl in bidding me good night.

Dawn had many characteristics that made one love her, and a few in spite of which one bore her affection. Her method of dealing with her native tongue came among the latter. It was reprehensible of her too, seeing the money her grandmother had spent in giving her a chance to be a lady—that is, the type of lady who affects a blindness concerning the stern, plain facts of existence, and who considers that to speak so that she cannot be heard distinctly is an outward sign of innate refinement. She had made poor use of her opportunities in this respect, but if to be honest, healthy, and wholesome is lady-like, then Dawn was one of the most vigorous and thoroughly lady-like folk I have known, and what really constitutes a lady is a mootable point based largely upon the point of view.

FIVE.

MISS FLIPP'S UNCLE.

I DID not sleep that night. Dawn and her grandma had given me too much food for cogitation. I felt I had incurred a responsibility in regard to the former, upon which I chewed tough cud at the expense of sleep.

While there was hard common-sense in the old grandmother's point of view, it was also easy to be at one with the girl's desire for something brighter and more stirring than old Noonoon afforded. The fertile valley was beautiful in all truth, but with the beauty that appeals only to the storm-wrecked mariner, worn with a glut of human strife and glad to be at anchor for a time rebuilding a jaded constitution.

Upon a first impression this girl did not seem abnormally anxious for the mere plaudits or the notoriety part of the stage-struck's fever, nor was she alight with that fire called genius which will burn a hole through all obstacles till it reaches its goal; she appeared rather to regard the stage as a means to an end—a pleasant easy way, in the notion of the inexperienced, of obtaining the fine linen and silver spoon she desired. Had she been a boy, doubtless she would have set out to work for her ambition, but being a girl she sought to climb

by the most approved and usual ladder within reach—
the stage ; for actresses all married the lovely, rich (often
titled) young gentlemen who sat in rows in the front
seats and admired the high-class "stars" and worshipped
the ballerinas and chorus girls, or so at least a great
many people believed, being led astray by certain
columns in gossip newspapers, which doubtless have
a colouring of truth inasmuch that the women of the
stage are idealised creatures—idealised by limelight, and
advertised by a pushing management for the benefit of
the box-office.

Now Dawn had ample ability and appearance for
success on the stage if her parents had been there
before her, so that she could have grown up in touch
with it, but whether she had sufficient iron and salt to
push her way against the barriers in her pathway I
doubted. Only sheer genius can get to the front in
any line of art with which it is not in touch, and even
giant talent is often so mangled in the struggle that
when it wrests recognition it is too spent to maintain
the altitude it has attained at the expense of heart-sweat
and blood.

The girl worried me, and it worried me more to think
that after all my experience I was so foolish and senti-
mental that I could be worried regarding her. She had
a comfortable home, a loving guardian, youth, health,
good appearance, and, to a certain extent, fitted her sur-
roundings. There was nothing of the ethereally æsthetic
about her, and no stretch of sickly imagination could
picture her as pining to be understood. Notwithstand-
ing this, there was I longing to help her so much that,
in spite of my health and an acquaintance that was only
twelve hours old, I was contemplating entering society

for her sweet sake. The fact was, this little orphan girl who had taken up the life her mother had laid down at dawn of day nineteen years ago, had collected my scalp, and was at leave to string it on her belt as that of an ardent faithful lover who never entertained one unworthy thought of her, or wavered in affection from the hour she first flashed upon her.

I desired to save her from such savage disappointment as had blighted my life, not that she would ever have the capacity to feel my frenzy of griefs, but remembering my own experience, I was ever anxious to save other youngsters from the possibilities of a similar fate.

The best disposal to be made of Dawn was to settle her in marriage with some decent and well-to-do man on the sunny side of thirty; but where was such an one?

Thus I lay awake, and heard the hours chime and the trains go roaring by, till all the household but Miss Flipp had returned. She entered from the outside, did not come in till after midnight, and was not alone. Her uncle accompanied her. My room had French lights opening into the garden in the same way as Miss Flipp's, and as my ailment was a heart affection it was sometimes necessary for me to go outside to get sufficient air, and in this instance I had the door-windows wide open and the bed pulled almost to the opening. Miss Flipp apparently had her window open too, for despite the conversation in her room being in subdued tones, I heard it where I lay.

It contained startling disclosures anent these two persons' relations and characters, and when Mr Pornsch went his way with the uneven footsteps of the overfed and of accumulating years, he left me in a painful state of perturbation.

What course should I pursue ?

Casting on a pair of slippers and a heavy cloak, I took a little path leading from my window through the garden to the pier where the boats were moored, and here I sat down to consider. Experience had taught me to be chary of entering matters that did not concern me, but it had not made me sufficiently callous to preserve my equanimity in face of a discovery so serious as this.

Miss Flipp had sinned the sin which, if discovered, put a great gulf 'twixt her and Grandma Clay, Dawn, Carry, and myself, but which would not prevent her fellow - sinner from associating with us on more than terms of equality. Should Grandma Clay become aware of what I knew, she certainly would bundle the girl out neck and crop, as she would be justified in doing. But the girl was in a ghastly predicament, and more sinned against than sinning, when one heard her grief and remembered the age of her betrayer, which should have made him the protector instead of the seducer of young women.

Times out of number the dramatic critics have termed me an artist of the first rank, and it is this temperament which furnishes the faculty of regarding all shades and consequences of life's issues unabashed, and with the power to distil knowledge from good and bad and use it experimentally, rather than, as a judge, condemnatory.

I determined to keep the girl's secret, and show myself sympathetically friendly otherwise, hoping she would extend me her confidence, so that in a humble way I might be privileged to stand between her and perdition.

It was a beautiful night, one of those when the moon relinquishes her court to the little stars. Vehicular traffic had ceased, and the only sound breaking the still-

ness of the great frostless, silver-spangled darkness was
the panting of the steam-engines and the murmur of the
river where half a mile down it took a slight fall over
boulders. The electric lights of the town twinkled in the
near distance, and farther east was a faint glow beyond
the horizon, rightly or wrongly attributed to the lights
of the metropolis. After a time it grew chilly, and I
was glad to return to my bed. Dawn was separated from
me by a thin wooden partition, and her strong healthy
breathing was plainly discernible as she lay like an
opening rose in maiden slumber, but there was now no
sound from the room of the other poor girl—a rose
devoured by the worm in its core.

Next morning, however, she appeared at breakfast, for
Clay's was not a house wherein one felt encouraged to
coddle themselves without exceptional reason, and to all
but a suspicious or hypercritical observer she seemed as
usual.

Carry was going to church.

"I haven't been able to go this three weeks because
my dress wasn't finished, and next Sunday will be my
week in the kitchen, so if I don't go now I won't be
able to show it for a fortnight," she announced.

"Well, I ain't going," said grandma. "Gimme back your
porridge, I forgot to dose it"—this to Andrew, on whose
oatmeal she had omitted to put sugar and milk. "I've
always found church is a good deal of bother when you
have any important work. I contribute to the stipend;
that ought to be enough for 'em. If one spent all their
time running to church they would have no money to
give to it, an' I never yet see praying make a living
for any one but the parsons."

Thus, Dawn being engaged in the kitchen, and her

Uncle Jake keeping her company there while he perused the 'Noonoon Advertiser,' which descended to him on Sunday morning, Andrew having gone away with Jack Bray, and Miss Flipp being invisible, grandma and I were left together to enjoy a small fire in the dining-room, so I took this opportunity of inquiring how Jim Clay had managed to capture her. This sort of thing interested me; I liked life in the actuality where there was no counterfeit or make-believe to offend the sense of just proportions. Not that I do not love books and pictures, but they have to be so very very good before they can in any way appease one, while the meanest life is absorbingly interesting, invested as it must ever be with the dignity of reality.

SIX.

GRANDMA CLAY'S LOVE-STORY.

"OH, you don't want to hear it now," she said in response to my request, but she gave a pleased laugh, betraying her willingness to tell it. "Sometimes I get running on about old times an' don't know where to stop, an' Dawn says people only pretend to be interested in me out of politeness. I think I hinted to you that mine was a love match—the only sort of marriage there ought to be; any other sort, in my mind, is only fit for pigs."

"But sometimes love matches would be utterly absurd," I remarked.

"Well, then, people that are utterly absurd ought to be locked up in a asylum. Anybody that's *fit* to love wouldn't love a fool, because there must be reason in everything. *Some* people I know would love a monkey, but they ain't fit to be counted with the people that keeps the world going. Well, I got as far as we kep' a accommodation house on the Sydney road,—fine road it was too, level and strong, and in many places flagged by the convicts, an' it stands good to this day. It ain't like these God-forsaken roads about here,"—grandma showed symptoms of convulsions, — "but *some* people is only good for to be stuffed in a—a—asylum, and that's where the Noonoon Municipal Council ought to be, an' I say it though Jake there, me own brother, is one of them."

"Did Jim Clay——" I said, by way of keeping to the subject.

"I told you how I used to sneak out to buckle the horses on ; an' w'en Jack Clay, a great chum of me father's, used to be driving the 'Up' coach, me father, w'en he'd be slack of passengers,—which wasn't often, there being more life and people moving in the colony then,—an' w'en I'd be good, would put me up on the box an' take me on to the next stage, an' I'd come back with Jack Clay—that was me husband's father.

"As it used to be in the night, it usedn't to take from me time, an' I'd be up again next day as if I'd slep' forty hours. I wasn't like the girls these days, if they go to a blessed ball an' are up a few hours they nearly have to stay in bed a week after it. In that way I come to be a great hand with the reins, an' me father took a deal of pride in me because all the young men up that way began to talk about me. Me father had the best team of horses on the road. He used to always drive them hisself. He was always a kind man to every one and everythink about him. He drove three blood coachers abreast and two lighter ones, Butterfly and Fairy, in the lead. Weren't them days ! That great coach swingin' round the curves and sidlings in the dark, I fancy I can feel the reins between me fingers now ! And there was always a lot of jolly fellows, and usedn't they to cheer me w'en the horses 'u'd play up a bit. It was considered wonderful for me to manage such a team. I was only a slight slip of a girl, not near so fat as Dawn ; she takes more after her grandfather. Me and me sisters had no lack of sweethearts, and we didn't run

after them neither. Some people make me that mad the
way they run after people and lick their boots. W'en
I'd be drivin' with me father, Jim Clay used to be with
his, but he was some years older than me. He wanted to
enter the drivin' business soon as opportunity came, an'
him an' me were sort of rivals like. Many of the young
swells used to bring me necklaces and brooches, but some-
how when Jim Clay only brought me a pocket-handker-
chief or a lump of ribbon I liked it better an' kep' it
away in a little scented box, an' I was supposed to be in
love with a good many in them days. *Some people* always
knows other's business better than they do theirselves.
Me two sisters got married soon as they were eighteen—
one to a thrivin' young squatter, an' the other to a rich
old banker. Seein' how she got on is what makes me
agen old men marryin' young girls. It ain't natural. A
man might marry a girl a few years younger than hisself,
but there must be reason in everythink. I was older
than me sisters, an' people began to twit me an' say I'd
be left on the shelf, but before this, w'en I was sixteen
an' Jim Clay twenty, me father broke his leg and was put
by. All his trouble was his horses ; he fretted an' fretted
that they'd be spoilt by a careless driver, an' he had 'em
trained so they knew nothing but kindness. I was only
too willin', and I up an' undertook to drive the coach
right through. Old Jack Clay said he'd come with me a
turn or two an' leave Jim to take his team, but just then
he had some terrible new horses that no one could handle
but hisself,—he was a wonderful hand with horses was
Jim's father,—so Jim was sent with me. My, wasn't
there a cheer when I first brought the mail in all on me
own !" The old face flashed forth a radiance as she
told her tale.

"Some of the old gents in the town of Gool-Gool come out an' shook hands with me, an' the ladies kissed me w'en I got down off of the box. There was a lawyer feller considered a great lady-killer in them days. He had a long beard shaved in the Dundreary,—Dawn always says he must have been a howler with a beard of that description; but times change, an' these clean-faced women-lookin' fellers the girls think is very smart now will look just as strange by-an'-by. However, he was runnin' strong with me, an' me mother considered him favourable, —him bein' a swell an' makin' his way. Soon as ever I started runnin' the coach he was took with a lot of business down the road, an' used to be nearly always a passenger."

"It appears that sweetheart tactics have not changed if the style in beards has," I remarked with a smile.

"No, an' they'll never change, seein' a man is a man an' a girl a girl, no matter what fashions come an' go. I never can see why they make such a fuss and get so frightened because wimmen does a thing or two now they usedn't to. Nothing short of a earthquake can make them not men an' wimmen, an' that's the main thing. Well, to go back to me yarn, lots of other passengers got took the same way, an' there was great bidding for the box seat: that was a perquisite belongin' to the driver, an' me father used to get a sovereign for it often. I used to dispose of it by a sort of tender, an' £5 was nothink for it; an' once in the gold-rush times, w'en money was laying around like water, a big miner, just to show off, gave me two tenners for it. They used to be wantin' to drive, but I took me father's advice an' never let go the reins. Well, among all these fine chaps Jim Clay wasn't noticed. He was always a terrible quiet feller. *I* did all

the jorin'. He'd always say, 'Come now, Martha, there's
reason in everythink,' just w'en I'd be mad because I
couldn't see no reason in nothink. He was sittin' in the
back of the coach, an' it was one wet night, an' only a few
passengers for a wonder, who was glad to take refuge
inside. Only the lawyer feller was out on the box with
me, an' makin' love heavier than it was rainin'. I staved
him off all I could, an' with him an' the horses me hands
was full. You never see the like of the roads in them
days. It was only in later years the Sydney road, I was
remarkin', was made good. In them times there was no
made roads, and you can imagine the bogs! Why, some-
times you'd think the whole coach was going out of sight
in 'em, and chargin' round the stumps up to the axle was
considered nothink. We had more pluck in them days!
Well, that night the roads was that slippery the brake
gave me all I could do, an' a new horse in the back had
no more notion of hangin' in the breechin' than a cow; so
I took no notice to the lawyer, only told him to hold his
mag once or twice an' not be such a blitherer, but it was
no use, he took a mean advantage off of me. You can
imagine it was easy w'en I had five horses in a coach
goin' round slippery sidlin's pitch dark an' rainin'. He
put his arms 'round me waist an' that raised me blood, an'
I tell you things hummed a little. You'll see Dawn in a
tantrum one of these days, but she ain't a patch on me
w'en me dander was up in me young days." Looking at
the fine old flashing eyes and the steel in her still, it was
easy to see the truth of this.

"I jored him to take his hands off me or I'd pull up
the coach an' call the inside passengers out to knock
him off. He gamed me to do it, an' laughed an' squeezed
me harder, an' the cowardly crawler actually made to

kiss me; but I bit him on the nose and spat at him, an
took the horses over a bad gutter round a fallen tree
at the same time—an' some people is afraid to let their
blessed daughters out in a doll's sulky with a tiddy little
pony no bigger than a dog. If I had children like that
I'd give 'em all the chances goin' of breaking their neck,
as they wouldn't be worth savin' for anythink but sausage
meat. Well, this cur still kep' on at his larks, so soon
as I got the team on the level,—it was at Sapling Sidin',
runnin' into Ti-tree creek; I could hear the creek gur-
gling above the sound of the rain, and the white froth
on the water I can see it plain now,—I pulled sudden
and said 'Woa!' an' it was beautiful the way they'd
stop dead. The passengers all suspected there must
be a accident, or the bushrangers must have bailed us
up, for they was around in full blast in them days. Well,
w'en I pulled up I got nervous an' ashamed, an' bust out
crying, an' the passengers didn't know what to make of
it; but Jim Clay, it appears, had his eye an' ear cocked
all the time, an' before any one knew what had happened
he had the lawyer feller welted off of the coach an' was
goin' into him right an' left. That's what give me a
feelin' to Jim Clay all of a sudden, like I never had to
no one else before or since. He was always such a
terrible quiet feller that no one seemed to notice, an'
he'd never made love to me before, but he got besides
hisself then and shouts, 'If ever you touch my girl
again I'll hammer you to smithereens.' Then he got
back on the box an' wiped me eyes on his handker-
chief an' protected me. The men inside—mostly diggers
makin' through to Victoria—w'en they got the hang of
things bust out roarin' an' cheerin', an' said, 'Leave the
dawg on the road an' giv him a stummick ache.' He

tried to get up, but they pushed him off.   He made great
threats about the law, but miners is the gamest men alive
an' loves fair play.   It ain't any use in talking law to them
if it ain't fair play, an' they give him to understand if he
said anythink to me about it, or told any one an' didn't
take his lickin' like a man, they'd break every bone in
his body, an' they meant it too.   Then they lerruped up
the team and left him in the rain an' pitch dark miles
from anywhere.   That was the only time I give up the
reins.   I couldn't see for tears, so Jim drove; an' the men
took me inside so he could attend to his work, they
said, an' they cheered an' joked an' asked w'en the weddin'
was comin' off, an' said they'd all come an' give us a
rattlin' spree if we'd let 'em know.   I didn't know what
come over me; I never was much for whimperin', but I
cried an' cried as if me heart was broke; an' it wasn't,
because every time I thought of the way Jim Clay stuck
up for me it give me the best feelin' I ever knew, an' the
men was all on my side, an' there was no harm done, an'
I ought to have been smilin', but I could do nothink but
sob, an' I always think now w'en I see girls cryin' on
similar occasions to let 'em alone.   Girls can't tell what's
up with them, and a cry is good, because they ain't got
the outlets that men has w'en they're worked up.   We
came to the end stage, an' w'en we got off the men all
shook hands, an' one or two kissed me, an' pulled me
curls, an' slapped Jim Clay on the back, an' called him my
sweetheart.   W'en we delivered the mail Jim drove me
to where I stayed, an' it was terrible embarrassin' w'en
we was left alone with no extra people to take the down
off of the affair.   Jim was painful shy, but he faced
it manful; an' he said it didn't matter what they said
about us bein' lovers, if it was disagreeable to me he'd

never mention it nor think nothink about it, an' it would
be forgot in a day or two, as he was a feller of no
importance. That was the way he put it; he never was
for puttin' hisself up half enough. So crying again I just
snuggled up to him an' said I didn't want to forget it,
I wanted to remember it more an' more, an' with that
he took the hint an' kissed me; an' that's how we got
engaged without no proposing or nothink. I didn't tell
me mother, or there would have been a uproar, an' just
then Jim Clay got a coach on the Cooma line, an' went
right away. I told him I'd wait for him. He was
away two years, an' w'en he came home we found it was
still the same with us. I was eighteen then, an' him
twenty-two.

He went away to Queensland for two years more, an'
in that time the sister next me was married, an' Jake
there was comin' on; but he was never no good on the
box—he pottered round and grew forage. Me mother
began to suggest I ought to marry this one an' that one,
but I waited for Jim Clay, an' w'en I was gettin' on for
twenty-one, old Jack Clay reckoned he was gettin' too
old for drivin' in all weathers, an' Jim come home an'
took his place. A fine great feller he was, all tanned and
brown, with his white teeth showin' among his black
beard. He said he'd seen no girl that wasn't as tame
as ditch water after me, an' as for me, no one else could
ever give me the feelin' he could, so we reckoned to be
publicly engaged. It raised the most terrible bobberie,
and me mother nearly took a fit. She had me laid out
for a swell like me sisters, an' she said I must be mad to
throw myself away like that. Me brother-in-laws got
ashamed of their wives' parents bein' in such a trade,
an' as they had made a comfortable bit, they was goin'

to give it best and rare a few sheep an' cattle, an' me
sisters came down on me an' said I would disgrace them
now they had rose theirselves up in the stirrups. Mother
said she'd never give her consent, an' I told her very saucy
I'd do without it. That's why I know it don't do to
press Dawn over far; she must have the same fight in
her, an' if drove in a corner there'd be no doing any-
think with her. Things was very strained at home then;
they thought to wean me of him, an' Jim Clay he hung
back some, sayin' I'd better think twice before I threw
myself away on him. That made me all the determinder.
Jim was the only man for me. I never did have patience
with them as can't make up their mind. So I waited,
an' the day I was twenty-one—me two sisters was twins
and married, one at nineteen and the other at eighteen—
I gathered up a few things, and I had two hundred in
the bank, and I went to a point of the road, Fern-tree
Gully it was named, an' w'en Jim come down the hill
with his horses I waved—we had it all made up—an'
he stopped till I clambered aboard, an' the box seat was
reserved for me that day for nothink, and at the end of
the stage we was married. I stayed with Jim's mother
for a week or two till we seen a opening, an' I kep' a
accommodation while Jim drove a coach. Jim was always
steady, an' we was both very popular, though I never
pandered to no one, or put up with nothink that didn't
please me. Our story was a sort of romance in them
days, an' money was changin' hands freely, an' we was
all right. The old folk died by-and-by; they didn't
live very long, and Jake there come to me. He wasn't
good enough for his sisters, an' somehow that's made us
always cling together. I ain't blind, I can see he's no
miracle; he has his faults. Who hasn't?" the old lady

fiercely demanded. I assured her I knew none, and
somewhat appeased by this she proceeded.

"Well, as I say, Jake there ain't a wonder of smartness,
but he's the only one belonging to the old days left to
me, an' you couldn't understand what that means till you
get to be my age. If I went to any one of your age, or
old enough to be your mother, an' said, 'Do you remem-
ber this or that,' how far back could they go with me, do
you think?"

"And then did you and Jim Clay——"

"Me an' Jim Clay was the happiest pair I think ever
lived under a weddin' ring, an' it was a love match. He
was quiet an' easy-goin' like, an' I was the one to bustle,
consequently there would be times w'en there would be a
little controversy in the house; but Jim, he'd always put
his arm round me an' kiss me, an' that's the sort of thing
a woman likes. She doesn't like all the love-makin' to
be over in the courtin' days, as if it was only a bit of
fishin' to ketch her. Tho' of course I'd tell him to leave
me alone, that I couldn't bear him maulin' me; but women
has to be that way, it bein' rared into them to pretend
they don't like what they do. An' you see Jim always
remembered how I had stuck to him straight, an' flung
up swell matches for him, which must have showed I
loved him. That's what gets over a man, he never forgets
that in a girl, an' always thinks more of her than the one
with prawperty who marries a poor girl and is always
suspicioning she took him for what he has. Of course,
there are some crawlers of men ain't to be pleased any-
how, but they can be left out of it. In givin' advice to
young wives, I always tell 'em w'en they get sick of their
husbands, which they all do at times, especially at the start
before you get seasoned to endure them, never to let him

suspect it, for men, in spite of all their wonderful smart-
ness, has a lot of the child in 'em after all, an' can take
a terrible lot of love. (When it comes to givin' any in
return, of course that's a horse of another colour.) But
of course this is only dealin' with a man that's worth
anythink; as I said, there are some crawlers you could
make a door-mat of yourself for, an' they'd dance on you
an' think nothink of it; but as I said before, there must
be reason in everythink to begin with. After Jim died I
didn't care for livin' in the old place, an' thought I'd like
to get somewhere near the city. Old people ought to have
sense. They don't want to crawl round like Methuselah
at forty, but they know w'en they git up to seventy they
ain't goin' to live for ever, nor get any suppler in the
joints, an' ought to make some provision to get nearer
churches an' doctors an' all that's necessary to old people;
so I sold out an' bought this place down here."

"What family have you?"

"Only Dawn's mother and Andrew's, and two sons away
in America. I was misfortunate with me daughters; they
both died young, one as I told you, an' the other of typhoid;
and so after bein' done with me own family I started with
others. I used to think once I'd be content to live till I
see me little ones grown up an' settled, an' then I wanted
to live till I see Dawn able to take care of herself, an' now
I suppose, if I didn't take care, I'd want to be waitin' to
see Dawn's children around me. That's the way; w'en we
get along one step we want to go another, an' it's good
some matters ain't left for us to decide. But it's all for
Dawn and Andrew I bother now, only for them me work
would be done; but it's good to have them, they keep me
from feelin' like a old wore-out dress just hangin' up
waitin' to be eat by the moths."

"Grandma!" said the voice of Dawn in the doorway, "I can't get this beastly old stove to draw, and I'm blest if I can cook the dinner. I never saw such a place, one has to work under such terrible difficulties. It's something fearful." Her voice was cross, and her facial expression bore further testimony to a state of extreme irritation.

Grandma rose to combat, she never meekly sat down under any circumstances, great or small.

"Terrible place, indeed; see if *you* had to provide a home what you'd have in it. You was never done squarkin' for that stove; some one else had one like it, an' you was goin' to do strokes w'en you got it. It's always easy to complain about things w'en you are not the one responsible!"

Grandma and I decided to go to the kitchen and prescribe for the stove.

From an idle onlooker's point of view it seemed an excellent domestic implement in good health; but the beautiful cook averred it would produce no heat.

"It must be like Bray's," said grandma, "they thought it was no good, and it was only because of some damper that had to be fixed."

"Yes; and they had a man there to fix it for them; that's the terrible want about this place, there being no *man* about it to do anything," Dawn said pointedly, looking at Uncle Jake, who was calmly sitting in his big chair in the corner. He was not disconcerted. A man who could live for years on a widowed sister without making himself worth his salt is not of the calibre to be upset by a few hints.

"I've busted up me pants again," cheerfully announced Andrew from the doorway — misfortunes never come singly. "Dawn, just get a needle and cotton and stitch 'em together."

"I never knew you when they weren't 'busted up,' and you can get another pair or hold a towel round you till Carry comes home; she's got to do the mending, it's her week in the house. I've got enough to worry me, goodness knows!"

"Dear me!" said grandma, walking away as I once more volunteered to be a friend in need to Andrew, "w'en people is young, an' a little thing goes wrong, they think they have the troubles of a empire upon them, but the real troubles of life teaches 'em different. You are a good-for-nothink lump anyhow, Andrew. Where have you been on a Sunday morning tearing round the country?"

Andrew threw no light on the question, and his grandma repeated it.

"Where have you been, I say—answer me at once?"

"Oh, where haven't I been!" returned Andrew a trifle roughly, "I couldn't be tellin' you where I've been. A feller might as well be in a bloomin' glass case as carry a pocket-book around an' make a map of where he's been."

The old lady's eyes flashed.

"None of yer cheek to me, young man! You're getting too big for yer boots since you left school. If in five minutes you don't tell me where you've been an' who you was with, I'll screw the neck off of you. Nice thing while you're a child an' looking to me for everythink that goes into your stummick an' is put on your back, an' I'm responsible for you, that you can't answer me civil. Your actions can't bear lookin' into, it seems. I'll go over an' see Mr Bray about it this afternoon if you don't tell me at once."

"I ain't been anywhere, only pokin' up an' down the lanes with Jack Bray."

"Well, why couldn't you say so at once without raisin' this rumpus. Them as has rared any boys don't know what it is to die of idleness an' want of vexation."

"It wasn't *me* rose the rumpus. Some people always blames others for what they do themselves: it 'u'd give a bloke th' pip," grumbled Andrew, as I put the last stitch in his trousers and his grandma departed. Her black Sunday dress rustled aggressively, and her plain bibless holland apron, which she never took off except when her bonnet went on for street appearance or when she went to bed, and her little Quaker collars and cuffs of muslin edged with lace, were even more immaculate than on week-days. She scorned a cap, and her features were so well cut that she looked well with the grey hair— wonderfully plentiful and wavy for one of her years, —simply parted and tidily coiled at the back. This costume or toilet, always fresh and never shabby, was invariably completed by a style of light house-boots, introduced to me as "lastings"; and there was an un-impaired vigour of intellect in their wearer good to contemplate in a woman of the people aged seventy-five.

It came on to rain after dinner and confined us all to the house.

Dawn borrowed an exciting love-story from Miss Flipp; grandma read a "good" book; Uncle Jake still pored over the 'Noonoon Advertiser,' while Andrew repaired a large amount of fishing-tackle, with which during the time I knew him I never knew him to catch a fish, and Carry grumbled about the rain.

"Poor Carry!" sympathised Andrew, "she can't git out

to do a spoon with Larry, an' the poor bloke can't come in—he's so sweet, you know, a drop of rain would melt him."

"It would take something to melt you," retorted Carry. "The only thing I can see good in the rain is that it will keep Mrs Bray away."

And thus passed my first full day at Clay's.

SEVEN.

THE LITTLE TOWN OF NOONOON.

THE little town, situated whereaway it does not particularly matter, and whose name is a palindrome, is one of the oldest and most old-fashioned in Australia. Less than three dozen miles per road, and not many more minutes by train from the greatest city in the Southern hemisphere, yet many of its native population are more unpolished in appearance than the bush-whackers from beyond Bourke, the Cooper, and the far Paroo. It is an agricultural region, and this in some measure accounts for the slouching appearance of its people. Men cannot wrest a first-hand living from the soil and at the same time cultivate a Piccadilly club-land style and air.

It is a valley of small holdings, being divided into farms and orchards, varying in size from several to two or three hundred acres. Many grants were apportioned there in the early days. Representatives of the original families in some instances still hold portions of them, and the stationary population has drifted into a tiny world of their own, and for want of new blood have ideas caked down like most of the ground, and evinced in many little characteristics distinct from the general run of the people of the State.

Though they were, when I knew them, possessed of
the usual human failings in an average degree, they
were for the most part a splendid class of population
—honest, industrious producers, who, in Grandma Clay's
words, "Keep the world going." There was only a small
percentage of idlers and parasites among them, but they
did duty with a very small-minded unprogressive set of
ideas.

There is a place in New South Wales named Grabben-
Gullen, where the best potatoes in the world are grown.
Great, solid, flowery beauties, weighing two pounds avoir-
dupois, are but ordinary specimens in this locality, and
the allegorical bush statement for illustrating their un-
common size has it that they grow under the fences and
trip the horses as they travel the lanes between the pad-
docks. Similarly, to explain the wonderful growth of
vegetation in the fertile valley of Tumut, its inhabitants
assure travellers that pumpkin and melon vines grow so
rapidly there that the pumpkins and melons are worn
out in being dragged after them.

Now, as I strolled around the lanes of Noonoon, I felt
the old slow ways, like Grabben-Gullen potatoes, pro-
truding to stifle one's mental flights ; but there was
nothing representative of the Tumut pumpkin and
melon vines to wear one out in a rush of progress.
The land was rich and beautiful and in as genial and
salubrious a climate as the heart of the most exacting
could desire ; but the residents had drifted into un-
enterprising methods of existence, and progress had
stopped dead at the foot of the Great Dividing Range.
The great road winding over it bore the mark of the
convicts, and other traces of their solid workmanship
were to be found in occasional buildings within a radius

of twenty miles; but their day had passed as that of
the bullock - dray and mail - coach, superseded by the
haughty "passenger - mail" and giant two - engined
"goods" trains,—while for quicker communication with
the city than these afforded, the West depended upon
the telegraph wires.

In days gone by the swells had patronised Noonoon
as a week - end resort, and some of their homes were
now used as boarding - houses, — while their one - time
occupants had other tenement, and their successors
patronised the cooler altitudes farther up the Blue
Mountains, or had followed the governor to Moss
Vale.

Once upon a time Noonoon had rushed into an elab-
orate, unbalanced water scheme, and had lighted itself
with electricity. To do this it had been forced to
borrow heavily, so that now all the rates went to the
usurer, and no means were available for current affairs.
The sanitation was condemned, and the streets and roads
for miles, as far as the municipality extended, were a dis-
grace to it.

Exceedingly level, they possessed characteristics of
some of the best thoroughfares; but the wheel-ways were
formed of round river stones which neither powdered nor
set, and to drive along them was cruel to horses, ruinous
to vehicles, and as trying on the nerves of travellers as
crossing a stony stream-bed. There seemed to be nothing
possible in the matter but to abuse the municipal council
as numskulls and crawlers, and this was done on every
hand with unfailing enthusiasm.

Though so near the metropolis, Noonoon was less in
touch with it than many western towns,—in most re-
spects was a veritable great-grandmother for stagnation

and bucolic rusticity, and in individuality suggested one of the little quiet eddies near the emptying of a stream, and which, being called into existence by a back-flow, contains no current. But while thus falling to the rear in the ranks of some departments of progress, the little town retained a certain degree of importance as one of the busiest railway centres in the state, and its engine-sheds were the home of many locomotives. Here they were coaled, cleaned, and oiled ere taking their stiff two-engine haul over the mountains to the wide, straight, pastoral and wheat-growing West, and their calling and rumbling made cheery music all the year round, excepting a short space on Sundays; while at night, as they climbed the crests of the mountain-spurs, every time they fired, the red light belching from their engine doors could be seen for miles down the valley. Thus Noonoon's train service was excellent, and a great percentage of the town population consisted of railway employés.

What is the typical Australian girl, is a subject frequently discussed. To find her it is necessary to study those reared in the unbroken bush,—those who are strangers to town life and its influences. City girls are more cosmopolitan. Sydney girls are frequently mistaken for New Yorkers, while Bostonian ladies are as often claimed to be Englishwomen; and it is only the bush-reared girl—at home with horse, gun, and stock-whip, able to bake the family bread, make her own dresses, take her brother's or father's place out of doors in an emergency, while at the same time competent to grace a drawing-room and show herself conversant with the poets — who can rightfully lay claim to be more typically Australia's than any other country's daughter. Of course the city Australians are Australians too.

Australia is the land they put down as theirs on the
census paper. She is their native land; but ah! their
country has never opened her treasure-troves to them
as to those with sympathetic and appreciative under-
standing of her characteristics, and many of them are
as hazy as a foreigner as to whether it is the kooka-
burra that laughs and the moke-poke that calls, or the
other way about. They are incapable of completely
enjoying the full heat of noonday summer sun on the
plains, and the evening haze stealing across the gullies
does not mean all it should. The exquisite rapturous
enjoyment of the odour of the endless bush-land when
dimly lit by the blazing Southern stars, or the com-
panionship of a sure-footed nag taking the lead round
stony sidlings, or the music of his hoof-beats echoing
across the ridges as he carries a dear one home at
close of day, are all in a magic storehouse which may
never be entered by the Goths who attempt to measure
this unique and wonderful land by any standard save
its own,—a standard made by those whose love of it,
engendered by heredity or close companionship, has
fired their blood.

These observations lead up to the fact that Noonoon
folk boasted their own individuality, smacking somewhat
of town and country and yet of neither. Some of the
older ones patronised the flowing beards and sartorial
styles "all the go way up in Ironbark," yet if put
Out-Back would have been as much new chums as city
people, and were wont to regard honest unvarnished
statements of bush happenings as "snake yarns"; while
the youths of these parts combined the appearance of
the far bush yokel and the city larrikin, and were to be
seen following the plough with cigarettes in their mouths.

The small holdings were cut into smaller paddocks, the style of fence mostly patronised being two or three strands of savage barbed wire stretched from post to post. This insufficient separation of stock was made adequate by the cattle themselves carrying the remainder of the white man's burden of fencing around their necks, in the form of a hampering yoke made of a forked tree-limb with a piece of plain fencing-wire to close the open ends. This prevented them pushing between the wires, and it was a pathetically ludicrous sight to see the calves at a very tender age turned out an exact replica of their elders. All the places opened on to the roads like streets; and to go across country was a sore ordeal, as one had to uncomfortably cross roughly upturned crop-land, and every few hundred yards roll under a line of barbed wire about a foot from the ground, at the risk of reefing one's clothes and the certainty of dishevelment. To walk out on the main roads and stumble over the loose stones ankle-deep in the dust was torture. Some averred they had known no repairs for ten years, and that they were as good as they were, because to have been worse was impossible. Walking in this case being no pleasure, I bethought me of riding for gentle exercise, and inquired of Grandma Clay the possibilities in that respect.

"Ride! there ain't nothink to ride in this district, only great elephant draughts or little tiddy ponies the size of dogs," she said with unlimited scorn; "I never see such crawlers, they go about in them pokin' little sulkies, and even the men can't ride. In my young days if a feller couldn't ride a buck-jumper the girls wouldn't look at him, an' yet down here at one of the shows last year in the prize for the hunters, the horses had to be all rode by one man; there wasn't another young feller in the district fit to take a blessed moke over a fence. I felt like goin' out an' tacklin' it meself, I was that disgusted. I never was a advocate for this *great* ridin' that racks people's insides out an' cripples them, there ain't a bit of necessity for it, but there is reason in everythink, an' they're goin' to the other extreme, and will have to be carried about on feather-beds in a ambulance soon if they keep on as they are. There's nothink as good as it was in the old days. As for a woman ridin' here, all the town would go out to gape like as she was somethink in the travellin' show business. I used to ride w'en I come down here first,— that was sixteen year ago,—but every one asked me such questions, an' looked at me like a Punch an' Judy show, that I got sick of it. I rode into Trashe's at the store there one day, an' w'en I was comin' out he says, 'Will you have a chair to get on?' an' as he didn't seem to be man enough to sling me on, I said I supposed so. He goes for one of them tallest chairs—it would be as easy to get on the horse as it—an' I sez, 'Thanks, I'm not ridin' a elephant, one of them little chairs would do.' But even that didn't seem to content him; he put it high on the pavement an' put the horse in the gutter. Then, instead of puttin' the reins over the horse's head proper, he left them on the hook, an' with both hands an' all his might holds the beast short by them in front of its jaw, like as it was the wildest bull from the Bogongs. The idiot! Supposin' the beast was flash an' pulled away from him, where would I be without the reins? That about finished me, I was sick of it, as I could not have believed any man, even out of a asylum, could be so simple about puttin' a person on a horse."

For this kind of exercise there seemed no promising outlet, and I was put to it to think of some other. As grandma said, with few exceptions, the only horses in the district were draughts and ponies. Every effect has a cause, and the reason of this was that these big horses were the only ones properly adapted to agriculture, and the smallness of the holdings did not admit of hacks being kept for mere pleasure, so the cheapest knock-about horse to maintain was a pony, as not only did it take less fodder and serve for the little saddle use of this place, but tethered to a sulky, took the wives and children abroad. It was the land of sulkies,—made in all sizes to fit the pony that had to draw them, and of quality in accordance with the purse that paid for them,—and a pair of horses and a buggy was a rare sight.

Andrew suggested that I should go rowing, and glow-ingly recommended a little two-man craft named the *Alice*, and as I could row well in my young days, I determined to test her capacity by going up stream very gently, as my time was unlimited and my strength pain-fully the reverse. It was a crisp day towards the end of April, so I was feeling brisker than usual, and the *Alice* was deserving of her good reputation. The Noonoon was one of the noblest and most beautiful streams in the State, and above the substantial and unique old bridge its deep, calm waters stretched for about two miles as straight as a ribbon, in a reach made historic because it has been the racecourse of some of the greatest sculling matches the world has known. Orange- and willow-trees were reflected in the clear depths of the rippleless flow, and lured by its beauty, the responsiveness of my craft, and an unusual cheerfulness, I foolishly overdid my strength. I was thinking of Dawn. Her girlish confidence regarding the desire of her hot young heart had so appealed to me that I was exercised to discover a suitable knight, for this and not a career I felt was the needful element to complete her life and anchor her restless girlish energy. To tell her so, however, would ruin all. Time must be held till the appearance of the hero of the romance I intended to shape. With this end in view I thought of recommending her grandma to let her voice be trained. Two years at the very least would thus be gained, and if properly floated and advertised in the matrimonial field, what may not be accomplished in that time by a beautiful and vivacious girl of eighteen or nineteen? I was recalled from such speculations by finding that it was beyond me to row another stroke, and I was in a fix. A slight wind turned the boat, and she drifted on to a fallen tree a little below the surface, and, though not upsetting, stuck there, and was too much for me to get off.

At that time of the year, except very occasionally, the river was free from boaters and the fishers who told of the fish that used to be got there in other times, so there was nothing to do but wait until my absence caused anxiety, when some one would surely come after me. Not a very alarming plight if one were well, but I felt one of my old cruel attacks was at hand, which was not encouraging. No one was within sight, but in case there should be a ploughman over a rise within hearing, I coo-eed long and well. My voice had been trained. I coo-eed three times, allowing an interval to elapse, and then settled into the bottom of the boat to await developments. Soon I was disturbed by the plunk! plunk! of a swimmer, and saw a young man approaching by strong rapid strokes. It is strange how hard it is to recognise any one when only their face is above water and one meets them in an unexpected place, and though this face seemed familiar there was nothing unusual in that, as I knew so many theatre patrons' faces in a half fashion. My rescuer having ascertained the simple nature of my dilemma, and easily gaining the boat by reason of the log, exclaimed—

"Why, it's never you! What on earth are you doing here?" and I responded—

"Ernest Breslaw! It's never you! What are *you* doing here? *I'm* stuck on this log."

"And I've come to get you off it," he laughed.

"Yes, but otherwise? This may be a suitable cove for a damaged hull, but what can a newly-launched cruiser like you be doing here?"

"I'm in training, and was just taking a plunge; it's first-class!" he said enthusiastically, and looking at his splendid muscles, enough to delight the eye of even such a connoisseur in physique as myself, and well displayed by a neat bathing-suit, there was no need to inquire for what he was in training. 'Twas no drivelling pen-and-ink examination such as I could have passed myself, but something needing a Greek statue's strength of thew.

"Are you feeling ill?" he considerately inquired, and as I assured him to the contrary, though I was feeling far from normal, he put me out on the bank while he rowed up stream for his clothes and returned to take me home. Having encased himself in some serviceable tweeds and a blue guernsey, he rolled me in his coat ere beginning to demolish the homeward mile—an infinitesimal bagatelle to such a magnificent pair of arms. I enjoyed the play of the broad shoulders and ruddy cheeks, and did not talk, neither did he. He was an athlete, not a conversationalist, while I was a conversationalist lacking sufficient athletic strength to keep up my reputation just then.

"It was very silly of you to come out alone or attempt to row in your state of health! It might have been your death," he presently remarked in a grandfatherly style. "Where are you putting up?"

"At Clay's."

"I know; the old place with the boats," he replied as the *Alice* whizzed along.

"I was aching for diversion," I said, in excuse for the rashness of my act.

"Well, I can take you for a pull now. I'll be here for a few weeks. Will you come to-morrow afternoon? Would three o'clock suit you?" he inquired as he moored. "The scenery is magnificent farther up the river."

"Yes, if I'm not here at three o'clock you'll know that I'm not able to come. You are very good, Ernest, to waste time with me."

"I'm only too proud to be able to row you about and expend a little despised brute force in returning all the entertainment with brains in it you have given me in the past."

"Yes, at the cost of anything under 7s. 6d. an evening, —am I to pay you that for rowing me?"

"Put it in the hospital-box," he said with a laugh that displayed his strong white teeth between his firm bold lips. He was altogether a sight that was more than good in my eyes.

I found I was not strong enough to spring ashore, but young Breslaw managed that and my transit up the steep bank to the house with an ease and gentleness so dear to woman's heart, that the strength to accomplish it is the secret of an athlete being in ninety per cent of cases a woman's ideal.

"Oh, I say," as he was leaving me at the gate, "if you

mention me, speak of me as R. Ernest, as I've dropped the
Breslaw where I'm staying. I don't want wind of my
being here to get into the papers. I'm practising in the
dark, as I'd like to give some of the cracks a surprise
licking."

"Very well, I'm under an alias too, so please don't
forget. To all except a few theatre patrons I'm as dead
as ditch-water ; but some one might recognise the old
name, and it would be very unpleasant."

"Right O ! To-morrow at three, then, I'll give you a
pull," he said, doffing his cap from his heavy ruddy locks,
now drying into waves and gleaming a rival hue in the
setting sun, as he bounded down the bank and made his
way along the river-edge to the bridge, as his place of
sojourn was farther up than Clay's and on the other side.

The excitement of thus meeting him had somewhat
revived me, for here at once, as though in response to my
wish, was a fitting knight to play a leading *rôle* with my
young lady, the desire for whose wellbeing had taken grip
of me. For her sweet sake, and the sake of the fragrant
manliness of the stalwart and deserving knight, I straight-
way resolved to enter the thankless and precarious busi-
ness of matchmaking, one in which I had not had one
iota of experience; but as women have to face marriage,
domesticity, and mostly all the issues of life assigned
them, without training, I did not give up heart. As a
first effort I determined that Dawn should chaperon me
when I went for my row on the morrow. As I looked at
the sun sinking behind the blue hills and shedding a
wonderfully mellow light over the broad valley, I thought
of my own life, in which there had been none to pull a
heart-easing string, and the bitterness of those to whom

that for which they had fought has been won so late as to be Dead Sea fruit, took possession of me.

The doctors had several long and fee-inspiring terms for my malady, but I knew it to be an old-fashioned ailment known as heart-break—the result of disappointment, want of affection, and over-work. The old bitterness gripped the organ of life then; it brought me to my knees. I tried to call out, but it was unavailing. Sharp, fiendish pain, and then oblivion.

EIGHT.

GRANDMA TURNS NURSE.

WHEN I came to it was dark enough for lights, Dawn's well-moulded hands were supporting my head, Grandma Clay's voice was sternly engineering affairs, and Andrew was blubbering at the foot of the bed on which I was resting.

I tried to tell them there was no cause for alarm, and to beg grandma's pardon for turning her house into a "sick hospital," but though not quite unconscious, I appeared entirely so.

"I wish you had sense to have gone for Dr Tinker when Dr Smalley wasn't in," said the old lady, with nothing but solicitude in her voice.

The sternness in evidence when I had been trying to gain entrance to her house was entirely absent.

"I'm afraid she's dead," said Dawn.

"Oh, she ain't; is she, Dawn?" sobbed Andrew. "She was a decent sort of person. A pity some of those other old scotty-boots that was here in the summer didn't die instead." And that cemented a firm friendship between the lad and myself. An individual utterly alone in the world prizes above all things a little real affection.

Presently there was a clearance in the room, effected

by the doctor, who, after a short examination, pronounced
my malady a complication of heart troubles, gave a few
instructions, and further remarked, "Send up for the
mixture. She isn't dead, but she may snuff out before
morning. She's bound to go at a moment's notice, some-
time. Give her plenty of air. If she has any friends she
ought to be sent to them if she pulls through this."

Grandma gave the meagre details she knew concerning
me, and as the practitioner, whom I took to be a veterinary
surgeon called in for the emergency, went out, he said—

"If she dies to-night you can send me word in the
morning; that will be soon enough; and if I don't hear
from you I'll call again to-morrow."

"She ain't goin' to die if I can stop her," said grandma
when he had departed. "I'll bring her to with a powltice.
I ain't given to be cumflummixed by what a doctor says;
many a one they give up is walking about as strong as
bull-beef to-day. I never see them do no good in a
serious case. They are right enough to set a bone or sew
up a cut, but when you come to think of it, what could
be expected of them? They know a little more than us
because they've hacked up a few bodies an' know how the
pieces fit together, but as for knowin' what's goin' on, they
ain't the Almighty, and ain't to be took notice of. The
way they know about the body is the same as you and
Carry know the kitchen, an' could go in the dark an' feel
for anythink while all was well, but if anythink strange
was there you couldn't make it out," and setting to work,
brewing potions and applying remedies of her own, the
practical old lady soon brought me around so that I was
able to make my apologies.

"Good Heavens! What do you take us for?" she
exclaimed. "It would be a fine kind of a world if we

wasn't a little considerate to each other. It does the
young people good to learn 'em a little kindness. I
couldn't be askin' people like Carry there to wait on
people, but it's Dawn's week in the house an' she'll look
after you, an' you needn't be wantin' to clear out to the
hospital. You won't be no better looked after there than
here."

Never was more tactful kindness on shorter acquaint-
ance.

Little Miss Flipp undertook to sit by my bed during
the early watches of the night, for they could not be
persuaded to leave me alone. Her eyes bore evidence of
many more sleepless watches, but the poor little thing did
not unburden her heart to me. Dawn appeared to relieve
her at 2 A.M., and the engaging child manfully struggled
against the sleep that leadened the pretty blue eyes till
morning, when grandma, brisk as a cricket, took her turn.

At eleven I was interested by the doctor's entrance.
He came on tiptoe, but like a great proportion of male
tiptoeing it defeated its intention and made more noise
than walking. Bearing down upon grandma, he inquired
in a huge whisper, " How is she ? "

At this juncture I opened my eyes, so he cheerfully
remarked, in a strong twang known by some supercilious
English as the " beastly colonial accent "—

" So you didn't peg out after all ! "

This being the language applied to stock, confirmed me
in the notion that he was a veterinary. I had once before
heard it applied to a human being in a far bush place,
where a man who lived unhappily with his wife one
morning remarked to a neighbour that " The missus
nearly pegged out last night," and it was considered
a fitting remark for such a monster as this man was

supposed to have been, but this doctor said it quite naturally.

I found him a friendly and communicative fellow, and as he gave in an hour's gossip with grandma and me for one fee, I was willing to take it to pass away a dull morning.

"What on earth did you go rowing for?" he asked me.

"The roads are too bad to go walking."

"That's only within range of the municipality. The council wants bursting up. They can't do anything with everything mortgaged to old Dr Tinker. He holds the whole thing. It's a pity he wouldn't peg out one of these nights, and we might get something done. But it's not him who has the money—it's the old woman."

"That's her Mrs Bray was tellin' us walloped the girl for bein' admired by the old doctor," explained grandma.

"Money, that's what he married her for," continued the doctor. "I don't know where he could have picked her up. Some say she is a publican's widow, but Jackson, the solicitor here, has a different hypothesis. He says he's seen her running along carrying five cups and saucers of tea at once, and no one but a ship's waitress could do that. At any rate she's a great man of a woman; can swear like a trooper if things don't go right. She's got the old man completely cowed."

"Am I to infer that cowing her spouse and swearing outrageously makes her *man*-like?" I laconically inquired. But the doctor's understanding didn't seem to go in for small satirical detail, he conversed on a more wholesale fashion, rattling on for a good half-hour to a patient for whom quietude was necessary, lest she should "peg out."

"Ain't he a bosker?" enthusiastically commented

Andrew, coming in to see what I had thought of this
doctor, who was the idol of Noonoon.

"Has he a large practice?" I cautiously inquired,
seeking to discover was he really a doctor.

"My word! Nearly all the people go to him, he's so
friendly and don't stick on the jam—speaks to you every-
where, and has jokes about everything."

"He's a fine man!" corroborated grandma.

"Yes; must be more than six feet high," I responded.

"An' such a gentleman, he's never above having a yarn
with you about anythink and everythink."

"Oh, well," I said, "any time I take these turns just
send for him."

One doctor was as harmless as another to me. I knew
it would relieve the household to have a medico, and
he could not injure me, seeing I accorded his medicine
and advice about as much deference as the hum of a
mosquito.

"Is he a family man?" I asked.

"Yes; so there are all your chances gone in one slap,"
said Carry, appearing to inquire my state.

I did not tell her there was the most insuperable of all
barriers in the way of my marrying any one, and that
I had no desire if I could. The first I did not want
known, and the second would not be believed if it were,
because, though woman is somewhat escaping from her
shackles, the skin of old crawl subjection still clings
sufficiently tight for it to be beyond ordinary belief that
one could be other than constantly on the look-out to
secure a berth by appending herself to some man, and
more especially does this suspicion hang over a spinster
with her hair as grey as mine, and who takes up a position
at a boarding-house which is supposed to be the common

hunting-ground of women forced on to the matrimonial warpath.

"He has seven little children, and one's a baby, an' his wife is a poor broken-down little thing near always in the hospital. You'd wonder how he married her, *he's* such a fine-looking man," vouchsafed Andrew.

"Such a fine man that you'd wonder concerning several other patent facts about him," I responded.

There was quite a chorus in favour of him now. He was evidently a true gentleman in his patients' eyes, because he was not above stopping to talk to them in their own vernacular about local gossip, and had the reputation of great good nature in regard to the bills of the poor, and they loved his jokes. They were of the class within grasp of the elementary sense of humour of his audience. This type of gentleman he undoubtedly was, but to that possessed of graceful tact and expressing itself in good diction — by some considered necessary attributes of a gentleman — he could lay no claim. Neither could he to that ideal enshrined in my heart, who would not have had seven little children — one of them a baby—and a poor little broken-down wife at the same time ; but as to what is really a gentleman depends on the attitude of mind.

NINE.

THE KNIGHT HAS A STOLEN VIEW OF THE LADY.

GRANDMA CLAY kept me in bed that day, so I forgot all about my appointment on the river until some time after three, when Andrew announced from the doorway—

"A man wants to know can he see you?"

"Who can he be?"

"He's a puddin'-faced, red-headed bloke, wearin' a blue sweater under his coat like the bike riders," was Andrew's very unknightly description of the knight whom I had chosen to play lead in the drama of the beautiful young lady at Clay's.

"That's a particular friend of mine, you may show him in," I said.

"Oughtn't Dawn to be woke up first and told to scoot out of that?" said he.

Dawn was one of those young beings so thoroughly inured to easy living that the few hours' sleep she had lost the night before had made her so dozy when she had come to keep me company now, that I had persuaded her to rest beside me on the broad bed, where, much against Andrew's sense of propriety, she was fast asleep.

"I'll hide her thus," I said, covering her with the counterpane, for it would not be good stage management

to allow the lady to escape when a fitting knight was on
the threshold.   This satisfied Andrew, who withdrew to
usher in the "puddin'-faced, red-headed bloke," who sat
in the doctor's chair, and made a few ordinary remarks
about the weather and some equally kind about my state
of health.

When in the company of ladies the only brilliance in
evidence about my young friend was the colour of his
hair, so there was little danger of his waking Dawn with
his chatter, as he sat inwardly consumed with a desire to
escape.   As I lay with my hand where I could feel the
girl's healthy breathing, I wondered would she too dismiss
my chosen knight as pudding-faced and red-headed, or
would she see him with my eyes!   His locks certainly
were of that most attractive shade hair can be, and his
good looks were further enhanced by a clear tanned skin
and dark eyes.   His large clean-shaven features had the
fulness and roundness of unspent youth in full bloom,
and he was far from the small bullet-headed type, which
accounted for Andrew's designation of "puddin'-faced."
I had always found him one of the most virile and upright
young creatures I had ever seen, and he had endeared
himself to me by his simple, untainted manliness, and the
fragrant evidence of health his presence distilled.   Dawn,
too, was so robust that there was a likelihood of her being
attracted by her opposite, and inclined to favour a carpet
knight before one of the open field.

Some men have brain and muscle, but this is a com-
bination as rare as beauty and high intellect in women,
and almost as startling in its power for good or evil; but
apart from the combination the wholesome athlete is
generally the more lovable.   When his brawn is coupled
with a good disposition, he sees in woman a fragile flower

that he longs to protect, and measuring her weakness by his beautiful strength, is easily imposed upon. His muscle is an engine a woman can unfailingly command for her own purposes, whereas brilliance of intellect, though it may command a great public position in the reflected glory of which some women love to bask, nevertheless, under pressure in the domestic arena, is liable to be too sharply turned against wives, mothers, and daughters to be a comfortable piece of household furniture. On the other hand, the athlete may have the muscles of a Samson, and yet, being slow of thought and speech, be utterly defenceless in a woman's hands. No matter how aggravatingly wrong she may be, he cannot bring brute force to bear to vanquish a creature so delicate, and being possessed of no other weapon, he is compelled to cultivate patience and good temper. Also, health and strength are conducive to equability of temper, and hence the domestic popularity of the man of brawn above the one of brain, who is not infrequently exacting and crossly egotistical in his family relations where the other would be lenient and go-easy.

The silence of my guest and myself was presently broken by Dawn turning about under the counterpane.

"Good gracious! what have you got there?" inquired Ernest. "Is it that old terrier you used to have?"

"Terrier, indeed! I have here a far more beautiful pet. Because you are such a good child I will allow you just one glance. Come now, be careful."

The girl's dress was unbuttoned at the throat, displaying a perfect curve of round white neck; her tumbled brown curls strayed over the dimpled oval face; the long jetty lashes resting on the flushed cheeks fringed some eyelid curves that would have delighted an artist;

the curling lips were slightly parted showing the tips of her pretty teeth, and the lifted coverlet disclosed to view as lovely a sleeping beauty as any of the armoured knights of old ever fought and died for. The latter-day one, politely curious regarding my pet, bent over to accord a casual glance, but the vision meeting his eyes sent the blood in a crimson wave over his tanned cheeks and caused him to draw back with a start. It was inconsistent that he should have been so completely abashed at sight of a fully-dressed sleeping girl who was placidly unconscious of his gaze, when it was his custom to regularly occupy the stalls and enjoy the choruses and ballets composed of young ladies very wide awake, and wearing only as much covering as compelled by the law; but where is consistency?

"I had no idea it would—er—be a young lady," he stammered, keeping his eyes religiously lowered, and fidgeting in a palsy of shyness such as used to be an indispensable accomplishment of young ladies in past generations.

"Just take a good look, she'll bear inspection," I said.

"I'd rather not, the young lady might not like it."

"But I'm giving you permission, she's mine, and then run before she discovers you have pirated a glance. I will keep the secret."

He lifted his eyes, but so swiftly and hesitatingly that I could not be sure that he had discerned the beauty that was blushing half unseen, instead of being displayed under limelight and drawn attention to by brass trumpets in accordance with the style of this advertisemal age.

As Ernest went out Andrew came in and awakened Dawn with a request to make him some dough-nuts for tea, but she ordered him to go to Carry as it was her week in the kitchen.

"Bust this week in the kitchen! A feller can hear nothing else, it's enough to give him the pip; it ought to be put up like a notice so it could be known," he grumbled as he departed.

That evening Mrs Bray made one of her calls, which were always more good - natured regarding the length of time she gave us than the tone of her remarks about people.

The famous Mrs Tinker, it appeared, from the latest account of her vagaries, had enlivened the lives of Noonoon inhabitants by swearing in a hair-lifting manner at one of the local shows because her horses had not been awarded first prize, &c., &c.

Whether, as Carry averred, it was this conversation that did the mischief or not, the fact remains that I became too faint to speak, and the girls would not leave me all night. I lay that way all the next day too, so that when Ernest called to make inquiries and discovered my state he took a turn at making himself useful, prevailing upon Grandma Clay to allow him to do so by explaining that he was a very firm friend of mine, and had had some experience of invalids owing to his mother having been one for some years before her death, both of which statements were perfectly true.

As I improved, I was anxious to discover what impression he had made on the household, and cautiously sounded them.

"He seems to be a chap with some heart in him," said grandma. "He'd put some of these fine lah-de-dahs to shame. I always like a man that ain't above attending on a sick person. Like Jim Clay, he could put a powltice on an' lift up a sick person better'n all the women I ever see."

"It's always Jim Clay," said Dawn in an irreverent aside; "I never heard of a man yet, whether he was tall or short, or squat or lean, or young or old, but he was like Jim Clay, if he did any good. I'm about dead sick of him."

"You don't seem to remember Jim Clay was your grandfather," I said, as his relict left the room, "and that he is very dear in your grandmother's memory. It is pleasing how she recalls him. Wait till your hair is grey, my dear, and if you have some one as dearly enshrined in your heart it will be a good sign that your life has not been without savour."

"Yes, of course, I do forget to think of him as my grandfather, never hearing of him only as this everlasting Jim Clay, and if he was like that red-headed fellow it would take a lot of him to be remembered as anything but a big pug-looking creature that I'd be ashamed to be seen with."

This was not a propitious first impression, and as she was inclined to be censorious I considered it diplomatic to point out his detractions, knowing that the combative propensity of the young lady would then seek for recommendations.

"Yes, he is a great, unattractive, red-headed-looking lump, isn't he?"

"Oh, I wouldn't say that. He looks fine and healthy at all events, and I do like to see a man that doesn't make one afraid he'll drop to pieces if you look at him."

"But he's hopelessly red-headed," I opined.

"But it isn't that sandy, insipid sort of red. It's very dark and thick, and his skin is clear and brown, not that mangy-looking sample that usually goes with red hair," contended Dawn; and being willing that she should retain this opinion, I let the point go.

There is one advantage in a heart trouble, that it often departs as suddenly as it attacks, and ere it was again Carry's week in the house, I was once more able to stroll round and depend upon Andrew for entertainment.

He invited me to the dairy to see him turn the hand cream-separator, and I remained to dry the discs out of its bowl while he washed them. He had a conversational turn, and in his choice of subjects was a patriot. He never went out of his realm for imported themes, but entirely confined his patronage to those at hand. This day his discourse was of blow-flies; I cared not though it had been of manure. I had knocked around the sharp corners of life sufficiently to have got a sensible adjustment of weights and measures, refinements and vulgarities. Besides, I gratefully remembered the tears Andrew had shed during my illness, and bore in mind that many a dandy who could please me by his phraseology of choice anecdotes could not be more than "bored" though I might die in torture at his feet.

"My word! I'm thankful for the winter for one thing," he began, "and that's because there ain't any blow-flies. They'd give you the pip in the summer. They used to be here blowin' everything they come across. They'd blow the cream if we left it a day. They'd blow you if you didn't look sharp. I had Whiskey taught to ketch 'em. Here, Whiskey! Whiskey!" and as that mongrel appeared, his master tossed him pellets of curds dipped in cream, and grinned delightedly as they were fiercely snapped. "He thinks it's blow-flies. Great little Whiskey! good little Whiskey, catch 'em blow - flies.

By Jove! I've had enough of farming," continued he, "it's the God-forsakenest game, but me grandma won't let me chuck it. I notice no one with any sense stays farmin'. They all get a job on the railway, or take to auctioneering, or something with money in it. You're always scratchin' on a farm. You should have been here in the summer when the tomatoes was ripe. Couldn't get rid of 'em for a song—couldn't get cases enough. They rotted in the field till the stink of them was worse than a chow's camp, an' what didn't rot was just cooked in the sun. Peaches the same, an' great big melons for a shilling a dozen. That's farming for you! The only time you could sell things would be when you haven't got 'em. Whiskey can eat melon like a good 'un, and grapes too." Andrew now threw out the wash-up water, pitching it on to Whiskey, who went away whimpering aggrievedly, much to the delight of his master, and illustrating that even the favourite pet of a youth has something to put up with in this imperfect life.

TEN.

PROVINCIAL POLITICS AND SEMI-SUBURBAN DENTISTS.

MAY dawned over the world, and throughout New South
Wales awoke a stir, reaching even to the sleepy heart
of Noonoon. This was owing to the fact that the State
Parliament was near the end of its term, and political
candidates for the ensuing election were already in the
field.

Though not many decades settled, the country had
progressed to nationhood, England allowing the preco-
cious youngster this freedom of self-government, and
sending her Crown Prince to open her first Common-
wealth Parliament. Then the fledgling nation, bravely
in the van of progress, had invested its women with
the tangible hall-mark of full being or citizenship, by
giving them a right to a voice in the laws by which
they were governed; and now, watched by the older
countries whose women were still in bondage, the women
of this Australian State were about to take part in a
political election. Not for the first time either, — let
them curtsey to the liberality of their countrymen!

The Federal elections, for which women were entitled
to stand as senatorial candidates, had come previously,
and though old prejudice had been too strong to the

extent of many votes to grasp that a woman might really be a senatrix, and that a vote cast for her would not be wasted, still one woman candidate had polled 51,497 votes where the winning candidate had gone in on 85,387, and this had been no "shrieking sister" such as the clever woman is depicted by those who fear progress, but a beautiful, refined, educated, and particularly womanly young lady in the heyday of youth. The cowardly old sneer that disappointment had driven her to this had no footing here, as she had every qualification, except empty - headedness, to have ensured success as a belle in the social world, had she been disposed to pad her own life by means of a wealthy marriage instead of endeavouring to benefit her generation in becoming a legislator. She was a fitting daughter of the land of the Southern Sun, whose sons were among the first to admit their sisters to equal citizenship with themselves, and she brilliantly proved her fitness for her right by her wonderful ability on the hustings, which had been free from any vocal shortcoming and unacquainted with hesitation in replying to the knottiest question regarding the most intricate bill.

The Federal election, however, in a sense had been farther away—fought at long-range, while that of the State was brought right to one's back door.

The Federal campaign had been freer from the provincial bickering which was a prominent feature of the State election, and made it more a hand-to-hand contest, where every elector was worthy of consideration; and though women were debarred from entering the State Parliament, yet they were now beings worth fawning upon for a vote, and their addition to the ranks of the electors gave matters a decided fillip.

The first intimation that the campaign had actually started reached me one afternoon when Dawn drove me into town to see a dentist. The whole Clay household had risen up against me patronising a local dentist.

" They're only blacksmiths," said Andrew. " I could tinker up a tooth as good as they can with a bit of sealing-wax."

However, I could get no doctor to give me a longer lease of life than twelve months, and as it was not a very important tooth, I considered the local practitioners were sufficient to the evil.

The afternoon before, when Ernest had dropped in to see *me*, I had *casually* mentioned that Dawn and I were going up town next day, so therefore, what more natural than, as we entered the main street, to see him very busily inspecting wares in a saddler's shop—articles for which he could have no use, and which if he had, a man of his means could obtain of superior quality from Sydney. I diplomatically, and Dawn ostentatiously, failed to notice him as we drove past to where was displayed the legend— S. Messre, Chemist and Dentist, late C. C. Rock-Snake, and where Dawn halted, saying, at the eleventh hour, " You ought to go to Sydney, Charlie Rock-Snake was all right, but I don't care for the look of this fellow."

Going to Sydney, however, would not serve my ends nearly so well as consulting S. Messre; for while I was with him Dawn would remain outside, and what more certain than that Mr R. Ernest Breslaw, walking up the street and quite unexpectedly espying her, and being such a friend of mine, should dawdle with her awaiting my reappearance, while growing inwardly wishful that it might be long delayed.

I knocked on the counter of the dusty, dirty shop,

and after a time an extraordinary person appeared behind it.

" Are you Mr Messre ? "

" I believe so.   Hold hard a bit."

Probably he went to ascertain who he really was, for I was left sitting alone until a splendidly muscular figure in a fashionable pattern of tweeds halted opposite the vehicle holding my driver.   I was quite satisfied with Mr S. Messre's methods, though his initial, as Andrew averred, might very well have stood for silly.

The golfing cap came off the heavy red locks, while the bright brown ones under the smart felt hat with the pom-poms, bobbed in response, and Mr S. Messre came upon me again, wiping his fingers on a soiled towel, and tugging each one separately after the manner of childhood.

" Did you want a tooth pulled ? "

" Well, I wished to consult you dentally, but not in public," I said, as two urchins came in and listened with all their features.

" Well, hold hard a bit and I'll take you inside."

I held or rather sat hard on the tall hard chair, and heard Ernest explaining to Dawn that he had been swimming in the sun, which made his face as red as his hair, for he gave her to understand that such was not his usual complexion.   His red locks, very dark and handsome, which lent him a distinction and endeared him to me, were such a sensitive point with him that his mind was continually reverting to them, and that audacious Dawn unkindly replied—

" It wouldn't do to be all red.   If my hair were red I'd dye it green or blue, but red I would not have."

"But it's a good serviceable colour for a *man*," meekly protested the knight.

"Perhaps for a *fighting* man," retorted the young minx with no contradictory twinkle in her eye; "but I could never trust a red-headed person: all that I know are deceitful."

I was dismayed. How would a gentle young athlete weather this? To a perky little man of more wits than muscle, or to a gay old Lothario, it would have been an incentive to the chase, but I feared Dawn was too horribly, uncompromisingly given to speaking what she felt, irrespective of grace, to expand this young Romeo to love; but much merciless fire will be stood from beauty, and he made a valiant defence.

"There are exceptions to every rule, Miss Dawn. I never was known as deceitful; ask any one who knows me."

"I don't know any one who knows you."

"Ask your friend inside, I think she'll give me a good character."

"Quite the reverse. If you heard what she says about you, you'd never be seen in Noonoon again;" but this assertion was made with such a roguish smile on eye and lip that Ernest took up a closer position by stepping into the gutter and placing one foot on the step of the sulky and a corresponding hand on the dashboard railing; and in that position I left them, with yellow-haired Miss Jimmeny from the corner pub. walking by on the broken asphalt under the verandahs, and casting a contemptuous and condemnatory glance at the forward Dawn who favoured the men.

Mr S. Messre led the way to a place at the back of the shop which was layered with dust and strewn with cotton-wool and dental appliances, some of them smeared from the preceding victims, evidently. He did not seem to know how to dispose of me, so I placed myself in the professional chair and invited him to examine the broken molar.

"The light is bad here," he remarked, fumbling with my head, and making towards my face with one of the soiled instruments.

"That is not my fault," I replied.

"This is him!" he further remarked, tapping my cheek with a finger.

"Yes."

"He wants patching."

"So *he* leads me to imagine."

"The nerve would want killing."

"Quite so, and to attend to its wants I'm here."

"I'd take eight shillings to kill the nerve."

"Would you use them as an apparatus to execute it?"

"Then I'd take twelve or thirteen shillings to fill it," he continued.

I was interested in the uniqueness of his methods.

"Would you purpose to powder the shillings or use them whole — I would have thought an alligator's or shark's tooth would scarcely require that quantity of material?"

Mr Messre stared at me in a dazed manner.

"I wouldn't touch the tooth under that," he continued.

"Is there another tooth under it? then extract this one and give the other a fair chance."

"It would be a lot of trouble," he kept on, without specially replying to my remark.

"Perhaps so; when one comes to think of it, teeth, I suppose, are not filled without some exercise on the part of the dentist."

"I wouldn't think of touching that tooth for less than a guinea; why it would take at least an hour to do it."

"This is the first intimation I've had that dentists calculated to mend teeth without spending any time on them," I said.

Mr Messre didn't seem to grasp the drift of my remarks, and as I felt unequal to maintaining the conversation for a more extended period, I announced my intention of thinking about what he had said. He said it would be as well, and I emerged to find Ernest had so far progressed as to be seated in the sulky holding my parasol over Dawn.

Youth and beauty is privileged to command an athlete to hold its sunshade, while old age has difficulty in finding so much as a small boy to carry its basket across the street. Mayhap this is why it is largely the elderly and frequently the unattractive people who fight for honest rights for their class and sex, while it is from pretty young women's lips issues most of the silly rubbish anent it being entirely women's fault that men will not conform to their "influence" in all matters. Only a very small percentage can regard conditions from any but a selfish point of view or conceive of any but their own shoe-pinch.

"I happened to see Miss Dawn here and waited to ask you how you are," said Ernest.

"Just what you should have done," I replied; "and now if you can wait till I investigate another dentist I want your opinion on a purchase I am making."

"Oh, certainly," he hastened to reply; "I'm doing a loaf

this afternoon.   I thought I heard my oar crack this morning, so came for some leather to tack round it."

This in elaborate explanation of his presence there.

The second dentist proved the antithesis of his contemporary, being short, pleasant, and bright.

"I'll tell you what," he said, laughing engagingly, "the best thing to be done with that tooth is to dress it with carbolic acid.   Now this is a secret."

"One of those that only a few don't know, I suppose."

"Perhaps so," he said, laughing still more pleasantly.

"You can do this tooth just as well as I can.   Get three penno'worth of acid and put some in once or twice a-day and the nerve will be dead in two or three. days, and I'll do the rest."

As he proved such an amiable individual, though probably an exceedingly suburban dentist, I got rid of half an hour in desultory chat, as I could see from the window that the knight and the lady, if not progressing like a house on fire, were at least enjoying themselves in a casual way.

"Did you have only one tooth to be attended to?" inquired Dawn when I appeared.

"Yes; and I fear that it will be one too many for Noonoon dentists," I replied.   I could think of nothing upon which to ask Ernest's advice, so I feigned that I was not feeling well enough for any further worry that afternoon, but would command his services at a future date.

I now held the pony while Dawn disappeared into a shop and reappeared with an acquaintance who invited us to attend a political meeting that night.   The electors, alarmed at the prodigal propensities of the sitting government, were forming an Opposition League to remedy matters, and the first step was to choose one of the two candidates offering themselves as representatives of this party for Noonoon.   The first one was to speak that night in the Citizens' Hall, and by paying a shilling one could become a member of the League, and vote for this candidate or the other.

"Oh, if I only had a vote!" regretfully exclaimed Dawn.

"He's a young chap named Walker, from Sydney,— very rich, I believe.   Do you know him?" Mrs Pollaticks inquired of me.

"I've heard of him," I said, exchanging glances with Ernest, "and should like to hear him, if convenient."

"I'll drive you in," volunteered Dawn.

"If you're around you might act as groom," I suggested to Ernest, and he gladly responding, it was agreed that we should begin electioneering that night.

"I knew Ernest would be delighted to be with us, he takes great pleasure in my company," I remarked with assumed complacence as we drove home; and I watched Dawn smile at my conceit in imagining any one took pleasure in my company while she was present, and that any normal male under ninety should do so would have been so phenomenal that she had reason for that derisive little smile.

"You said he was hopelessly red-headed," she remarked; "why, I think he has a handsome kind of red hair.   I never thought red hair could be nice, but Mr Ernest's is different."

I smiled to myself.

"I never thought much of men, but this one is different," has been said by more than one bride; and, "I never could suffer infants, but this kid is different to all I've seen," is an expression often heard from proud young fathers.

"His young lady thinks so at all events," I innocently remarked, and we fell into silence complete.

ELEVEN.

ANDREW DISGRACES HIS "RARIN'."

THE silence that fell upon Dawn and myself was un-
broken when we went to tea and seemed to have affected
the whole company, or else it was the conversational
powers of Andrew, who was absent, which were wanting
to enliven us.

"He ought to be home," said grandma. "He's got no
business away, and the place can't be kep' in a uproar for
him when the girls want to go out."

The old lady had determined to take a vigorous interest
in politics, and spoke of going to hear the meetings later
on herself.

It presently transpired that Andrew had not been look-
ing to his grandma for all that went into his "stummick"
so religiously as he should have been. Just as he was
under discussion he made a dramatic entry, and fell
breathlessly in his grandma's arm-chair near the fireplace.
The usual occupant glared at him in astonishment and
demanded "a explanation," which came immediately, but
not from Andrew. Instead there was a loud and impera-
tive knocking at a side door, and when Carry, after
cursing the white ants which had made the door hard to

open by throwing it out of plumb with their ravages, at last got it open, there appeared an irate old man carrying a stout stick. It was plain that he too had been running,—in short, was in pursuit of Andrew, who had quite collapsed in the chair.

"I've come, missus, to warn you to keep your boy out of my orange orchard," he gulped. "Six or seven times I've nearly caught him an' young Bray in it, but to-night I run 'em down, an' only they escaped me I'd have give 'em the father of a skelpin'. If I ketch them there again I'll bring 'em before the court an' give 'em three months; but you being a neebur, I'd like to give you a show of keepin' him out first."

The old dame, à la herself, had been in the act of pouring milk and sprinkling sugar on some boiled rice which frequently appeared on the menu during Carry's week in the kitchen, previous to handing it to Miss Flipp, but she waved her hand, thereby indicating that in so dire an extremity we were to be trusted with the sugar-basin ourselves, — in fact, that any laxity in this item would have to be let slide for once.

After the manner of finely-strung temperaments with the steel in them, which wear so well, and to the last remain as sensitive as a youth or maiden, Mrs Martha Clay then rose from her seat, visibly trembling, but with a flashing battle-light in her eyes.

"What have you got to say to this?" she demanded, turning on her grandson.

"I never touched none of his bloomin' old oranges. It was Jack Bray, it wasn't me."

"Yes," said she; "and if you was listening to Jack Bray it would be you done it all, an' he who never done nothink. What's the charge, and what damages have you laid on it ?" she demanded of the accuser, fixing him with a fiery glance.

"I ain't goin' to lay any damages this time, I only thought you'd rather me warn you than not; I know I would with a youngster. I suppose after all he ain't done no more than you an' me done in our young days, an' my oranges bein' ripe so extra early was a great temptation," familiarly said the man.

"Well, I don't know what *you* done in your young days, but I know I never took a pin that didn't belong to me, none of me children or people neither; and as for Jim Clay, he wouldn't think of touchin' a thing—he was too much the other way to get on in the world. An' it ain't any fault of my rarin' that me grandson is hounded down a vagabond," said the old lady in a tragic manner.

Seeing her fierce agitation, the lad's pursuer was alarmed and sought to pacify her by further remarking—

"He ain't done nothink out of the way, an' I admit the oranges was a great temptation."

The old lady snorted, and the colour of her face heralded something verging on an apoplectic seizure.

"Temptation ! If people was only honest and decent by keepin' from the things that ain't any temptation, we'd be all fit for jail or a asylum. Pretty thing, if he's only to leave alone that which ain't any temptation to him ! You could put other people's things before me, I wouldn't take 'em, not if me tongue was hanging out a yard for 'em. That's the kind of honesty that I've always practised to me neighbours and rared into any one under me, and that's the only kind of honesty that is honesty at all," she splendidly finished. "An' I'm very thankful to you for informin' me. I wish you had caught him an' skelped the hide off of him. It's what I'll do meself soon as I sift the matter."

The old man bade good-night and departed with his stick.

"He's always sneakin' about the lanes, an' only poked his tongue out at me w'en I wanted to know where he was," maliciously said Uncle Jake in reference to his grand-nephew.

"Mean old hide, always likes to sit on any one when they're down," whispered Dawn and Carry to each other. "A pity Andrew hadn't two tongues to stick out at him."

Miss Flipp was too dull to be aroused by even this disturbance. The only time she showed any feeling was when her "uncle" paid her clandestine visits. Her life seemed to be in a terrible tangle—more than that, in a syrtis,—but I did not take a hand in further crushing her. She had been kind to me during my indisposition, and except in extreme cases, "live and let live" was an axiom I had learned to carefully regard. Knowledge of the slight chance of circumstances or opportunity—which too frequently is the only difference between a good person and a bad one, success and failure—reminds one to be very lenient regarding human frailty.

"Now, me young shaver! I'll deal with you," said grandma, turning to Andrew, in whom there appeared to be left no defence. Never have I seen so old a woman in such a towering rage, and rarely have I seen one of seventy-five with vigour sufficiently unimpaired to feel so extremely as she gave evidence of doing.

"This is the first time anythink like this ever happened in my family, and if I thought it wouldn't be the last I believe I'd kill you where you are."

Andrew emitted no sound, he had given himself up

with that calmness one evinces when the worst is upon them—when there is nothing further beyond.

"Go off to bed as you are without a bit to eat," she continued, plucking at her little collar as though to get air. "To-morrow I'll see the Brays about this, and I'll skelp the skin off of you. I'd do it now, only there's no knowing where I'd end, I feel that terrible upset. What would Jim Clay think now, I wonder? You God-forsaken young vagabond, bringin' disgrace upon me at this time of me life. I'd be ashamed to walk up town and give me vote as I was lookin' forward to, and me grandson nearly in jail for stealing. *Stealing!* It's a nice sounding word in connection with one of your own that you've rared strict, ain't it? You snuffed up mighty smart when I asked you your doings, now it comes out why you couldn't account for 'em. 'Might as well be in a bloomin' glass case as have to carry a pocket-book round an' make a map of where he's been,' sez he. It appears a map of your doin's wouldn't pass examination by the police. How would you have been makin' a honest way in the world if I wasn't here to be responsible for you?"

"Oh, grandma!" said Dawn, seeking to calm her, lest the excitement would be too much. "After all it mightn't be so bad. Lots of boys take a few paltry oranges out of the gardens and no one makes such a fuss but that old creature. He just wants to be officious." This was an injudicious attempt at peace.

"Is that you speakin', Dawn? '*Lots of boys do it.*' Perhaps you will also say, 'Lots of girls come home with a baby in their arms.' Once you get the idea in your head that there's no harm because lots do it, you're on a express train to the devil. Lots of people do things and some don't, and that's the only difference between the vagabonds I've never been, and the decent folk I'd cut me throat if I wasn't among. An' you're the last person I ever would have thought would have upheld a *thief!*"

"Well, grandma!" protested Dawn, "I don't uphold him. I'm ashamed to be related to him, but don't make yourself ill now. Sleep on it, and to-morrow give him rats."

"Remember this," continued grandma, "an' carry the knowledge through life with you, that I can't make your character for you. Each one has to make their own, but seeing the foundation you've been give, makes you a disgrace to it. It takes you all your time for years an' years puttin' in good bricks to make a good character, but you can get rid of it for ever in one act, don't forget that; an' remember that belongin' to a respectable family won't stop you from bein' a thief. You are very quick to talk about some of these poor rag-tag about town, an' I suppose you an' Jack Bray thought you couldn't be the same, but you've found out your mistake! Go to bed now, and I'll leather you well to-morrer," she concluded encouragingly; and Andrew lost no time in taking this remand, looking, to use his own expression, as though he had the "pip."

"Dear me!" sighed the old lady, "them as has rared any boys don't know what it is to die of idleness an' want of vexation. If it ain't somethink beyond belief, one might be that respectable theirself they could be put in a glass case, an' yet here would be a young vagabond bringin' them to shame before the whole district."

"But I don't see that he has done anything very terrible," hazily interposed Miss Flipp.

"Good gracious! If he had been cheekin' some one or playin' a far-fetched joke, I might be able to forgive him, but there must be reason in everythink, an' to go an' meddle with other's property is carryin' things too far. 'Heed the spark or you may dread the fire,' is a piece of wisdom I've always took to heart in rarin' *my* family, and I notice them as are inclined to look leniently on evil, no matter how small, never come out the clean potato in the finish," trenchantly concluded the old woman; and Miss Flipp was so disconcerted that she immediately retired to her room, but noticed by no one but me. Probably the poor girl, if gifted with any capacity for retrospection, wished that she had heeded the spark that she might not now be in danger of being consumed by the fire.

TWELVE.

SOME SIDE-PLAY.

As Andrew was banished, and grandma determined to retire to ponder upon his sin, she waived it being Carry's week in the kitchen and consequently her duty to prepare supper coffee, and suggested that we younger women should all go to the meeting, but Miss Flipp refused on the score of a headache.

"Poor creature!" observed grandma, "I think she's afraid of a attack of her old complaint, she looks that terrible bad, and don't take interest in anythink. She wants rousin' out of herself more. She ain't a girl that will confide anythink to one, but her uncle is comin' up again to-morrer, an' I think I'll speak to him."

When Carry, Dawn, and I arrived at the Citizens' Hall, Ernest was already waiting to act groom, while Larry Witcom also accidentally hovered near. He quite as casually took possession of Carry, so there was nothing for a common individual like myself but to become extremely self-absorbed, so that my keen observation might not be an interception of any interest likely to circulate between the knight and the lady. The latter seemed to be in one of her contrary moods, so attached herself to me like a barnacle, settled me in a seat one from the

wall, and peremptorily indicating to Ernest that he was
to take the one against it, put herself carefully away from
him on the outside. A wag would have arranged the
party to suit himself, but that was beyond Ernest. He
meekly sat down beside me, with a helplessness possible
only to the sturdiest athlete in the room when in the
hands of a fair and wilful maid. I could have come to
his rescue, but deemed it wiser not to thrust him upon
Dawn for the present. We had arrived very early, so
there was time for conversation. Encouraged by me,
Ernest leant forward and addressed a few remarks to
Dawn, which she received so coolly that he distraitly
talked to me instead, and as people began to gather,
above the majority towered the fair head and striking
profile of him I had first seen dealing in pumpkins, and
who was colloquially known as " Dora " Eweword. Dawn
beckoned him to the seat beside her, which he took with
alacrity, a rollicking laugh and a crimsoning face, which,
in conjunction with a double chin, bespoke the further
partnership of a large and well-satisfied appetite.

"I haven't seen you for an age," said Dawn with
unusual graciousness.

"Are you sure you wanted to see me?" he inquired,
with an amorous look.

Dawn used her bewitching eyes of blue in a laughing
glance.

"You know you only have to give me the wink and
you'll see me as often as you want," straightforwardly
confessed " Dora "; but Dawn having encouraged him to
a certain distance, had a mind to bring him no nearer.

"I don't care if I never saw you again," she said
bluntly, "but grandma likes yarning with you, that's
why I inquired."

"Dora" looked very red in the face indeed.

"How's Miss Cowper?" mercilessly pursued Dawn, going to the point about which she was curious, as is characteristic of swains and maids of her degree. "I hope she's well."

"So do I," said Eweword.

"You used to ask after her health about twice a-day. I thought you would be taking her to Lucerne Farm to relieve your anxiety;" and in response to this "Dora" sealed his fate, as far as my feeling any compunction whether he singed his wings or not in the light of Dawn's bright candle, for he said with a touch of bravado—

"Oh, I was only pulling her leg."

To do the man justice he did not seem down to the full unmanliness of this statement; it appeared more one of those nasty and idle remarks to which all are prone when in a tight corner, and speaking on the spur of the moment.

"Oh, was that all!" said Dawn mockingly. "It was very nice of you. Are you always so kind and thoughtful?"

"I'm thinking of clearing out to Sydney in a day or two, I've spent enough time loafing. The only thing that has kept me here so long is that I wanted to hear how Les. got on in his maiden speech. We're not much to each other, but when a fellow has no one belonging to him he feels a claim on the most distant connection," said Ernest on the other side of me. His interest in Leslie Walker's maiden speech had been developed as suddenly as his opinion that he had spent enough time in a boat on the river Noonoon.

The connection he mentioned between himself and the candidate about to speak was that old Walker, whose only son the latter was, had married a widow with one son, by name Ernest Breslaw. Both these parents were now dead, leaving the step-brothers as their only offspring. The lads had been reared together, and though of utterly different tastes and callings, a mutual regard existed between them. Walker had passed his examinations at the bar, and Breslaw had been trained to electrical engineering, but both being wealthy, neither followed their professions except in a nominal way. Walker had put in his time in society, motoring, flirting, travelling, dabbling in the arts, and building a fine town mansion, while Ernest had spent all his time in athletic training, with the result that Walker had fallen a prize in the marriage arena, while Ernest was yet in full possession of his bachelorhood.

Any further conversation was out of the question, as the candidate—a smart, clean-shaven man with clearly cut features—now appeared, and announced himself by removing his new straw "decker," and calling out—

"Ladies and gentlemen, before we begin I would like to follow the democratic principle of asking you to choose a chairman from among yourselves."

"We propose Mr Oscar Lawyer!" called several voices, naming a popular townsman, and this being seconded, the candidate and the people's chairman, two very gentlemanly-looking men for the hustings, ascended to the stage side by side.

The chairman took up a position behind a little red table supporting a water-bottle and smudgy tumbler, while Leslie Walker sat on another chair at the end of it.

Many members of parliament, having risen to their position from coal-heaving or hotel-keeping, when going on the war-path a second time, take great pains to get

themselves *up* in accordance with their idea of the dignity
of their office. Many old fellows, roaring "Gimme your
votes, I'm the only bloke to save the country and see
you git yer rights," dress this modest *rôle* in a long-tailed
satin-faced frock-coat, a good thing in the trouser line,
and a stylish button-hole; but Leslie Walker, one of the
champagne set, had made equally palpable efforts to dress
himself *down* to his present *début*.

For sure! his suit, which comprised an alpaca coat
with a crumpled tail, must have been the shabbiest he
had, while the glistening new white sailor hat had prob-
ably been procured at the last moment in the vain
imagination that, dress as he would, it was not evident
at a first glance that he had had the bread-and-butter
problem solved for him by a provident parent before his
birth, and that he had lived what is designated the
cultured life, far and autocratically above sympathy
with the vulgar and despised herds, upon whose sweat
his class build the pretty villas fronting the harbour,
charge haughtily along the roads in automobiles, and sail
the graceful yachts on the idyllic waters of Port Jackson.

"By Jove! Les. has different ambitions from mine,"
said Ernest. "I'd rather have to stand up to a mill with
the champion pug. than face what he's on for to-night.
Doesn't he look a case in that get up? Supposing he
gets in, what the devil good will it do then, and it takes
such crawling to get into parliament nowadays. There
are too many at the game. I could never face the way
one has to flatter some of these old creatures for their
vote. I'd rather plug them under the jaw."

Mr Oscar Lawyer having introduced the speaker, he
came forward, and after explaining it was his first appear-
ance in politics, charmingly proceeded, "I hope I shall not

bore you with my remarks as I endeavour to outline the various planks in the platform of the party to which I have the honour to belong."

Quite superfluous for him to explain that he was a new chum in politics. Only a fledgling from a Brussels or Axminster carpeted reception-room would stand on the hustings and publish a fear that he might be boring his audience. One familiar with the trade of electioneering, as it has always been conducted by men, would strut and shout and brag, never for a moment worrying whether or not he came anywhere near the truth or feeling the slightest qualm, though he deafened his hearers with his trumpeting or bored them to complete extinction, and would refuse to be silenced even by "eggs of great antiquity."

"Les. ought to stick to society," observed his step-brother; "flipping around a drawing-room and making all the girls think they were equally in the running was more in his line."

"He's a nice, clean, good-looking young fellow at any rate, and doesn't look as if he gorged himself—hasn't that red-faced, stuffed look," said Dawn. "If I had a vote I'd give it to him just for that, as I'm sick of these red-nosed old members of parliament with corporations."

"He's the real lah-de-dah Johnny, isn't he?" laughed "Dora" Eweword.

"Don't you say he's any relation of mine," said Ernest. "It would give me away, and he thinks I'm in Melbourne. I told every one that's where I was bound. I hope he won't catch sight of me."

There was little fear of this; one has to be accustomed to facing a crowd before they can distinguish faces.

After the meeting, which dispersed early, Ernest and I

hurried out into the galvanised iron-walled yard, in which those coming from a distance put their horses and vehicles.

Having noted the disconsolate manner in which a pair of dark eyes below a thatch of generous hue surreptitiously glanced towards a tormentatious maiden with ribbons of blue matching her eyes and fluttering on her bosom, I thought it time to come to his rescue.

"If you would care to talk to your friend, he can drive you home while I walk with 'Dora'; he says he has something to say to me," said Dawn in an aside.

"Are you sure you want to hear it?" I asked.

"How could I tell until I hear it?"

"That is not a fair answer, Dawn."

"Well, it wasn't a fair question," she pouted.

"Very well, I will not press you more, but you'll tell me of it after, will you not?"

"Well, what would you like me to do?" she asked.

"Oh, I'd like you to be naughty. Mr *Dora's* complacence inspires me to inveigle him into having to drive me home while you walk with some one else."

"Very well, anything for fun," she responded with dancing eyes; and as Ernest had the horse in I got into the sulky and said—

"There is room for three here, Mr Eweword, and we would be glad of you to put the horse out when we get home."

He took the reins and a seat, and moved aside to make room for the loitering Dawn, but she said—

"No, I'll walk; I must keep Carry company, and she doesn't want to come just yet."

"Drive on," I commanded, and there was nothing for the entrapped "Dora" to do but obey.

I saw Carry go on with another escort. "Will you permit me to see you to your gate?" I heard Ernest saying as we went, and Dawn asserting that it was unnecessary.

It was a beautiful starry night, with a prospect of a slight frost, as we turned down the tree-lined streets of the friendly old town, whose folk on their homeward way dawdled in knots to discuss the interposition of the women's vote.

"Now the women will do strokes," said one.

"The men have things in such a jolly muddle it will take a long time to improve them," another retorted.

"The women will make bloomin' fools of themselves!"

"Couldn't be worse than the men!"

"The women'll all go for this chap because he's good-looking."

"Just as good a reason as going for another because he shouted grog for you," and similar remarks, drifted to my ears, but "Dora's" mind did not seem to be running on politics.

"Who was that red-headed fellow sitting the other side of you?" he inquired.

"Which one?"

"A short block of a fellow with a clean face."

"Oh, he's a man I know."

"Pretty cool of us leaving Dawn. The old dame won't like it."

"She won't mind, considering Dawn has about the most reliable escort procurable."

"I suppose it's all right if you know him, but to me he looked like a bagman or bike-rider or something in the spieler line."

"Oh no," and pulling my boa about me I smiled to think of the chagrin of Dora. He was so beautifully transparent too, but to do him justice did not seem to resent the scurvy trick I had played him, as soon his equanimity was restored, and we laboured cheerfully but unavailingly to promote a conversation.

"Do you really like farming—take a pleasure in it?" I inquired.

"When I'm knocking a decent amount of money out of it I do. There's not much fun in anything when it doesn't pay."

"Quite true."

"There might be a frost to-night, but they're nothing here—always disappear as soon as the sun is up. Great Scott! aren't these roads? The council want stuffing in the Noonoon. It would be an all right place only for the roads."

This brought us to Clay's gate, and no further conversational effort was necessary. I lingered outside till Eweword had disposed of the pony and trap, and by that time Ernest and Dawn, bearing evidence of quick walking, appeared, and we went into grandma and Uncle Jake in a body.

"The women are going to form a committee to work for Mr Walker if he's selected," announced Dawn, "and I want to join it, grandma. I am not old enough to vote, but I'd like to work for Mr Walker. He looks worth a vote. He's nice and thin, and speaks beautifully without shouting and roaring,—not like these old beer-swipers who buy their votes with drink."

"He is a decent-looking fellow," said Eweword.

"Oh, well, he'll go in then; that's all the women will care about," said Uncle Jake in one of his half-audible sneers.

"Well," contended Dawn, "men always sneer at women

for doing in a small degree what men do fifty times worse. If a pretty barmaid comes to town all the men are after her like bees, and if a pretty woman stood for parliament the men would go off their heads about her, and yet they get their hair off terribly if a woman happens to prefer a nice gentlemanly man to a big, old, fat beer-barrel, with his teeth black from tobacco and his neck gouging over his collar from eating too much. Can I join the committee, grandma?"

"If it's proper, and he's my man, you can, an' work instead of me, but I must hear them both first."

"If Walker could get you to make a speech for him, we'd all vote for him in a body," laughed Eweword; but Dawn replied—

"Oh, you, I suppose you say that to every girl."

Eweword sizzled in his blushes, while Ernest's face slightly cleared at this rebuff dealt out to another.

Grandma brought in the coffee and grumbled to Dawn about Carry's absence.

"That Larry Witcom ain't no monk, and while a girl is in my house I feel I ought to look after her. I believe in every one having liberty, but there's reason in everythink."

The girl did not appear till after the young men had gone and Dawn and I had withdrawn, but we heard grandma's remonstrance.

"That feller, I told you straight, was took up about a affair in a divorce case, an' it would be as well not to make yourself too cheap to him. I don't say as most men ain't as bad, only they're not caught and bowled out; but w'en they are made a public example of, we have to take notice of it. Marry him if you want—use your own judgment; he'll be the sort of feller who'll always have a good home, and in after years these

things is always forgot, and it would be better to be
married to a man that had that against him (seein'
they're all the same, only they ain't found out) and
could keep you comfortable, than one who was *supposed*
to be different an' couldn't keep you. But if you ain't
goin' to marry him, don't fool about with him. An'
unless he gets to business an' wants marriage at once,
don't take too much notice to his soft soap, as you ain't
the only girl he's got on the string by a long way."

"He acknowledges about the fault he did in his young
days, and he says it's terribly hard that it's always coming
against him now," said Carry.

"Well, if a woman does a fault she has to pay for
it, hasn't she? — that's the order of things," said
grandma.

"But this was when he was young and foolish," con-
tinued Carry.

"Yes, the poor child, he was terribly innocent, wasn't
he? an' was got hold of by some fierce designing hussy—
they always are—and it was all her fault. It always is
a woman's fault—only for the women the men would be
all angels and flew away long ago," said grandma sarcas-
tically. "They'll give you plenty of that kind of yarn
if you listen to 'em; an' if you are built so you can
believe it, well an' good, but the facts was always too
much of a eye-opener for me," and with that the con-
tention ended.

"Yes, Carry's the terriblest silly about that Larry
Witcom," said Dawn; "she swallows all he says. She
said to me yesterday, 'He seems to be terribly gone on
me.' 'Yes,' I said. 'You keep cool about his goneness.
Wait till he gets down on his knees and bellows and
roars about his love, and take my tip for it he could

forget you then in less than a week.' I've seen men
pretending to be mad with love, and the next month
married to some one else. Men's love is a thing you
want to take with more discount than everything you
know. You might be conceited enough to believe them
if you went by your own lovers, but you want to look
on at other people's love affairs, and see how much is to
be depended on there, and measure your own by them,
and it will keep your head cool," said this girl, who had
the most sensible head I ever saw in conjunction with
her degree of beauty.

She had contracted the habit of slipping into my room
for a talk before going to bed, and as her bright presence
there was a delight to me, I encouraged her in it. The
gorgeous kimono was a great attraction; she loved it so
that I had given it her after the first night, but did not
tell her so, or she would have carried it away to her own
room, where I would have been deprived of the pleasure
of seeing it nightly enhance the loveliness of her firm
white throat and arms.

"How did you and Dora get on together?" she pres-
ently inquired.

"Well, you see we didn't elope; how did you and
Ernest manage?"

"Well, you see we didn't elope," she laughed.

"No, but you might have arranged such a thing."

"Arranged for such a thing!" she said scornfully.
I'm not in the habit of trucking with other people's
belongings."

"What do you mean?"

"It was you who said something about his young lady
this afternoon—as far as I can see he doesn't behave
much as if he had one."

So it was my chance remark that had run her wheel out of groove during the last few hours !

"Does he not?" I replied. "I think he appears more as though he has a young lady now than he did during my previous knowledge of him."

"Well, I don't know how you see it," she said, as she tore down her pretty hair.

"What!" I ejaculated in feigned consternation. "He has not been making love to you, has he, Dawn? I always had such faith in his manliness."

"Well, he doesn't *say* anything," said Dawn, with a blush. "But he glares at me in the way men do, and when I mention anything I like or want, he wants to get it for me, and all that sort of business."

"Perhaps he's falling in love unawares. Young men are often stupid, and do not recognise their distemper till it is very ripe. He ought to be removed from danger."

"Well, if I ever had a lover, and he liked another girl better, I'd be pretty sure he hadn't cared for me, and would not want him any more," she said off-handedly.

"But would it not be better to let him go away and be happy with the maid who loves him than to spoil his life by wasting his affection on you, when you only think him a great pug-looking creature that you'd be ashamed to be seen with?"

"Yes, I don't care for him," she said still more off-handedly; "but he doesn't look so queer now I've got used to him. I suppose any one who liked him wouldn't think him such a horror."

"No; I for one think him handsome."

"Handsome?"

"Yes, *handsome*."

"Well, I'll go to bed after that and think how some people's tastes differ."

"Well, take care you don't think about Ernest."

"Thank you; I don't want the nightmare," she retorted, tossing her head.

THIRTEEN.

VARIOUS EVENTS.

THE following day was eventful. To begin with, after Andrew had discharged his early morning duties, he was to appear before his grandma for the execution of the sentence she had passed upon him the night before. I was assisting him to dry the parts of the cream-separator, a task which had become chronic with me, when Carry shouted from the kitchen, where she was putting in her week—

"Your grandma says not to be long; she's waiting for you."

Andrew unburdened his soul to me.

"Lord, ain't I just in for it! I'll hear how me grandma rared me since I was born! I'm dead sick of this born and rared business. It would give a bloke the pip. I didn't make meself born, nor want any one else to do it; there ain't much in bein' alive," he said with that pessimism which, like measles and whooping-cough, is indigenous to extreme youth.

"How could I help being rared? I didn't ask 'em to rare me. I didn't make meself a little baby that couldn't help itself, and they needn't have rared me unless they liked. Goodness knows, I'd have rather died like a little

pup before his eyes were opened," he continued so tragic-
ally that I took the opportunity of smiling behind his
back as he threw out the dish-water.

"Hurry up! your grannie is waiting!" called Carry
once more.

"Blow you! you'll have to wait till I'm done," retorted
the boy in a tone the reverse of genial.

"People is always chuckin' at their kids how much
they owe them. I'm blowed if ever I can see it. I didn't
want 'em to have me, and don't see why it should be
everlasting threw at me."

It is a wise provision that youth cannot see what it
owes the previous generation. This is a chicken that
comes back to roost in heavier years.

"I wish I had a grandma like Jack Bray's ma. He
nicked over to me w'en I was after the cows, an' Mrs
Bray ain't goin' to kick up any row about the oranges.
She says she never knew of a boy that didn't go into
orchards in their young days, and that his dad did, and
people don't think no more of a boy pickin' up a little
fruit than they do of pickin' up a stick. Yet grandma
will tan the hide off of me. She done it once before, and
I was stiff for a week."

"Take a tip from me, Andrew! March into your
grandma bravely; she's the best woman I've seen; you
ought to be proud to have such a grandma! She's in the
right and Mrs Bray's in the wrong. Let her hammer you
for all she's worth, and every whack you get feel proud
that she's able to give it at her time of life, and I bet
when you're a man you'll be telling every one that you
had a grandma who was worth owning. When she leaves
off tell her that this is the last time she'll ever have to do
it for anything like that, and see if you don't feel more

a man than you ever did before. Promise me that's what you'll do."

"Is that what you'd do if you was me?" he inquired with surprise.

"That's what *you'd* do if you were me," I replied with a smile. "Just try that. Never mind if your grandma does go for you hot and strong."

Andrew wiped the table, wrung out his dishcloth in the back-handed manner peculiar to his sex, hung it on a nail behind the door, dried his hands on his trousers, which for once were not "busted up," and with a less rueful expression than he had exhibited for several hours, went forth to meet his grandma.

About ten minutes later he returned blubbering, but it was a sunshiny shower, and I did not despise the lad for his tears, for he had a soft nature, and was quite a child despite his big stature and sixteen years.

"Well?" I inquired, recognising that he was anxious to relate his experience.

"She banged away with the strap of the breechin' till she was winded, and then I said I hoped she'd never have to beat me again for acting the goat in other people's gardens that didn't concern me, an' she didn't beat me no more then, but I had plenty as it was," he said, rubbing his seat and the calves of his legs.

"Well done, stick to that, and be thankful for such a grandma!"

"She ain't a bad old sort when you come to consider," he said with that patronage, also an attribute of extreme youth or unsubdued snobbishness, and when compared, snobbishness and youth have some similar characteristics.

Next item on the programme was Mr Pornsch, whom grandma invited to remain to midday dinner, and the old

lady being sufficiently human to denounce a swell far
more fiercely behind his back than to his face, in con-
sideration of this one's presence, once more entrusted us
to sugar our own puddings, regardless of consequences.

After luncheon she interviewed him about his niece's
health. Mr Pornsch seemed really concerned, and said
perhaps she needed to be diverted, and that he would see
about a further change, which might prove beneficial.
He then put up his eyeglass to inspect Dawn's beauty,
and ogling her, attempted to engage her in conversation;
but the girl didn't seem at all attracted by him or thank-
ful for the favours he brought her in the form of an
exquisite box of bonbons and the latest song.

"I don't accept presents, thank you," she said uncom-
promisingly.

"Do you never make exceptions?"

"Only from people I like *very* much."

"Well, I trust I may some day be among the excep-
tions," he said, in a gruesome attempt to be ingratiating;
but the girl replied—

"Then you hope for impossibilities."

Somewhat disconcerted though not the least abashed,
Mr Pornsch persevered by asking if she ever went to
Sydney, and stated the pleasure it would be to him to
provide her with tickets for any of the plays; but even
this could not overcome her unconquerable horror of the
various intemperances suggested by his person, so he had
to retreat.

Dawn's grandmother remonstrated with her afterwards.

"You ought to be a little more genteeler, Dawn, and
you could refuse presents just as well. Even if he isn't
the takin'est old chap, that is not any reason for you to be
ungenteel."

"Well, I don't care," replied Dawn, whose exquisitely
moulded chin, despite an irresistible dimple, was expressive
of determination.   "If I was a great old podge and had a
blue nose from swilling and gorging, and was fifty if I was
a day, and then went goggling after a young fellow of
eighteen, he wouldn't be very civil to me, or be lectured
if he spoke to me the way I deserved, and I think these
old creatures of men ought to be discouraged by all the
girls.   What's sauce for the goose is the same for the
gander."

Mr Pornsch had not long departed when Mrs Bray
favoured us with a call, so grandma was spared a pilgrim-
age to her house.   She and Carry exchanged a stiffly
formal greeting, but the visitor beamed upon the re-
mainder of us and seated herself in our midst.

"Oh, I say, ain't it a blessed nark to the men us going
to have a vote?   He! he!   Ha! ha!   It fairly maddens
'em to see us getting a bit of freedom—makes 'em that
wild they don't know how to be sneerin' an' nasty enough.
Every one of us will just roll up an' use our power now
we've got it,—they've kep' our necks under their heel long
enough."

"I wasn't thinkin' of the vote at present," said
Grandma Clay.   "I was just off to see you about what
our noble nibbs have been doin' in that old Gawling's
orchard; but I beat Andrew already in case.   What
did you think of 'em?"

Mrs Bray put back her handsome head, decorated by
an extremely fashionable hat, and laughed boisterously.

"Fancy the old toad runnin' 'em down,—gave 'em a bit
of a scare, didn't it?   Old mongrel, to kick up a fuss over
a few paltry oranges!   As if we don't all know what boys
is; why, there'd be no chance of rarin' them without

touchin' nothing, unless you carted them off to the back-blocks where there wasn't no one within reach. I told him what I thought of him. 'How dare you!' says I. 'Bring witnesses of this,' said I."

Grandma Clay arose.

"Well, if that's your idea of rarin' a family, it ain't mine. Why, can't you hear the parson's everlastin' preaching and giving examples how taking a pin has been the start of a feller coming to the gallows; and this is a much worse beginning than a pin! If the only way of rarin' them not to steal was to put 'em where there was no possibility of stealing nothink, a pretty sort of honesty that would be; you might as well say the only way to rare a girl modest was to let her never have a chance of being nothink else. Some people, of course, has different views, but I believe in holding to mine; they've brought me up to this time very well."

"Oh, you are terrible strict; you wouldn't have no peace of your life rarin' boys if you cut things so fine as that. Now w'en women gets the rule it might become the fashion for men to be more proper. Look here, the men are that mad——"

Uncle Jake here interrupted her by appearing for four o'clock tea.

"Well, Mr Sorrel, now the women has come to show you how to do things, there might be something done in the country."

"Nice fools they'll make of themselves," he sneeringly replied.

"They couldn't make no greater fools of themselves than the men has always done,—lying in the gutter an' breakin' their faces," said Mrs Bray.

"Wait till the women go at it, they'll fight like cats," continued Uncle Jake, whose power to annoy depended not so much upon what he said as his way of saying it.

Dawn chipped into the rescue at this point.

"I'm dead sick of that yarn about women fighting. It's a mean lie. They never fight half as much as men; and girls always love each other more, and are more friendly together than men. The only women who fight with their own sex and call them cats are a few nasty things who are trying to please men by helping them to keep women down and make little of them; and the fools! that sort of meanness never pleases any men, only those that are not worth pleasing."

"Well, now that women has the vote they ought to plough, an' drive the trains, and let the men sit down inside," continued Jake. But Mrs Bray descended upon him.

"Yes; an' the men ought to come inside an' sweep, an' sew, and have their health ruined for a man's selfishness, an' be tied to a baby and four or five toddlers from six in the mornin' till ten at night, day in and day out, like the women do. What do you think, Mr Eweword?" she inquired of this individual, who had joined the company and awaited the conclusion of her remarks ere he greeted us.

"I think the women ought to vote if they want to. There's nothing to stop 'em voting and doing their housework as well; and the Lord knows it doesn't matter who they vote for, as all the members are only a pack of 'skytes,' after a good billet for themselves. Think I'll have a go for it to see if it would pay better than farmin'," he said, with his mouth extended in a laugh that redeemed the weakness of this feature by exhibiting the beauty of a perfect set of teeth.

"What about women havin' to keep theirselves in subjection?" persisted Uncle Jake. This subject apparently lay near his heart.

"I always think that means for them to take care of themselves, and not bust over the hard dragging work that men were meant for," said Mrs Bray; "for I've always noticed that any man who puts his wife to man's work never comes to no good in the finish. If a man can't float his own boat, and thinks a woman can keep his and her own end up at the same time, she might as well fold her hands from the start, as the little she can do will never keep things goin' and only pave the way for doctors' bills."

"You might try to argue it, but if you believe the Bible you can see there in every page that women ain't meant only to be under men," said the gallant Jake.

"It ain't a case of not believin' the Bible, it's only that we ain't fools enough to believe all the ways people twists it to suit theirselves; men as talks that way is always the sort would be in a benevolent asylum only for some woman keepin' 'em from it," said grandma, coming to the rescue. "Cowards always drag in the Bible to back theirselves up far more than proper people does; and there's always one thing as strikes me in the Bible, an' that is w'en God was going to send His son down in human form, He considered a woman fit to be His mother, but there wasn't a man livin' fit to be His father. I reckon that's a slap in the face from the Almighty hisself that ought to make men more carefuller when they try to make little of women."

Even Uncle Jake collapsed before this, and Mrs Bray ceased contention and veered her talk to gossip.

"Young Walker has been chose by the Opposition League in Noonoon, an' we're goin' to form a committee at once and work for him. Ada Grosvenor is goin' to form a society for educating women how to vote."

"Ada Grosvenor!" exclaimed grandma. "I thought she would be too much a upholder of the men to be the start of anythink like that."

"I don't see how educating one's self how to vote would be making them a putter down of the men," said Dawn.

"Well, it's much the same thing," said Mrs Bray. "For if a woman educates herself on anything it will show her that a lot of the men want puttin' down—a long way down too. You'll see the men will think it's against 'em, and try to squash her and her society, for they're always frightened if you begin to learn the least thing you will find out how you're bein' imposed upon; but they don't care how much you learn in the direction of wearin' yourself out an' slavin' to save money for them to spend on themselves."

"Oh, come now," laughed "Dora"; "we're not all so bad as that!"

"Not at your time of life w'en you're after the girls and pretendin' you're angels to catch 'em; it's after you've got 'em in your power that things change," said Mrs Bray.

The company was now further enlarged by the arrival of Ernest, soon followed by a young lady I had not previously met—a tall brown-eyed girl, with pleasant determination in every line of her well-cut face, and who

proved to be the young lady under discussion — Miss
Ada Grosvenor, daughter of the owner of the farm ad-
joining Bray's and Clay's.

Her errand was to invite Dawn to join the society she
was promoting.

She explained it was not for the support of a party, but
for the exchange and search of knowledge that should
direct electresses to exercise their long-withheld right in a
worthy manner. I listened with pleasure to the thought-
ful and earnest ideals to be discerned underlying the girl's
practically expressed ideas, and delighted in the humorous
intelligence flashing from her clear eyes, and was alto-
gether favourably impressed with her as a type of woman-
hood—one of the best extant.

She conversed with the elder members of the party and
Ernest, and this left "Dora" Eweword in charge of Carry
and Dawn. His giggle was much in evidence. Between
blasts of it he could be heard inviting the girls to a pull
on the river, and they presently set off round the corner
of Miss Flipp's bedroom leading to the flights of wooden
steps down to the boats under the naked willows. The
nature of the one swift glance that travelled after them
from Ernest's eyes did not escape my observation, so I
suggested that he, Miss Grosvenor, and myself should
follow a good example, and we did. I knew it would be
a relief to him to overtake Ewewood, pull past him with
ease, and leave him a speck in the distance, as he did.
I felt a satisfaction in noting Dawn watch his splendid
strokes, and Miss Grosvenor's animated conversation with
him and enthusiastically expressed admiration of his
rowing. She was not so exacting in the matter of de-
tail as Dawn, and red hair did not prevent her from
enjoying the company of a splendid specimen of the

opposite sex when she had the rare good fortune of encountering him.

"That's a fine stamp of a girl," he cordially remarked as, having at her request pulled the boat to the edge of the stream, she landed and sprang up the bank for ferns; but not by any inveiglement could I induce him to give an opinion of Dawn, which was propitious of her being his real lady. When we pulled down stream again between the fertile farm-lands spread with occasional orange and lemon groves, beautiful with their great crops of yellowing fruit, we found that the other party were already deserting their craft.

"We had to give it best. Mr Eweword soon got winded. I never saw any one pull a boat so splendidly as you do, Mr Ernest," called the outspoken Carry, who had not acquired the art of paying a compliment to one member of a party without running *amok* of the feelings of another. Eweword, despite his shapely and imposing bulk, had not developed his athletic possibilities so much as those of the gourmand, and, reddening to the roots of his stubbed hair, he looked the reverse of pleased with the tactless young woman,—an expression usually to be found on the countenance of one or more members of a company following the publication of her opinions.

Miss Grosvenor and Ernest continued to chat with such apparent enjoyment that Dawn said pointedly—

"Pooh! there's no art in pulling a boat; any galoot with a little brute force can do that,"—a remark having the desired effect, for the young Breslaw feigned not to hear, his face rivalled the colour of "Dora's," and his remarks grew absent.

"Oh, I don't know," persisted Carry, "I know plenty of galoots,—they're the only sort of men there are in the Noonoon district, and they can't row for sour apples."

Dawn singled out "Dora" Eweword, and went up the bank with him, leaving the remainder of us together. Miss Grosvenor favoured us with a cordial invitation to partake of the hospitality of her home during the following evening; and delighted with the intelligence and go of the girl, I was pleased to accept. Ernest said he would be delighted to escort me, but Carry said she had her work to do, and had no time to run about to people's places. Miss Grosvenor received this with a merry twinkle in her eye, and said to me—

"Well, Dawn will come to show you the way. It is an uncomfortable path if you don't know it;" and with this she bade good afternoon and ran around the orchard among the square weed and wild quince, across an area abounding in lines of barbed-wire.

Ernest too departed in a triangular direction leading to the curious old bridge spanning the stream.

"What makes him hang about here so long?" asked Carry. "Has he a girl in the district? Do you think he seems gone on Dawn?"

"Perhaps it's Carry?"

"No such luck. I wish he were. I suppose he has money. They say over where he boards he has a set of rooms to himself, and is very liberal. What would he be doing up here so long?"

"He doesn't publish his business. Perhaps he's staying in this nice quiet nook to write a book or something," I said idly, by way of accounting for his idleness, or the curious might have set to work to discover more of his doings than he wished to get abroad just then.

"He doesn't look much like the fools that write books,

but every one is writing one these days. I know of five or six about Noonoon even ; it seems to be a craze."

"Perhaps a cycle!"

"I often wonder who is going to read 'em all and do the work."

This brought us to Clay's, Carry supporting me on her arm, and thus ended her discourse.

Dora stayed for tea, but it was a dull meal, as Dawn now appeared desirous of repelling him.

Andrew, who on account of his drubbing had been very subdued during dinner, had regained his usual form, and when Uncle Jake, to whom the freeing of women seemed an unabating irritation, remarked—

"Who's this young Walker? All the women will be mad for him because he's good-looking and got a soft tongue. They ought to stick to the present member who is known, this other fellow hasn't been heard of;" his grand-nephew replied—

"Like Uncle Jake; he's been in the municipal council fifteen years and never got heard of ; he ought to put up an' see would the women go for him, because he's never been heard of an' is a bit good-lookin'."

"Well, there's one thing to his credit, an' that is, he's lived over sixty years an' never been heard of stealing fruit out of people's gardens, an' as for looks—' Han'some is who han'some does,'" said grandma, which effected the collapse of Andrew. In the Clay household there were ever current reminders of the truth of the old proverb, warning people in glass-houses to abstain from stone-throwing.

Dawn did not appear before me that night until I opened my door and called—

"Lady Fair, the kimono awaits thy perfumed presence!"

"I don't want to come to-night; I feel as scotty as a bear with a sore head."

"But I want you—youth must ever give way to grey hairs."

With that she appeared, and throwing herself backward on my bed, thrust her arms crossly above her head amid a tumble of soft bright hair.

"Youth, health, beauty, and lovers not lacking, what excuse have you for being out of tune? I want you to pilot me to tea at Grosvenor's to-morrow evening. Miss Grosvenor has invited you, Ernest, and myself."

"She just wants Ernest—she's terribly fond of the men."

"Well, did you ever see a normal girl who wasn't, and Mr Ernest is a man worth being fond of—I dearly love him myself."

"Pooh! I don't see anything nice about him," said Dawn aggressively.

"But you'll come to tea, won't you?"

"No, I can't. I never go to Grosvenors. Grandma doesn't care for them. She says he was only a pig buyer, and settled down there about the time she came here, and now they try to ape the swells and put on airs. They only come here to try to get on terms with some of the swell men. I wouldn't take him over there to please her if I were you."

"That's where you and I differ. I would just like to please them, and I'm sure it will do Ernest good to be in the company of such a pleasant and sensible girl as Ada Grosvenor."

"Yes, he'd want something to do him good, if I'm any judge."

Dawn's pretty mouth and chin were so querulous that I had to turn away to smile.

"So you won't come to tea?"

"I can't; I'd like to please you," she said somewhat softening, "but I've promised 'Dora' Eweword I'll go out rowing with him again to-morrow. He says he has something to say to me."

"He's been going to say this something a long time."

"Yes, but I stave him off. I know what it is right enough, and I don't want to hear it; but I suppose I had better please grandma."

"So you like him?"

"No, I detest him, and feel like smacking him on the mouth just where his underlip sticks out farther than the top one, every time he speaks; but what am I to do? I'd never be let go on the stage, and I might as well marry him as any one."

"Why marry any one? At nineteen, or ninety for that matter, there is no imperative hurry. To marry a man you dislike because you cannot attain your ambition is surely very silly indeed. Would you not love 'Dora' if you could go on the stage?"

"I wouldn't be seen in a forty-acred paddock with him. I'd like some man who had travelled, not an old Australian thing just living about here. I'd like an Englishman who'd take me home to England."

"You mustn't disparage your countrymen while I'm listening, as you'll find no better in any country or clime. Always remember they were among the first to enfranchise their women, and thus raise them above the status of chatteldom and merchandise."

"They only gave us the vote because they had to. Women have had to crawl to them for it, and pretend it was a great privilege the sweet darling almighties were allowing us, when all the time it has been our right, and they were selfish cowards who deserve no thanks for with-holding it so long. And they gave it that grudgingly and are that narked about it, it makes me sick."

"Of course, when the matter is stripped to bare facts, the truth of your remarks is irrefutable, but we must gauge things comparatively, and remember how many other nations won't even grudgingly free their women. If you don't like Eweword I can't see any pressing neces-sity to think of marriage at all."

"Oh, well, I'd have it done then and wouldn't be everlasting plagued on the subject," she said with the unreasonableness of irritability.

"Would it not be better though to wait a little while in hopes of a better choice?"

"But I suppose it will always be the same. Any man at all worth consideration is sure to be married or at any rate is engaged."

Here was the clue to her irritation. It was that im-aginary young lady of Ernest Breslaw's. Had she been a man, ere this she would have plunged into vigorous attempt to dislodge that or any other rival, no matter how assured his position, but being a woman and compelled to await "The idiot Chance her imperial Fate," the effect of such suppression on so robust and strenuous a nature was this form of hysteria.

"Well, what about a struggle for the desire of your heart? Undoubtedly you have, if well trained, sufficient voice to be a great asset on the stage, but it would take at the very least two years' hard work under a good master before it would be in the least fit for public use."

"I'd be twenty-one then."

"You are just at a good age to stand vigorous training."

"But what's the use of talking," she said hopelessly,

"you don't know how mad grandma is against the stage. She says she'd rather see me in my grave, and I feel I'd never prosper if I went against her."

"Very likely her point of view is founded on hard facts, but training your voice isn't going on the stage, and in two years, if you are able to sing decently, perhaps no one will be so anxious as your grandma that you should be heard,—I've heard of such a case before;" and I didn't add that two years was a long way ahead for an old woman of seventy-six, and also for a girl to whom study was not quite a fetich, and ample time for the or some knight to have come to the rescue. These thoughts were not for publication, as they might have made me appear a traitor to the prejudices of one party and the desire of the other, whereas I was loyal to them both.

"It would be lovely if you could get on the soft side of grandma, but I'm afraid it's impossible. Fancy being able to sing and please people, and travel about in nice cities away from dusty, dreary, slow old Noonoon," said the girl, the crossness melting from her pretty face and giving place to radiance.

She toyed with some silk scarves of mine, and between whiles said—

"Isn't it funny some people think one thing good and others don't. No one around here wants to be on the stage but me, or seems to understand that actresses are made out of ordinary people like you and me. 'Dora' doesn't know anything about the stage, but Mr Ernest does. He doesn't think them terrible women, and says that his best woman friend was an actress once. If you thought grandma could be brought round at all I wouldn't go out with Dora to-morrow, I'd go with you to get out of it. Mr Ernest seemed to be very pleased with

Ada Grosvenor; is she the same style as his young lady?"

This question wasn't asked because Dawn was transparent, but because I had led her to believe I was dense.

"No, not at all," I replied.

"What is she like?"

"She's about five feet five, and has a plump, dimpling figure. Her hair is bright brown, and her nose is an exquisitely cut little straight one. (Here I observed Dawn casting surreptitious glances in the mirror opposite.) Her eyes are bright blue with long dark lashes, and she has a mouth too pretty to describe, fitted up with a set of the loveliest natural teeth one could see in these days of the dentist; it is so perfect that it seems unnatural and a sad pity that it should sometimes be the outlet of censorious remarks about less beautiful sisters, but its owner is very young and not surrounded by the best of influences at present, and no doubt will have better sense as she grows older."

"What's her name?"

"Now you want to know too much, but I never knew another girl with such a beautiful one."

"She must be a beauty altogether," said Dawn rather satirically.

"She would be if she would only guard against being cross at times, but you must not breathe this to a soul as I'm only going on supposition. Young Ernest isn't engaged to her, but I've seen him with her once or twice, and he looked so pleased that I suspected him of kind regards, as no man could help admiring her."

"Is that all?" she said in a tone of relief; "he mightn't

care for her at all.   Just walking about with her and looking happy isn't any criterion.   Men are always doing that with every girl."

"Dora didn't look happy with me to-night then—how do you account for that?"

She accounted for it with a merry laugh, as curled in the silk kimono she remained in possession of my nightly couch.

I was espousing this girl's cause because I could not bear to see her honest, wholesome youth and beauty making fuel for disappointment and bitterness as mine had done.   There had been no one to help me attain the desire—the innocent, just, and normal desire of my girl-hood's heart,—no one to lend a hand, till my heart had broken with slavery and disappointment, and at less than thirty-five all that remained for me was a little barren waiting for its feeble fluctuating pumping to cease.

The girl presently fell asleep, so I covered her, kimono and all, and extinguishing the light, lay down beside what had once been a tiny baby, whose feeble life opening with the day had been nurtured on the milk of old Ladybird, the spotted cow with a dew-lap and a crumpled horn. She was now, I trusted, enjoying the reward of her earthly labours in that best of heavens we love to picture for the dear animals that have served us well, and but for whose presence the world would be dreary indeed, while the sleep of her beautiful foster-daughter had advanced to hold dreams of jewelled gowns, thrilling solos, travel, and splendid young husbands who could do no wrong, but she knew no room for thought of "Dora," who on the morrow was to row her on the Noonoon.   He might as well have relinquished the chase, for his chances here had grown as faint as those of pretty Dora Cowper—

whose leg he classically stated he had pulled—had grown with him.

Ah, well, there is a law of retribution in all things, direct or indirect, visible or invisible.

I lay awake a long time contemplating the best way of approaching Grandma Clay in regard to Dawn's singing lessons. One by one the passenger trains streamed into Noonoon, halted a panting five minutes at the station, then rumbled over the strange old iron-walled bridge, slowed down again to the little siding of Kangaroo on the other side, from whence up, up, the mountain-sides above the fertile valley, leaving the peaceful agriculturists soundly asleep after their toil. The heavy "goods" lumbered by unceasingly, the throbbing of their great engines, their signalling, shunting, and tooting proving a perennial delight to me, comforting me with the knowledge that I still could feel a pulsation from the great population centres where my fellows congregate.

It had lulled me to doziness, when I was aroused by the electric alarm-bell, the purpose of which was to warn folk when a train neared the bridge. A very necessary device, as there was but one bridge for all traffic, it being cut into two departments by three high iron walls that shut out an exquisite view of the river, and confined and intensified the rumble of trains in a manner well calculated to inspire the least imaginative of horses with the fear that the powers of evil had broken loose about them. The alarm-bell was humanly contrary in the discharge of its duty, and rang long and loudly when there was no train, and was not to be heard at all when they were rushing by in numbers. On this occasion, there being no train to drown its blatant voice, it so disturbed me that I was keenly alive to a dialogue that was proceeding in Miss Flipp's room.

"You must go away, I tell you," said Mr Pornsch. "A nice thing it would be if a man in *my* position were implicated."

"I didn't think a man of *your* class would be so cruel," sobbed the girl.

In rejoinder the man admitted one of the truths by which our civilisation is besmirched.

"There's only one class of men in dealing with women like you."

Then fell a silence, during which Dawn turned in her sleep, and I placed her head more comfortably lest she should awake and hear what was proceeding.

Not that it would in any way have sullied her, for her virtue, by sound heredity and hardy training, was no hot-house plant, liable to shrivel and die if not kept in a certain temperature, but was a sturdy tree, like the tall white-trunked young gums of her native forests, on which the winds of knowledge could blow and the rains of experience fall without in any way mutilating or impairing its reliability and beauty. It was for the sake of our poor sister wayfarer who was on a terrible thoroughfare, amid robbers and murderers, but who did not want her plight to be known, that I did not wish Dawn to awake.

FOURTEEN.

THE PASSING OF THE TRAINS.

NEXT morning, when Andrew and I had finished the separator, grandma came over to inspect the work. She sniffed round the dishes and cans, which barely passed muster, and then descended upon the table by running her slender old forefinger along the eaves, with the result that it came up soiled with the greasy slush that careless wiping had left there.

"Look at that, you dirty good - for - nothink young shaver; if the inspector came round we'd most likely lose our licence for it, an' it's no fault of mine. If a great lump your age can't be depended on for nothink, I don't know what the world is coming to. I have to be responsible for everythink that goes on your back and into your stummick, and yet you can't do a single thing. You think I'm everlastin' joring, but I have to be. Some day, if ever you have a house of your own, you'll know how hard it is."

"I'm goin' to take jolly fine care I never have no house of me own. The game ain't worth the candle," responded Andrew; "I reckon them as comes and lives in the place, like some of them summer-boarders, and orders us about as if they was Lord Muck an' we wasn't anybody, has the best of it."

"That ain't the point. I'm ashamed of that table. W'en I was young no one ever had to speak to me about things once, before I knew. Once I left drips round the end of my table, and me mother come along and 'Martha,' says she——"

"It's a wonder the wonderful Jim Clay didn't say it," muttered the irreverent representative of the degenerate rising generation *sotto voce.*

"'If that's the way you wash a table,' says she, 'no blind man would choose you for his wife,' for that was the way they told if their sweetheart was a good housekeeper, by feelin' along the table w'en they was done washin' up."

"An' what did you say?" interestedly inquired Andrew.

"I didn't say nothink. In them days young people didn't be gabbing back to their elders w'en they was spoke to, but held their mag an' done their work proper," she crushingly replied.

"But I was thinkin'," said Andrew quite unabashed, "that you was a terrible fool to be took in with that yarn. For who'd want to be married by a blind man, an' I reckon that blind men oughtn't be let to marry at all, and I think anyhow he ought to have been glad to get any woman, without sneakin' around an' putting on airs about being particular," he earnestly contended.

"But that ain't the point, anyhow," said she.

"Well, what did you tell it to me for, grandma?"

"Hold your tongue," said the old lady irately; "sometimes you might argue with me, but there's reason in everythink, an' if you don't have that table scrubbed and cleaned proper by the next time I come round you'll hear about it."

With this she walked farther on towards the pig-sty and cow-bails, and considering this a good opportunity for private conversation I went with her, remarking in a casual manner—

"Your granddaughter has a very good voice."

"Yes; a good deal better than *some people* that think they can sing like Patti, and set theirselves up about it."

"Yes; but she badly needs training."

"She sings twice as well as some that has been trained and fussed with."

"Probably; but she requires training to preserve the voice. She produces it unnaturally, and in a few years the voice will be cracked and spoilt."

"All the better, an' then she'll give up wanting to go on the stage with it."

"Is there anything frightful in that?" I said gently. "A great many mothers would give all they possessed to get their daughters on the stage. It is an exploded idea to think the stage a bad place."

"A lot is always tellin' me that, an' I believed them till I went to see for meself, and the facts was too much of a eye-opener for me. I'll keep to me own opinions for the future. It will be three years ago this month, Dawn prevailed upon me to go to a play there was a lot of blow about, an' I was never so ashamed in me life. I didn't expect much considerin' the way I was rared regardin' theayters, but it beat all I ever see."

"What was it?"

"I don't know the name, but it was a character of

a play. There was women in it must have been forty
by the figure of them, and they had all their bosoms
bare, and showed their knees in little short skirts.
They stood in rows and grinned—the hussies! They
ought to have set down an' hid theirselves for shame!
I thought we must have made a mistake and got into
a fast show, but we read in the paper after that among
the audience was all the big bugs, an' they seemed to
be enjoyin' theirselves an' laughing as if it was a in-
tellectual, respectable entertainment. I wanted to get
up an' leave, but Dawn coaxed me an' I give in, an'
thought the next might be better, but it was worse. I
give you my word for it, there was hussies there on
that stage, before respectable people's eyes, trying all
they knew to make men be bad. They was fast pure
and simple, just the same as some Jim Clay told me
about once when he went to Sydney on his own. The
way he described their carryin's on was just like them
actresses on the stage, an' me a respectable married
woman who's rared a family, havin' paid to look at
them! I was ashamed to hold me head up after it for
a long time. 'It's only actin', grandma,' says Dawn,
but to think that people would act things like that;
no good modest woman would ever do it, an' the Bible
strictly warns us to abstain from the appearance of
evil. An' even that wasn't all; they come out an'
kissed one another — married women supposed to be
kissing other men. What sort of a example was that to
be setting other men an' women? It was the lowerin'est
thing I ever see. I told Dawn she was not to breathe
where we had been, an' from that day to this I never
would have a actor or a actress in my house. I'd just
as soon have a *real* loud woman as one who gets out

on a stage where every one is lookin' at her and pre-
tends to be one. She'd have no shame to stand between
her and the bad. Oh no! there must be reason in
everythink. I was prepared for a terrible lot of fools
and rot, but that I should be so lowered was a eye-
opener."

"I feel exactly the same in regard to the stage, Mrs
Clay, but I like concerts, when the singers just come
out and sing—do you not?"

"That ain't so bad, I admit."

"You would not object to Dawn singing on a plat-
form, would you?"

"No; doesn't she often sing on the platform in Noo-
noon? They're always after her for some concert or
another. It's a bad plan to sing too much for them.
They don't thank you for it. They'd only say we're
tired of him or her, and the one who'd be sour an'
wouldn't sing often would be considered great."

"Well, let her have lessons, so she could sing with
greater ease at these concerts."

"She can sing well enough for that. It would be
throwing away money for nothink."

"But if trained she could sometimes command a fee."

"I've got plenty to keep her without that," said the
old lady, bridling, "and it might give her stronger notions
for the stage."

I was thankful that I had never published my calling.

"I had me own ideas of them before—walkin' about,
and everythink they do or say they're wonderin' what
people is thinkin' of them, and if they're observin' what
great bein's they are. An' I've seen 'em here—goin'
in fer drink an' all bad practices, and w'en I remonstrate
with 'em, 'It's me temperament,' says they, an' led me

to believe by the airs of them that this temperament makes 'em superior to the likes of ordinary human bein's like me an' you; an' this temperament that makes 'em not fit to do honest common work, but is makin' 'em low crawlers, is the thing that at the same time makes 'em superior. I don't see meself how the two things can be reconciled. There must be reason in everythink."

"If you want to turn your granddaughter from the stage, let her start vocal training. You'll see that before twelve months she'll have enough of it. It would keep her content for the present, and in the meantime she might marry," I contended.

"If I could be sure she wouldn't come in contact with them actin' and writin' fools; if she was to marry one of them it would be all up with her. Do you know anythink about teachers?"

"Yes; I would be only too pleased to see to that part of it. Your granddaughter is a great pleasure to me. She gives me some interest in life which, having no relations and being unfit for permanent occupation, I would otherwise lack."

"Well, I'm sure Dawn would interest anybody, and I think you're a good companion for her. She seems to have took up with you, and you've evidently been a person that's seen somethink, an' can tell her this, that, an' the other, but as for that she don't want no tellin' to be better than most. *Some people!* —— " Grandma always worked herself up to a pitch of congested choler when these unworthy individuals were mentioned.

"I'll think about the singin' lessons if they ain't beyond reason. She's been terrible good lately, and

deserves somethink. Here's Larry Witcom arrove, an'
there's Carry gone out to him. I want to see him me-
self; he's been a little too strong with his prices lately,
but he's the obliginest feller in many ways. I don't hear
anythink about it not bein' Carry's week in the kitchen
w'en Larry comes. She's always ready to give Dawn a
hand then. But we was all young once; I can remember
w'en I worked a point, whether it was me turn or not,
to get near Jim Clay."

"Dawn, I think the battle for the singing lessons is
half won," I said to that individual when I met her
privately a few minutes later.

"Really, it can't be true!" said the girl with an in-
tonation of delight, as she drew a tea-towel she had been
washing through her shapely hands and wrung it dry.

Uncle Jake then entered, and cut short further private
discussion.

"There, Dawn!" he said; tossing a pair of trousers on
the kitchen-table, "the seat of them is out, an' I want
to put 'em on to do a little blacksmithin'—they're dirty."

"That's easy to be seen and known too, as some
people's things are always dirty," said she. "When do
you want them?"

"At once."

"At once! You'd come in the middle of cooking some
pastry and want a woman to put patches on a dirty old
pair of trousers, and then want to know why the dinner
wasn't up to tick; and besides, it's Carry's week in the
house."

For Dawn's sake I would have offered to do the patching,
but feared Uncle Jake might suspect me of matrimonial
designs upon him, such being the conceit of old men.

"I never go to Carry," he snapped, "an' it's a pity your

mother wasn't alive instead of you, she could put a patch
on in five minutes any time you asked her, but she never
spent her time in roarin' and bellerin' round after a vote;"
and so saying Uncle Jake disappeared, leaving his grand-
niece with her pretty pink cheeks deepened to scarlet,
and a spark in her blue eyes.

"The old dog! if he wasn't grandma's brother I'd hate
him. It's always these crawling old things who can do
nothing themselves, and have to be kept by a woman,
who are always the worst at trying to make women's
position lower, and talk about them as inferior. He's
always after a woman to do this and to do that, and com-
paring her — I'd like to see the woman, mother or
father — who could put a patch on those pants in five
minutes."

"There's one way it could be done in the time," I said,
calling to mind a prank related by a gay little friend—
"clap it on with cobbler's wax."

Dawn's eyes danced, and the irritation receded from
the corners of the pretty mouth as, procuring a piece of
cloth and a lump of cobbler's wax, she did the deed in
less than five minutes, and Uncle Jake contentedly re-
ceived his trousers, while I departed to put in some
more time with my friend Andrew, without telling her
there might be a sequel to patching trousers with
cobbler's wax.

"Well, Andrew, how goes the scrubbing?"

"Oh, great! Look at that!" said he, drawing back to
exhibit a really clean table; and as it would not have
conduced to our friendship had I pointed out that it
had been arrived at at the expense of slushing the lime-
washed wall and the stand of the separator, I wisely
kept silent.

"There! I reckon me grandma nor Jim Clay neither never done a table better," he said with enviable self-appreciation. "You know I reckon them old yarns about the people bein' so good w'en they was young is a little too thin to stand washin'—don't you? You've only got to take the things the wonderful Jim Clay and me grandma done w'en they was courtin',—you get her on a string to tell you,—an' if Dawn done the same with any of the blokes now, she'd jolly soon hear about it; an' as for old Jake there, I reckon I'd be able to put him through meself at his own age—don't you? Anyhow, I'm full of farmin'. It's only fools an' horses sweat themselves, all the others go in for auctioneering, or parliament, or something, and have a fine screw comin' in for nothing."

"But think of those water-melons," I said; for as a subject of conversation he most frequently and most lovingly referred to these.

"But I could buy a waggon-load of 'em for one day's pay, an' not have any tuggin' and scratchin' with 'em. Melons ain't too stinkin', but lor', tomatoes is a stunner! They rotted till you couldn't stand the smell of them, and it would give a billy-goat the pip to hear them mentioned. There was no sale, and the blow-flies took to 'em. One man down here had thirty acres. I'm goin' to be somethink, so I can make a bit of money. No one thinks anythink of you if you ain't got plenty money. You know how you feel if a person has plenty money, you think twice as much of him as if he hasn't any. There's nothink to be made at farmin', delvin' and scrapin' your eyeballs out for no return," said this youngster, who did barely enough to keep him in exercise, who had been fed to repletion, and comfortably clothed and bedded all his sixteen years.

Luncheon or dinner was enlivened by an altercation between Dawn and her uncle.

The blacksmithing to which he had referred was the act of sitting down beside the forge, where he had grown so warm that the sequel to mending trousers with cobbler's wax had eventuated. The melted wax had attached the garment to the old man's person, and he had sat—his sitting capacity was incalculable—until it had cooled again, and on rising suffered an amount of discomfort it would be graceful to leave to the imagination. Uncle Jake however was not so considerate, and aired his grievance in a manner too brutally real for imagination.

To do her justice Dawn did not think of the joke going thus far, so I attempted to take the blame, but she would not have this.

"I want him to think I knew how it would turn out. I'd do it to him every day if I could."

Grandma fortunately took her part, and the mirth of Andrew and Carry was very genuine.

"I reckon I was as smart as my mother that time," giggled Dawn, as she carried in the dinner.

"It would have been a funny joke if you played it on some good-humoured young feller," said grandma, "but Jake there is entitled to some kind of consideration, because he is old and crotchety."

"I'd play it on 'Dora' Eweword," said Dawn, "only that he might stick here so that he'd never move at all if I didn't take care."

The first moment we had in private she took opportunity of saying—

"I think I'll go over to Grosvenor's with you this

evening, but not to tea. I'll go over to bring you home, if you'll help me make some excuse to get out of going rowing with 'Dora.'"

"Why not come to tea? that would be sufficient excuse."

"Oh, but they try to ape the swells, and grandma doesn't like them; but I'll be sure to go for you after it, and that will save Mr Ernest coming round with you."

I thanked her, though her escort was not at all necessary, seeing that instead of saving Ernest it would only make his presence surer. There being nothing else to do during the afternoon, I awaited the time of setting out for the Grosvenor's, who tried to ape the swells—the swells of Noonoon! These being, as far as I could gather, the doctors, the lawyer, a couple of bank managers on a salary somewhere about £250 per annum, the Stip. Magistrate, and one or two others—surely an ordinarily harmless and averagely respectable section of the community, in aping whom one would be in little danger of being called upon to act up to an etiquette as intricate and tyrannous as that in use at court.

In the old days the town had been the terminus of the train, and it had squatted at the foot of the mountains, while strings of teams carried the goods up the great western road out to Bathurst and beyond, to Mudgee, Dubbo, and Orange. Nearly all the old houses—grandma's and Grosvenor's among them—had been hotels in those days, when the miles had been ticked off by the square stones with the Roman lettering, erected by our poor old convict pioneers, who blazed many a first track. Every house had found sufficient trade in giving D.T.'s to the burly, roystering teamsters who lived on the roads, dealt in no small quantities, and who did not see their wives and sweethearts every week in the year.

As the afternoon advanced, true to appointment, "Dora" Eweword arrived to take Dawn for a row. His chin was red from the razor, and he looked well in a navy-blue guernsey brightened by a scarlet tie knotted at the open collar, displaying a columnar throat which, if strength were measured by size, announced him capable of supporting not only a Dawn, but a Sunset. He sat on an Austrian chair, for which he was some sizes too large and too substantial, and reddened as he laughed and talked with Carry, till I appeared and spent some time in talking and admiring his appearance until Dawn came upon the scene.

"Well, Dawn," he said, "I'm waiting for this row; are you ready?"

Dawn glanced at me.

"Dawn has promised to chaperon me to-night," I said. Dawn decamped.

"Miss Grosvenor has invited Mr Ernest and me to tea, and to go without a representative of Mrs Grundy, I believe, is not correct in the social life of Noonoon."

Eweword laughed: but his face fell, and his reply showed him less obtuse than he appeared on the surface, seeing he was the first and only person to see through my matchmaking tactics.

"Touting for the red-haired bagman," he said, as Ernest could be seen swinging up the path.

"Supposing I am, what then?" I asked, regarding him with a level glance, and feeling more respect for his intelligence than I had heretofore experienced.

"Oh, well, I suppose all is fair in some things."

He would not say *love*, as that would have admitted too

much, and a lover admitting his passion and a drunkard confessing his disease are exceptions that prove the rule.

His remark was uttered with a broad good nature that would lead him to do and leave undone great things. In a desire to please the present girl he was not above saying he had been "pulling the leg" of the one absent, but he would also be capable of standing aside when he felt deeply—as deeply as he could feel—to allow a better man sea-room; and he was further capable of sufficient humility to think there could be a better man than himself, or so I adjudged him, and being the only narrator of this, the only history in which he is likely to receive mention, this delineation of his character will have to remain unchallenged.

Ernest had a geranium in his button-hole, and looked more immaculately spruce than ever, and even his red hair could not obliterate the fact of his being a goodly sight, and as such grandma recognised him.

"That's a fine sturdy chap," she afterwards observed. "It's a pity he ain't got somethink to do to keep him out of mischief. Is he a unemployed? He don't look like one of these Johnnies that has nothink to do but hang around a street corner and smoke a cigarette."

The two young men measured glances every whit as critically as girls do under similar conditions, and then equally as casually made reference to the weather. Ernest was somewhat overshadowed by Eweword, as the latter was superior in size and cast of features, being fully six feet, while Ernest was not more than five feet nine inches; but as a girl very rarely, if she has a choice, cares most for the handsomest of her admirers, I was not in the least cast down about this.

When it was time for me to depart, Ernest rose too,

but not Dawn. Ernest's face went down, Eweword's brightened.

"Miss Dawn is not coming over now, but later on," I said.

The men's glances reversed once more. As the former and I departed—Ernest carrying a wrap for me—I heard Eweword say—

"Well, come on, Dawn, you're not going to Grosvenor's after all. It seems that old party was only pulling my leg."

Ernest good-naturedly struggled to talk with me, but I spared him the ordeal, and, arrived at Grosvenor's, interestedly studied them to discover what manner of procedure "trying to ape the swells" might be—the swells of Noonoon—the doctor who thought I might "peg out" any minute, and the bank managers and the parsons.

The only difference to be observed between the tea-table at Clay's and Grosvenor's was that at the latter the equivalents of Uncle Jake and Andrew did not appear in a coatless condition, were treated to the luxury of table-napkins, and Mrs Grosvenor, who served, attended to people according to their rank instead of their position at the table, and entrusted them with the sugar-basin and milk-jug themselves. Farther than this there was no distinction, and this was not an alarming one. Certainly Miss Grosvenor, who had not enjoyed half Dawn's educational advantages, did not as glaringly flout syntax, and slang was not so conspicuous in her vocabulary. She and Ernest got on so well that none but my practised eyes could detect that as the evening advanced his brown ones occasionally wandered towards the entrance door, which showed that much as Miss Grosvenor had got him out of his shell, she had not obliterated Dawn.

That young lady arrived at about a quarter to ten, and we started homewards, determining to go a long way round, first by way of the Grosvenor's vehicle road to town, by this gaining the public highway, along which we would walk to the entrance to grandma's demesne. This was preferable to a short-cut and rolling under the barbed-wire fencing in the long grass sopping with dew, which at midnight or thereabouts would stiffen with the soft frosts of this region that would flee before the sun next morning.

Dawn's cheeks were scarlet from rowing on the river with " Dora " Eweword, and she spoke of her jaunt as soon as we got outside, apparently pregnant with the knowledge innate in the dullest of her sex, that the most efficacious way of giving impetus to the love of one lover is to have another.

This, however, is another art which, like good cooking, must be " done to the turn," and in this instance there was danger of it being done too soon, as Ernest's amour had not taken firm root yet; and a man, unless he be either of gigantic pluck or no honour at all, will not hurry to interfere with the secured property of another man.

They chatted in a desultory fashion while I manœuvred to relieve them of my presence. The night was lit by a million stars, paling towards the east, where behind the hills a waning moon was putting in an appearance. The electric lights of the town scintillated like artificial stars, and away down the long valley could be seen here and there the twinkle of a farmhouse light, showing where some held mild wassail or a convivial evening; for there were not many of the agriculturalists, tired from their heavy toil, who were otherwise out of bed at this ungodly hour of the night.

The crisp winter air agreed with me, and I felt un-
usually well.

"Let me walk behind, this night is too glorious to waste
in talking politics, so you young people get out of my
hearing and thresh out your candidate's merit and demerit
and leave me to think," I said, for politics were in the
air and they were touching upon them. They obeyed me,
and soon were lost to view in the dark of the osage and
quince hedges grown as breakwinds on the west of
Grosvenor's orangery. Soon I could not hear their
footfalls, for I stood still to watch the trains pass by.
'Twas the hour of the last division of the Western
passenger mail, bearing its daily cargo of news and
people to the great plains beyond the hills that loomed
faintly in the light of the half moon. Haughtily its huge
first-class engine roared along, and its carriage windows,
like so many warm red mouths, permitted a glimpse of
the folk inside comfortably ensconced for the night. It
slowed across the long viaduct approaching the bridge,
and crossed the bridge itself with a roar like thunder,
then it swerved round a curve to Kangaroo till the
window-lights gave place to its two red eyes at the rear.
As it climbed the first spur of the great range, and all
that could be seen was a belch of flame from the engine-
door as it coaled, something of the old longing awoke
within me for things that must always be far away. The
throbbing engines spoke to my heart, and forgetting its
brokenness, it stirred again to their measure—the rush-
ing, eager measure of ambition, strife, struggle! I was
young again, with youth's hot desire to love and be loved,
and as its old bitter-sweet clamourings rushed over me I
rebelled that my hair was grey and my propeller disabled.
The young folks ahead had put me out of their life as

young folks do, and, measuring the hearts of their seniors
by the white in their hair and the lines around their eyes,
would have been incredulous that I still had capacity for
their own phase. Only the royalty of youth is tendered
love in full measure ; those who fail to attain or
grasp it then find this door, from which comes enticing
perfume and sound of luring music, shut against them for
all time, and no matter how appealingly they may lean
against its portals, it will rarely open again, for they have
been laid by to be sold as remnants like the draper's
goods which have failed to attract a buyer during the brief
season they were displayed. I stood under the whispering
osage and listened to the now distant train puffing its way
over the wild mountains, also to be crossed by the great
road first cut by those whose now long dead limbs had
carried chains — members of a bygone brigade as I was
one of a passing company. But probably they each had
had their chance of love, and the old bitterness upsprung
that mine had not fallen athwart my pathway. Fierce
struggle had always shut me away from similar oppor-
tunity to that enjoyed by the young people ahead.

"Put back your cruel wheel, O Time!" I cried in my
heart, "and give me but one hour's youth again—sweet,
ecstatic youth with the bounding pulse, led by the purple
mirage of Hope, whose sirens whisper that the world's
sweets are sweet and its crowns worth winning. Let me
for a space be free from this dastard age creeping through
the veins, dulling the perspective of life and leadening the
brain, whose carping companions draw attention to the
bitters in the cups of Youth's Delights, and mutter that
the golden crowns we struggle for shall tarnish as soon as
they are placed on our tired brows!" Suddenly my bitter
reverie was broken by the knight and the lady calling in

startled tones. I replied, and presently they were upon me, Dawn very much out of breath.

"Oh, goodness, we thought you were ill again. You have given us such a shock. You should not have been left behind. I was a terrible brute that I didn't harness the pony and drive over for you;" and Ernest came in a slow second with—

"You should have taken my arm," and he wrapped my cloak about me with the high quality of gentleness peculiar to the best type of strong man.

Despite my assurance that I never had felt better, they insisted upon supporting me on either side; so slipping a hand through each of the young elbows conveniently bent, I playfully put the large hand on the right of me over the dimpling one on the left.

"There!" I said, taking advantage of the liberties extended a probable invalid, "I've made a breastwork of the hands of the two dearest young friends I have, so now I cannot fall;" and seeing I put it at that, at that they were content to let it remain, and the big hand very carefully retained the little one, so passive and warm, in its shy grasp. At the gate I dismissed Ernest, and Dawn condescended to remark that he wasn't *quite* such a fool as usual, which interpreted meant that he had not been so guardedly stand-off to her as he sometimes was.

The trains once more entertained my waking hours that night. Under Andrew's tutorage I had learned to distinguish the rumble of a "goods" from the rush of a "passenger," a two-engine haul from a single, and even the heavy voice of the big old "shunter" that lived about the Noonoon station had grown familiar; but the haughtiest of all was a travelling engine attended only by its tender, and speeding by with lightsome action, like a governor thankfully free from officialdom and hampered only by a valet.

Musing on what a little time had elapsed since the work of the passenger trains had been done by the coaches with their grey and bay teams of five, swinging through the town at a gallop, and with their occupants armed to the teeth against bushrangers, I dozed and dreamt. I dreamt that I was in one of the sleeping-cars which had superseded Cobb & Co.'s accommodation for travellers, and that from it I could see in a bird's-eye view not only the magnificent belt of mountains, the bluest in the world, but whirling down their westward slopes with a velocity outstripping the scented winds from sandal ridges and myall plains, I slid across that great western stretch of country where a portion of the railway line runs for a hundred and thirty-six miles without rise or fall or curve in the longest straight ribbon of steel that is known. But ere I reached its end I wakened with a start through something falling in Miss Flipp's room.

Surely I had not slept for more than half an hour, because the light which had shone in the adjoining room as we returned from Grosvenor's was still burning. Presently Miss Flipp put it out, and closing her door after her, stealthily made her way from the house. She trod cautiously and noiselessly, but her gown caught on the lower sprouts of the ragged old rose-bushes beside the walks, and though she took a long time to open the little gate opening towards the wharves and the narrow pathway running along the river-bank to the bridge, it creaked a little on its rusty hinges, so that I heard it and fell to awaiting the girl's return.

I waited and waited, and beguiled the time by counting the trains that passed with the quarter hours.   There were so many that I soon lost count. This line carried goods to the great wheat- and wool-growing west and brought its produce to the city. Many of the noisy trains were laden with "fifteen hundred" and "two thousand" lots of "fats," and the yearly statistics dealing with the sales at Homebush chronicled their total numbers as millions. From beyond Forbes, Bourke, and Brewarrina they came in trucks to cross the bridge spanning the noble stream at the mountain's base, but they never went back again to the great plains where they had basked in plenty or staggered through droughts as the fickle seasons rose and fell. The voracious, insatiable maw of the city was a grave for them all, and the commercial greed which falls so heavily on the poor dumb beasts in which it traffics, caged them so tightly for their last journey that by the time they reached Noonoon they were bruised and cramped and not a few trodden under foot. The empty trucks going west again made the longest trains, as they could be laden with nothing but a little wire-netting for settlers who were fighting the rabbits, and were easily distinguishable from other "goods," as when they clumsily and jerkily halted the clanking of their couplings and the bumping of their buffers could be heard for a mile or more down the valley. The splendid atmosphere intensified all sounds and carried them an unusual distance, and many a time at first I was wont to be aroused from sleep in the night with a notion that the thundering trains were going to run right over the house.

On the night in question I had not heard Miss Flipp return from her midnight tryst, though all the luggage trains had passed and it neared the time of the first division of the up or citywards mail from the west, which was the earliest train to arrive in town from the country

daily.   It passed Noonoon in the vicinity of 4 A.M.—a
radiant hour in the summer dawn, but then in winter, the
time when bed is most alluring, when the passengers'
breath congeals on the window-panes, they complain that
the foot-warmers have got cold, and give yet one more
twist to their comforters and another tug at their 'possum
or wallaby rugs.   This train passed with its shaking
thunder, drew into Noonoon for refreshments, then on
and on with noisy energy, but still Miss Flipp did not
return.

I concluded that she must have decided to leave us in
this fashion, or that I had missed her entry during the
rumble of a passing train, or mayhap I had snoozed for a
moment, or perhaps an hour, as the unsympathetic heavy
sleepers aver the insomnists must do; and ceasing to be
on the alert any longer, I really slept.

FIFTEEN.

ALAS! MISS FLIPP!

I HASTENED to appear at the half-past seven breakfast, as no excuse for non-appearance was taken, and the only concession made to Miss Flipp, who had not been present at it for some time, was that she could make herself a cup of cocoa when she chose to rise. For this meal grandma ladled out the porridge and flavoured it with milk and sugar in the usual way.

"I say, Dawn, which of them blokes, Ernest or Dora, is the best boat-puller?" inquired Andrew as he received his portion. "You were mighty stingy with the sugar, grandma!"

"Dora isn't in it," responded Carry. "Mr Ernest could get ahead of him every time."

"So he ought!" said Dawn. "His ears are the size of a pair of sails, and would pull him along."

Thus was published another defect in my knight, till I feared that it must be only my partial gaze that discerned a knight at all.

"Dear me," interposed grandma, "a man can't look or speak or walk but he's this, that, and the other. Things weren't so in my day. Of course there were some things that were took exception to, but there must be reason in everythink, an' I don't see what difference a man's ears being a little big makes. My father's ears—your great-grandfather's—was none too small, an' he was always a good kind man."

"I don't care if my own ears were big, it wouldn't make me like them," said the irrepressible Dawn; and grandma had just finished what she termed "dosing" the last plate of porridge, when we were interrupted by the appearance of policeman Danby at the French lights. There was nothing strange in this appearance of the embodiment of the law, even at that early hour of the morning; for the huge young man with the rollicking face and curly hair, though a good officer in attending to his work, was a better in admiring a girl, which, after all, taking matters at the base, is the chief and most vital business of life, as, were it neglected, there would be no police or populace.

Well, as I said, policeman Danby knew a pretty girl when he saw one, and there being two at Clay's, that household, in the way of the law, was very well looked after indeed; and for the purpose of escaping the annual registration fee, Andrew's little dog, "Whiskey," had remained a puppy as long as some young ladies tarry under thirty.

Carry on rising to admit the caller had the usual tussle with the door, while grandma reiterated uncomplimentary remarks about the "blessed feller" who should some time since have effected repairs, and Danby upon entering wore an extremely grave face, looked neither at Dawn nor Carry, but addressed himself straight to Mrs Martha Clay.

"I have to trouble you about a very unpleasant matter," he said, and cruelly all eyes went to poor

Andrew, as it was but recently he had to be chased home for breaking the law.

"Yes," said grandma, rising actively, and though a flurried colour came to the old withered cheek, the spark of battle flashed in the stern blue-grey eye.

"Could I see you privately?" said Danby.

"Certainly," said Mrs Clay: "but I'm not fond of secrecy; things is better open, and this is the first time in my life I've had to be seen secret by the police. Come this way."

We said nothing, but dropped our feeding tools and waited in suspense, till in less than a minute grandma thrust her head in the dining-room door.

"For mercy's sake, Dawn, look in Miss Flipp's room and see is she there."

Dawn rose in a hurry and boxed Andrew's ears as she passed, because he too rose and tumbled over his chair in her way.

"Some people ought to tie themselves up to be out of the way," she ejaculated.

"Miss Flipp is not in her room," she presently called, "and her bed is smooth and made up."

"God save us, then! Mr Danby says she's drownded in the river," exclaimed her grandma. "What's to be done?"

"We'll spare you all the trouble possible, Mrs Clay," said the man, with the respect always tendered the old dame; "but I'm afraid it's a suicide. Some men going to work on the new viaduct just noticed her clothes sticking up as they crossed the bridge at daylight and reported it, and I was sent down. We've taken the body to Jimmeny's pub., and sent for the coroner, at all events."

Dawn and Andrew howled together in a frightened

manner, while the sensible Carry, who never lost her head, admonished them—

"Don't be jackdaws. That won't mend matters. Perhaps it isn't half as bad as some make out. Things never are when you get the right hang of them."

"Things are bad enough anyhow, but the way to mend 'em ain't to be snivelling," rapped out grandma, giving Dawn and Andrew a shaking that braced them up.

Things were indeed bad enough, and nothing could mend them. They had gone beyond repair. It transpired that my senses had been correct, and poor Miss Flipp had *not* returned that moonlit night as I lay listening to the passing trains. She had ended her ruined life by weighting her feet and dropping into the pretty stretch of water under the bridge, where the locomotives rushed by like thunder, and from where could be seen the twinkling electric lights of one of the oldest towns in Australia.

The inquest, at which we all had to appear, elicited information that fairly stood poor grandma's hair on end. It was a great blow to find that she had been harbouring a woman who was not as Cæsar's wife, and that it was fear of the penalty of her divergence from what is accepted as virtue, had driven her to take her life ere she had transmitted the tribulation of being to a nameless child.

Nothing was cleared up regarding her antecedents. The person by whom she was supposed to be recommended to Mrs Clay knew of no such individual, and no one came to claim her.

Her uncle, it was discovered, had a day or two previously sailed for America on urgent business, and after the girl's death an affectionate letter for her arrived from him. She had left nothing to fix the blame where it belonged, but with a misdirected loyalty so common in her sex had paid all the debt her frail self.

The post on the day of her death brought me a pathetic little note, in which she stated that she wished to bear the whole blame; a woman always had to in any case, and as she could not face it she had decided upon death. She had written this to me because she felt I had had an inkling of how matters had been with her, and she thanked me that I had kept silent, in conjunction with the observation that it was not usual for such as she to meet with forbearance from those who had had sense to preserve their respectability. Ah, the regret that consumed me that I had not risked the unpopularity of interference and sought her confidence. I might have been able to have saved her from such an end!

I kept my knowledge to myself. It would scarcely have hurt Mr Pornsch. Under the British Constitution property is far more sacred than women. But having a fatality in belief that there is a law of retribution in all things, I hoped to be able to sheet this crime home to its perpetrator in a way that should put him to confusion when he least expected it.

There was ample money for burial among the girl's belongings, which were taken in charge by the police, and there let the cruelly common incident rest for the present.

The affair so upset Dawn that she refused to occupy her usual room any longer, and at her suggestion she and I determined to occupy a big upstairs room, up till that time filled with rubbish. This being agreed upon we forsook the apartments opening into the river garden, and betook ourselves to an altitude from which we had even a better view of the valley, river, and trains.

Dawn so perceptibly went " off colour " that I persuaded

her grandmother to let the singing lessons begin by way
of diverting her mind.

The old lady would not contemplate paying more than
two guineas per quarter, so I saw a six guinea teacher,
arranged with him to take the pupil at four, two of which
I privately paid myself, and Dawn at last set out for the
city for her first lesson in the arduous and unattractive
boo-ing and ah-ing that lie at the foundation of a singer's
art.

SIXTEEN.

ADVANCE, AUSTRALIA!

IN the career of a prodigy there invariably comes a time when it is compelled to relinquish being very clever for a child, and has to enter the business of life in competition with adults.

This crisis had arrived in the career of the prodigy Australia.

It is at the time of electing new or re-electing old representatives of the people to the legislature that the state of a country's affairs is more prominently before the public than at any other, and preceding the State election in which Grandma Clay was to exercise the rights of full citizenship for the first time, it was a lugubrious statement.

That the country had gone to the dogs was averred by each candidate for the three hundred a-year given ordinary State members, and each described himself as the instrument by which it could be restored to a state of paradisaical prosperity.

This is an old bogey, unfailingly revived at elections. The Ministerialists invariably roar how they have improved the public finances, while the Opposition as blatantly tries to drown them by bellowing that the retiring government has damned the country, and that the Opposition has the only recipe of satisfactory reconstruction, but in spite of this threadbare election scare the Commonwealth remained the freest and one of the wealthiest abiding-places in the world.

Just then its business affairs were undoubtedly badly managed, and mismanagement, if continued, inevitably leads to bankruptcy. Undeniably there was an unwholesome percentage of unemployed—inexcusable when there abounded vast areas of fertile territory quite unpeopled, mines as rich as any known to history all untouched; the sugar, grape, timber, and other industries crying aloud for further development, and countless resources on every hand requiring nothing but that these and men should meet on healthy and enterprising business terms. The population, instead of gaining in numbers, was foolishly leaving the country, like overindulged, spoiled children, imagining themselves illtreated, while others hesitated to come in because the Australian trumpet was not blown loudly enough nor in the right key.

The administration, like a young housewife tossed into an overflowing storehouse, had spent lavishly, but the bank of a multi-millionaire will come to an end in time, and so with the play-days of Australia.

The hour had arrived for her to be up and doing, to marshal her forces, advertise her wares, and take her place as a worker among the nations.

There are always old bush lawyers and city know-alls beside whom Chamberlain and Roberts are but small tomahawks as empire - builders, and these now were predicting that to make a nation of her Australia needed war and many other disasters to harden her people from the amusement-loving, sunny-eyed folk they were; but this was an extremist's outlook. She was in greater need of a land law that would sensibly and practically put the right people on the soil, and entice population of desirable class—independent producers—so that the development of the industries would follow in natural sequence. In short, Australia was languishing for a few patriotic sons with strong, clear, business heads to apply the science of statecraft, as distinguished from the self-seeking artifices of the mere job politician at present sapping her vitals, and all the elements for success were within her gates.

I had long had an eye open for the discernment of such an embryo statesman, and looked forward with interest to the study of the present crop of political candidates.

As soon as Leslie Walker—Ernest Breslaw's step-brother—had been elected as the Opposition candidate for Noonoon, canvassing, "spouting," war-whooping, and all manner of "barracking" began with such intense enthusiasm that fortunately Miss Flipp's sad fate was speedily driven out of our thoughts.

Dawn and Mrs Bray were on Walker's committee, and nearly every night there was an advocate of one party or the other gasconading in Citizens' Hall.

To Noonoon residents it became what the theatre is to city patrons of the drama, and more, for this was invested with the dignity of a certain amount of reality. To women being in the fray many attributed the unusual interest distinguishing this campaign, but the real cause was that public affairs had come to such a deadlock that legislature, as the medium through which they might be moved, had become a vital question to the veriest numskull, and all were mustering to ascertain who put forth the most favourable policy.

With politics and her newly started singing lessons, Dawn was too thoroughly engrossed for thought of any knight to pierce her armour of indifference, which was the outcome of full mental occupation. I invested in a nice little piano, that was carried upstairs to our big room, and had undertaken to superintend her practising, but she was a more enthusiastic politician than a vocal student, as I pointed out to her grandmother's satisfaction. These happenings had eventuated during the first fortnight of May, and in the third week of this month Leslie Walker imported a couple of experienced ranters to renew the attack and denounce the villainy of the present government in loud and blustering vote-catching war-whoops.

In the town itself, nearly every third person was employed on the railway, and their only care in casting their vote was to secure a representative who would not in any way reduce the expenditure of the railways. Thus a parliamentary candidate in Noonoon had to trim his sails to catch this large vote or be defeated. It was the same with other factions : any man with a common-sense platform, impartially for the good of the State at large, might as well have sat down at home and have saved himself the labour of stumping an electorate and bellowing himself hoarse for all the chance he had of being returned.

We turned out *en masse* from Clay's to hear the second speech of young Walker, assisted by two M.P.'s belonging to his party. Grandma and I drove in the sulky, while the girls and Andrew walked ahead, the latter under strict orders to behave with reason, and not make " a fool of hisself with the larrakins."

It was well we arrived early, as there was not sitting room for half the audience, though more than half the hall being reserved for the ladies, we got a front seat, and long before the time for the speakers to appear every corner was packed, and women as well as men were standing in rows fronting the stage. A great buzz of conversation at the front, and stampeding and cat-calling among the youths at the back, was terminated by the arrival of the three speakers of the evening, who were received amid deafening cock - a - doodling, cheering, stamping, and clapping. An old warrior of the class dressed *up* to the position of M.P. sat to one side, and next him was the barrister type so prolific in parliament, who had himself dressed *down* to the vulgar crowd, while third sat Leslie Walker.

Surely not the first Leslie Walker who had appeared a week or two previously! His bright, restless eye, though too sensitive for that of an old campaigner, now took in the crowd with complete assurance, and there was no hint of hesitation discernible. Having once smelt powder he was ready for the fray.

"By Jove! hasn't Les. bucked up!" whispered Ernest, who sat on one side of me, where he had landed after an ineffectual attempt to sit beside Dawn.

"Yes; if he can only roar and blow and wave his arms sufficiently he may have a chance."

"But he's still nervous," said the observant Andrew from the rear. "You watch him go for that flea in the leg of his pants!"

Sitting in full view of a "chyacking" audience is a severe ordeal to an inexperienced campaigner with a sensitive temperament, and this action, indeed peculiarly like an attempt to detain an annoying insect in a fold

of his lower garment, was one of those little mannerisms
adopted to give an appearance of ease.

Behind the speakers came, as chairman, one of the
swell class almost extinct in this region, and he, too,
had rather an effete attitude and physique, as he took
up his position behind the spindley table weighted by
the smeared tumblers and water-bottle. He rose with
the intention of flattering the speakers and audience in
the orthodox way, but the electors, among whom a spirit
of overflowing hilarity was at large, took his duties out
of his mouth.

"Don't smoodge, old cockroach, let the other blokes
blaze away, as we (the taxpayers) are paying dear for
this spouting."

The barrister man M.P. burst upon them first with
the latest trumpet blare with which speeches were being
opened. Having been primed as to the magnitude of
the railway vote in Noonoon, first move was to throw
a bone to it, and, metaphorically speaking, he got down
on his knees to this section of the electors, and howled
and squealed that all civil servants' wages would be
left as they were.

He took another canter to flatter the ladies regarding
the remarkably intelligent vote they had cast in the
Federal elections, and asserted his belief that they would
do likewise in the present crisis, and introduce a nobler
element into political life.

Creatures, a few months previously ranked lower than
an almost imbecile man, and with no more voice in the
laws they lived under than had lunatics or horses—it
was miraculous what a power they had suddenly grown!
The man at the back saw the point—

"Blow it all, don't smoodge so. It ain't long since

you was all rared up on yer hind legs showin' how things would go to fury if wimmen had the vote."

Having got past this prelude, he proceeded with a vigorous volley of abuse against the sitting government, and showed how Walker, the Opposition candidate, was the only man to vote for. He shook his fists, stamped and raved, and illustrated how much a voice could endure without cracking, the back people carefully waiting till he had to pull up to take a drink out of one of the glasses on the spindley table, when they got in with—

"You're mad! Keep cool! You'll bust a blood-vessel! When are you going to give Tomato Jimmy a show to blow his horn?" This being a reference to the calling of the other speaker, who was a middleman in the vegetable- and fruit-market. The first speaker, however, was not nearly exhausted yet—he had to thump his fists on the unfortunate spindley table, and work off several other oratorical poses and a deal of elocutionary voice-play, ere he was finished. I fairly rolled with enjoyment of the wonderful wit and humour of the crowd at the back, which, unless it be put down as the critical faculty, is an inexplicable phenomenon. Not one of the interrupters, if drafted on to the hustings, could have given a lucid or intelligent statement of his views, or indication that he was furnished with any, and yet not one slip on the part of a candidate, one inconsistent point, personal mannerism or peccadillo, but was remarked in an astonishingly humorous and satirical style.

The barrister man having finished "spouting," the common-sense individual, who always sits half-way down the hall, and who, when he asks a question, has to face the double ordeal of the crowd and the candidate, said—

"The speaker has shown us all the things the other fellows *can't do*, we'd like another speech now stating what *he can* do." The chairman rose to say this was out of order, but his voice was lost in the din.

"You sit down, old chap, we can manage this meetin' ourselves."

"But out of respect to the ladies present!"

"We'll look after the ladies too," was the good-humoured rejoinder. "Why, they're enjoyin' it as much as we are. They've got a vote now, you know, and are going to use it in an intelligent manner."

"Did you know Queen Anne was dead?" said another.

"The ladies won't be harmed. Any one that disrespects the ladies will be chucked out."

The ladies had to laugh at this, and the meeting went right merrily, and more merrily in that half the "blowing" from the stage was drowned by the interjectory din from the rear of the building, where lads and men stood chock-a-block, the former, and the latter too, making right royal use of their licence to be rowdy; but such a good-natured crowd could not often be seen. There were no altercations, only laughter and the crude repartee of such a gathering.

The first speaker having returned to his seat and sanity, the second took his place.

"Hullo, Tomatoes! What's the price of onions and spuds?"

"Now begin and tell the ladies how intelligent they are, so you'll get their vote."

"Tomatoes" did butter the ladies, next yelled that the civil servants would not be retrenched, and then upheld the virulent attack on the government. Keeping in time with the utterances of "Tomato Jimmy," the boys at the back grew so boisterous that at one time it appeared inevitable that the meeting must break up in disorder. The chairman, the candidates, the ladies, the whole house rose, and one man towards the front made himself heard amid the babel to the effect that the ladies ought to walk out to show their resentment of the insults that had been offered their presence by this disorderly behaviour.

"Ladies, don't go. *Dear* ladies, don't go," called some wags. "We're only educatin' you in politics,—learning you how to be like your superiors—men."

This evoked a round of laughter, and order was restored.

"That's right, ladies, don't go; if you was to turn dawg on us now, we'd be so crestfallen we couldn't think about politics and save the country at all."

Once more "Tomatoes" belched forth the infamy of the government, and louder and louder he yelled, till one marvelled at his endurance. Rougher and hotter grew his repartee till, by sheer abuse, he gained the ascendancy; but there was no sane statement of what he would propose as a remedy. Grandma Clay happened to rise as he neared the finish to see about a recticule she had dropped, and proved a target for those at the rear.

"Hello, grandma! are you going to contradict him? Give us a straight tip about women's rights while you're up;" and poor grandma sat down very precipitately with an exceedingly deep blush.

"If I could only get the chance," she gasped, "I'd give 'em a piece of me mind."

Third on the list came Leslie Walker, whose improvement was beyond belief. No notes or hesitation this time. Each sentence was crisp and clear, and in every detail he evinced the facility for enacting his *rôle* which is supposedly a feminine accomplishment.

The chairman, in closing the meeting, rose to say—

" In reference to the interjector who said the speaker was mad——"

"Oh, that's what every one said about *you* when you were in the council, and so you were too, and so are they all. Look at the roads we've got in the municipality," said a voice.

So the chairman had to let the meeting terminate with the candidates thanking the electors for the extraordinarily good hearing they had been accorded; it being part of the humour of politics that the worse a candidate is boo-hooed the more stress he lays upon the *good hearing* given him, and the more scurrilous he is regarding his opponent the more frantically he assures one that he is a bosom *personal* friend.

Andrew and I had the distinction of going home under grandma's tutelage, while Carry and Dawn stayed behind to go to the ladies' committee rooms, and Ernest lingered to escort them.

"I say, grandma, are you goin' to vote for that bloke ?" inquired Andrew.

"I'm goin' to hear the other side first, and give me opinion after. There wasn't one of the swells there, was there ?"

"Dr Smalley and Dr Tinker both was."

"Yes; but I mean the wimmen : an' how on earth did old Tinker ever get away from Mrs Tinker for that length of time ? You'll never see one of them kind of wimmen at anythink that makes for progress. That's the way they make theirselves superior to the likes of you an' me—by never doin' nothink only for theirselves. 'Oh, we've got all we want as it is, an' don't want the vote; a woman's place is home,' they say if you ask 'em. It's all very fine for them as has a man to keep them like in a band-box; they would have found it different if they had to act on their own like me. I'm sick of this intelligence in women they make a fuss about all of a sudden. I've rared a family and managed me business better than a man could; and what's there been all along to prevent a woman from stroking out a name on a paper I never could see. And it never seems to me much difference which name was struck out, for they're mostly a lot of impostors that only think of featherin' their own nests. You'll always hear of wimmen not bein' intelligent enough to do this and that, and these things is only what men like doin' best theirselves, and the things they make out God intended women to do is them the men don't like doin'. You don't ever hear of them thinkin' women ain't intelligent enough to do seven things at once." Grandma was in great form that night, and not only led but maintained the conversation.

"I rather like this young feller, but he ain't no sense much either. All he thinks of is buttoning for the railway people, and it's the people on the land that ought to be legislated for first. They are the foundation of everythink; other things would work right after. Every one can't live in Sydney, an' that's what they're all makin' for now. Every one is getting some little agency—parasite business. They've got sense to see the people on the land is the most despised and sat upon. You don't hear no squallin' about they'll protect the farmer. No, he's a despised old party that them scuts of fellers on the railway would grin at and think theirselves above, and scarcely give him a civil answer if he asked a question about his business what he's payin' them fellers there to do for him, and which only for the prodoocers wouldn't be there at all. Things is gettin' pretty tight on farms now. It means about sixteen hours hard graft a-day to make not half what a railwayman makes in eight hours. If you happen to have grapes or oranges, if they manage to escape the frost, an' hail, an' caterpillar, then the blight ketches 'em, or there's a drewth, and there ain't none; an' if there's any, there's so much that there ain't no sale for 'em; and the farmer's life I reckon ought to be stopped as gamblin', for a gambler's life ain't one bit more precarious."

"Then why the jooce do you want me to go on the land?" said Andrew.

"That ain't the point."

"It's the most sticking out point to me," protested the lad. "I reckon bein' on the land is a mug's game; scrapin' like a fool when a feller could be sittin' in an office an' gettin' all they want twice as easy."

"Here, you don't know what's good. It's more respectabler bein' on the land. You get the pony out, an' make the coffee, an' hold your tongue."

Andrew and I had undertaken to make the coffee for supper, and thus give Carry, whose week in the kitchen it was, a chance to go to the meeting.

They all arrived from it after a time—Dawn and the knight together, Carry and Larry Witcom following. Oh, where was "Dora"?

"Who's that with you, Carry?" asked Andrew.

"There was a young lady named Carry, who had a

sweetheart named Larry; at the gate they often would tarry, to talk about when they would marry."

But this remark of Andrew's to parry, Dawn good-naturedly plunged into an account of the meeting.

"What did they do?" asked grandma.

"Do?—they only blabbed. Mr Walker was there to-night. We asked that Jimmeny girl from the pub. to join, and she delivered a great parable at us, looking round all the time to see if the boot-licking tone of it was pleasing the men. She said that women ought to bring up their children to respect them——"

"The most commonest idea some people has of bringin' up their children to respect them," grandma chipped in, "is to let youngsters make toe-rags of their mother; and boys only as high as the table think they can cheek their mother because she's only a woman an' hasn't as much right to be livin' in the world as them, and when they are twenty-one the law confirms this beautiful sentiment. Leastways, until just lately," she concluded.

"And this Jimmeny piece," continued Dawn, "said women ought to treat their husbands decently, and she thinks a woman disgraces her sex by getting up on a platform to speak. I asked her if she thought they did not disgrace themselves and the other sex too by stand-ing behind a bar and serving out drinks and grinning at a lot of goods that ought to be at home with their families,—and that was a bit of a facer. Then she said it was only the ugly old women who wanted to shriek round and get rights,—that men would give the young pretty ones all they wanted without asking! Of all the old black gin ideas, I always think that the terriblest. A nice state of affairs, if people couldn't get honest civilised rights without being young and pretty; and *the fools!*" said the girl heatedly, "can't they look round and see how long the beauty and youth business will work! 'Men,' she says, 'ought to rule; they're the stronger vessel.'" And Dawn gave inimitable mimicry of Miss Jimmeny of the pub. "If you take my tip for it, those girls that sing out that men are the stronger vessel are the sort that have a dishcloth of a husband, and never let him off a string."

This attitude of mind was one of Dawn's distinctive characteristics. Having that beauty, which in the enslaved condition of women has always been an unfair asset to the possessor, to the exclusion of worthier traits, she was not like most beauties, content to sit down and trade upon it, but had wholesomer, honester, workaday ideals in regard to the position of her sex.

She was going to Sydney in the morning for her second singing lesson, and as Ernest, by a strange coincidence, happened to have business that would take him on the same journey by the same train, I accompanied him to the gate to warn him against inadvertently divulging that I had been an actress by trade.

"I want to take you into my confidence," I said, as we passed several naked cedar-trees, and halted in the shelter of some fine peppers that grew to perfection in this valley, where I related the trouble I had had to bring the old lady round to the idea of Dawn's singing lessons, and mentioned the girl's ambition regarding the stage.

"Now," I continued, "if the old dame were to discover I had been on the stage, she would think I was leading Dawn to the devil, and would not credit that no one is more anxious than I am to save her from the footlights, or that the best way to stave her off is this training. My

secret ambition regarding her," I said, critically observing
the strong knobby profile, " is that within the next five
years she should marry some nice youngster with means
to place her in a setting befitting her intelligence and
beauty."

"Have you got any one in your eye now?" he irrele-
vantly inquired. And, considering he stood where he
filled my entire vision, as he rose between me and the
light shed by the last division of the western pass-
enger mail as it self-importantly crossed the viaduct,
I answered—

"Yes; I think I know a man who would just fill the
bill."

He did not ask for further particulars, but remarked
warningly—

"Decent fellows with cash are scarce. They are in-
clined to get into mischief if they have too much time
and money on their hands."

"That's it; and I would not like to make a mess of
things now that I've taken up matchmaking. You'll
have to advise me when matters get out of hand; a little
practice may come in handy some day when you have
half a dozen daughters."

"It would come in still handier now."

"Pshaw, now! You'd only have to ask to receive, at
your time of life and with your qualifications."

"I'm not so sure. You're the only one who has such
an opinion of me," he said disconsolately. "Others look
upon me as a red-headed fool with big ears, &c.;" and thus
I knew Dawn's idle words had returned to his ears, as
these things invariably do, and had stung.

"Silly-billy! I'll take you in hand when I've settled
Dawn. I'm the one to advertise your wares, for could I

turn back the wheel of time eight or nine years and make us of an age, I'd make it leap-year and propose to you myself."

" I'd like to propose to you without altering the time," he gallantly responded, apparently not in such deadly fear of a breach of promise action as was Uncle Jake.

" If I don't move in the matter Dawn will be marrying that Eweword, and though he's a most handsome and worthy——"

" Soft as a turnip," contemptuously interposed Ernest ; " eats too much.   It would take twelve months hard training to make any sort of a man of him."

" It would be a pity to see Dawn just settling down into the dull, drudging life of a farmer's wife, going to an occasional show or tea-meeting in a home-made dress, with two or three children dragging at her skirts and looking a perfect wreck, as most of the mothers do."

" By Jove, yes ! "

" She has a right to be on the lawn on Cup Day or in the front circle on first nights.   She'd surprise some of the grandees, and with her vivacity and courage she'd make a furore for a time."

" She'd make a good sport if she were a man," assented Ernest.   " No running stiff or jamming a jock on the post or anything like that from her—she'd always hit straight out from the shoulder and above the belt."

" Yes ; she has particularly infatuated me, and I'd like to save her from Eweword."

" Marry him to the girl Grosvenor while you're about it and that will dispose of him and suit her, for she strikes me as anxious for matrimony."

" She hasn't been——" I began.

" Oh, no, I think she's a splendid woman in every way, but——"

"*But*, even the finest and most chivalrous man, while he thinks the only sphere for women is matrimony, yet is shocked if a woman betrays in the least way that her ambitions lie in the domestic line—strange inconsistency. However, you will not let Dawn know my ideas of disposing of her ; " and with the want of perspicacity of his sex, or else with a wonderful power of covering his thoughts excelling that of women, and of which women never suspect men, Ernest promised without sensing what I had in view.

SEVENTEEN.

MRS BRAY AND CARRY COME TO ISSUES.

CONTENTION arose in the Clay household next day, Dawn's singing lessons being at the root of the trouble. It was her week in the kitchen, and that she should be two days absent from the cooking, displeased Carry.

"Well, if you don't think the place fair, you can go!" said grandma. "But I think you're a fool, an' you're giving me a lot of worry. It's all very fine in other people's places, but some day w'en you have a home of your own you'll know the worry of it. Next time I make a arrangement with a girl she'll have to take a extra day in the kitchen without humbuggin'."

"I'll vote for me grandma on that bill," said Andrew, "for I've often been give the pip by who is in the kitchen an' who is out of it. Grandma, did you hear the latest? Young Jack Bray's been in another orange orchard and didn't do a get quick enough, and has got took up, and his father will have to pay money to keep him out of quod."

The old lady bristled.

"Didn't I tell you! Who knows how to receive these things best now? I've always believed in rarin' me family me own way, an' Mrs Bray is a fine woman, moral and decent, but she's got too many stones to throw at others and doesn't see to it sharp enough that less stones can't be threw at her. I thought she didn't take it serious enough. You'd have been in this too only for me dreadin' the spark. What are they goin' to do?"

"Pay the money, of course; an' Mr Bray is goin' to tan the hide off Jack."

"Some people don't get frightened of dishonesty unless it costs 'em something," said the old lady.

"Well, I'll vote for me grandma every time," said Andrew, "and Jim Clay every second time," as he went out the door, "and meself the most times of all," he concluded in the back yard.

Mrs Bray dropped in that afternoon for a chat, and grandma mentioned that we were without afternoon tea because Carry had "jacked up" about getting it, for reasons before mentioned.

"Just like her!" said Mrs Bray; "she gives herself as much side as if she was one of us. She's the sort of girl who wouldn't think twice of telling you to do a thing yourself, and you've made an awful fool of her by making so much of her. Them things of girls *earnin' their own livin'* ought to be kept in their place more," was the utterance of a woman who believed herself a staunch advocate for the freedom of her sex; but when Mrs Bray spoke of sex she meant self.

"That ain't the point," said grandma; "I never think it anythink but a credit to a girl to be earnin' her living, an' would never be narrer enough to make them feel it. I always make a practice of treatin' the girls as near equal as within reason, for Carry's every bit as fine-lookin' an' good a girl as me own, an' if I wasn't here, wouldn't Dawn have to be foragin' for herself too? but there's

reason in everythink, and Carry might be a bit ob-
ligin'."

"Of course she ought to be; but what could you expect
of her, took up with that Larry Witcom, an' does the ass
think he really wants her? He's only got her on a string
for his own amusement? He goes to see that Dora
Cowper at the same time; Jack seen him there. I
wonder will *he* be scared off by being thought a ketch
before the pot's boiled, so to speak. Good ketches, eh?
I don't see nothing in none of them. They're only thought
something because men is scarce here; they've all cleared
out to the far out places, and West Australia. It's like a
year the pumpkins is scarce, you can sell little things
you'd hardly throw to the pigs another time, and that's
the way it is with the few paltry fellers round here. It
makes me mad to see the girls after them—*the fools!* and
the men grinnin' behind their backs. There's that Ada
Grosvenor, if Eweword just calls up and talks to her she
tells you about it as if it was something, and inviting him
down there, an' then the blessed fellers gets to think
they're gods. It makes me sick!"

"Yes," said grandma; "I see the girls after fellers now,
—there's that Danby for instance, he's a fine lump of a
man, but w'en I was a girl I wouldn't have made toe-rags
of a policeman."

"Yes, a blessed feller strollin' up and down the street
lookin' at his toes or runnin' in a drunk. I say, did you
hear the latest about old Rooney-Molyneux? He didn't
believe in women having the vote, didn't consider they
had intellect to vote, so *he* says (not as much brain as he
has, don't you see, to marry a woman, and a baby to be
coming and nothing to put on its back, while he strolls
round and gets drunk), but now they've got the vote, he

says (the great Lord Muck Rooney-Molyneux says it,
remember) that it is their *duty* to use it, and he intends
to *make* (mind you, *make ;* I'd like to hear a man say he'd
make me do anything; I'd scald him, see if I wouldn't,
and that's what wants doing with half the men anyhow,
for the way they carry on to women), and he's going to
make his wife go round canvassing, *Now!* Men make
me sick; w'en they're boys they're that troublesome they
ought to be kep' under a tub, and we'n they get older
they're that cantankerous and self-important they all
want killin' off."

"I'll bet Mrs Rooney won't be workin' for a different
man to him. If her convictions led her that way, you'd
see he'd have a flute about her not bein' fit to be out of
her home," said grandma astutely.

"Yes, that's the way with 'em; first they thought the
world would tumble to pieces if women stirred out of the
house for a minute to vote, and now that we've got the
vote in spite of them, they'd make their wives walk round
after votes for their side whether they was able or not."

"They kicked agen us having the vote, and now we've
got it they think we ought to vote with them like as if we
was a appendage of theirs; men will be learnt different
to that by-and-by, but it's best to go gradual; they've
had as much as they can swaller for a time."

"Ain't it just the very devil to them to think women
is considered as important as themselves now, instead
of something they could just do as they like with? Old
Hollis there says he won't vote this year because the
women have one. Did you ever hear of an insult like
that? He says the monkeys will have a vote next, and
that shows you what men think of women,—like as if they
was some sort of animals."

"Well, if you ask me," said grandma, "the monkeys have been havin' a vote all along in the case of old Hollis."

Any further discussion in this line was terminated by the entrance of Carry, with her good-looking face flushed and hard set, as, rolling down her sleeve and buttoning it aggressively as the finishing touch to her toilet after completing her afternoon's work, she confronted Mrs Bray, on battle bent.

"Well, Mrs Bray, I'd like to have given my opinion of you to your teeth long ago, but I held my tongue as it wasn't my house, and some people have different tastes and have folk around that I'd be a long time having anything to do with. Now, I think things do concern me, and I'm going to have my say; I couldn't have it sooner because I'm a *thing* earning my living and had to finish my work. I haven't got a home of my own, and like some people, if I had, I'd be in it teaching my dirty rude brats not to be thieves. I wouldn't for everlasting be at other people's places scandalising people twice as good as myself. I didn't think Mrs Clay was the sort of person to go tittle-tattling—she can please herself; but it doesn't concern you if I do put on airs. I want to know what you mean by that I should be kept in my place. I'll swear I know how to carry my day as well as you do, and to keep in my place too well to be going round meddling with other people's business."

"I didn't say nothing but was correct, an' what right have you to come bullying me? It's like your impudence —you a hussy out to work for your living at a few shillings a-week, and calling yourself a *lady* help when you're a *servant*, that's what you are; to bully *me*, a woman with a good home, and the mother of a family."

Carry snorted contemptuously.

"That old 'mother of a family' racket needn't be brought forward. It doesn't hold as much water as it used to. Women are thought just as much of now who are good useful workers in the world, and not tied up to some man and the mother of a few weedy kids that aren't any credit to king or country."

"Mercy!" exclaimed grandma. "What am I to?"

"Let 'em fight it out," I laconically advised in an aside, and she seemed disposed to take my advice.

"You dare," blustered Mrs Bray. "And what else have you got to say?"

"I want an explanation of the aspersion on my character when you said I had taken up with Larry Witcom. I'm not going to stand anything on my character in that line if I *am* earning my living, and you *are* the mother of one or fourteen families, all as great a credit to you as the one Jack represents. And as for me earning my living, what are *you* doing? If a man wasn't keeping you to suit himself, how would you be earning your living? I could earn my living the same way as you are doing to-morrow if I liked; but of the two, I think my present occupation is the decentest and less dependent. Apart from your bullying selfishness, a nice sensible way you have of talking! If you killed off the men, who would you have to keep you? And that's a nice civilised way to speak about your fellow - creatures anyhow; whether they be men or black gins, they've just as much place in the scheme of creation as you have. We would have been a long time getting the vote or any other decent right if the men were like you. It's because you are the same stamp as so many of the men that we've been kept down so long as we have; and now, what about me taking up with Larry Witcom?"

" Well, it's well known what Larry is."

" Well, what is he ? "

" You ask him about Mrs Park's divorce case."

" I hope you don't think your old man is a saint, do you ? As big a fool as you are, you're surely not fool enough for that, are you ? Perhaps he isn't as clean a potato as Larry if it was all brought out."

" But he's a married man this many a year, with a married daughter, and his young days are lived down long ago."

" Well, so would Larry be married many a year and have things lived down in time, and not as many to live down either as your husband has at present, if things are true ; for all your everlasting shepherding he gets off the chain sometimes."

Hoity-toity ! this was putting a fuse to gunpowder.

" You hussy ! What have you got to say about my husband ? Prove it, and I'd make short work of him ; and if it's lies, I'll bring you into court for it."

" I'll leave it for you to prove ; you're one of those who thinks every yarn entertaining till they touch yourself."

" Two to one on Carry every time when me grandma's the umpire," grinned Andrew round the corner.

" Carry, you've had enough to say. I forbid any more in my house," said grandma, rising to order.

" I declare this a drawn fight," said Andrew.

" You can have it out with Mrs Bray in her own house if you want, but no more of it here," continued grandma.

" Don't you dare come to my house," said Mrs Bray.

" *Your* house ! no fear ; I never associate with scandal-mongers," contemptuously retorted Carry, as Mrs Bray made a precipitate departure, emitting something about a hussy who didn't know her place as she went.

"I'm surprised at you!" said grandma. "Her tongue does run on a little sometimes, but you ought to remember she's old enough to be your mother, and girls do owe somethink to women with families."

"And women with families and homes ought to remember they owe something to girls that aren't settled, because they haven't got a man caught yet to keep them."

"Well, this ain't my quarrel, an' don't you bring it up to me again. A woman that's rared a family, and two of them like I have done, has enough with her own dissensions."

It was rather a sullen party at tea that evening, so Dawn's return from Sydney immediately after, with her cheeks radiant from travel in the quick evening express, and herself brimming over with her day's adventures, formed a welcome relief.

"I had a great time coming home," said she. "Mr Ernest and Dora Eweword both went to Sydney this morning, and Mr Ernest and I raced into a carriage to escape Dora, and we did; and he must have asked the guard, for he found our carriage, but he had only a second-class ticket, and wouldn't be let in."

"And how came you to be in a first-class carriage?" inquired grandma. "I can't stand that; there's expense enough as it is, and your betters travel second."

"It wasn't my fault. Mr Ernest bought the tickets like a gentleman should (it says in the etiquette book), and I couldn't fight with him there and then,—you're always telling me to be more genteel."

"But I don't want strangers paying anything for my granddaughter."

"You needn't mind in this instance," I interposed.

"Mr Ernest probably wished to be gentlemanly to Dawn because she has been so good to me." Once more I saw the little derisive smile flit across the exquisite face, but she said—

"Yes; he said that you're looking so well it must be our nursing, and that he will try and get grandma to take him in if he falls ill."

"I wonder if he's going to get took bad—love-sick—like the other blokes," said Andrew.

Dawn cast a murderous glance at him, and covered the remark by making a bustle in sitting to her tea, and in retailing minute details of her singing lesson.

We retired early, and she produced from the basket in which she carried her music a most pretentious box of sweets and various society newspapers.

"Mr Ernest said you might like some of these, and I was to have a share because I carried them home, though he got the 'bus and brought me to the door, so I hadn't to walk a step."

"Good boy! What did he talk about to-day?"

"I asked him about all the actresses he has seen. He's going to give me the autographed photos he has of them. You wouldn't think he'd like to part with them, but he says he's tired of them all now—they're nearly all married, and are back numbers. Actresses are only thought of for a little while, he says."

"That is the natural order of things, and applies to others as well as actresses. Pretty young girls are not pretty for long. They should see to it that they are plucked by the right fingers while their bloom is attractive. The old order falls ill-fittingly on some, but is fair in the main,—we each have our fleeting hour."

"Yes; but where is there a desirable plucker?" said

the practical girl. "There are scarcely any good matches and the few there are have so many running after them that I wouldn't give 'em the satisfaction of thinking I wanted them too."

True, good matches are few. In these luxurious times the generality of girls' ideas of a good match being very advanced—in short, a man of sufficient wealth to keep them in petted idleness. There can be no shade of reproach on women for this ambition, it is but one outcome of the evolution of civilisation, and is merely a species of common-sense on their part; for the ordinary routine of marriage, as instanced by the testimony of thousands of women ranked among the comfortably and happily married, is so trying that girls do well to try for the most comfortable berths ere putting their heads in the noose.

"And Dora, where was he all this time?" I asked.

"Oh, he brought Ada Grosvenor home; thought that would spite me. She was in town too, and you should just hear her after this. The silly rabbit can't open her mouth but she tells you what this man did and that one said to her, when all the time it's nothing but some ordinary courtesy they ought to extend to even black gins."

EIGHTEEN.

THE FOUNDATION OF THE POULTRY INDUSTRY.

PEACE was restored in the Clay household through my
interviewing Carry and offering to teach her music and
allow her the use of my piano if she would do some of
Dawn's work for two days during every second week.
The next irritation arose from the male portion of the
family.

Now, we had all been so vigorously on political enter-
tainment bent, that no one had given a thought to Uncle
Jake and his doings or political opinions, or whether he
had any, but it transpired, though a "mere man," he had
been pursuing his course with as much attention to
electioneering technique as the most emancipated woman
among us.

On the afternoon following Carry's little difference
with Mrs Bray, Ada Grosvenor called to invite us to
accompany her to hear Olliver Henderson, the ministerial
candidate, who was to address the women at the hall first,
and the men at Jimmeny's pub. afterwards, and we all
went. Next morning at breakfast, when we had set to
work upon the "dosed" porridge, Andrew again catechised
his grandma concerning the casting of her vote.

"I'm goin' for young Walker of course; as for that

other feller!" said she cholericly, " I was that sick of his
stuttering and muttering, an' holdin' his meetin's at
Jimmeny's (we all know that that means free drinks), an'
after waitin' all my life fer it I'm not goin' to cast the
only vote that maybe I'll live to have, for a feller that
buys his votes with grog.   There's precious little to choose .
between them.   They only want the glory of bein' in
parliament for theirselves, and for the time bein' have
rose a flute about the country goin' to the dogs and them
bein' the people to save it; but once the election's over
that's all we'll hear of 'em, and though they'd lick our
boots now, they're so glad to know us, they'd forget all
about us then.   The one who can blow the loudest will get
in, and as it must be one it might as well be this feller
that can talk, an' could keep up his end of the stick in
parliament, as there's no doubt this talkin' an' blow
has become such a great trade one has to go to the wall
without it."

"Well, I'm going for Walker too, because he's some-
thing to look at," said Carry.

"The women was goin' to put in *clean* men an' do
strokes," sneered Uncle Jake, "an' it turns out they'd vote
for the best-lookin' man,—nice state of affairs that is."

"Ah! it's all very fine for a man to buck w'en a thing
treads on his own toes; it would be thought a terrible
thing for a woman to vote for a good-lookin' man an' pass
over merit, but that's what's been done to women all the
time.   The good-lookin' ones got all the honours, whether
they deserved 'em or not, and those complainin' agen this
was jeered at an' called 'Shrieking sisters,' but it's a
different tune now."

"Uncle, *darling*, who are you going to vote for?"
inquired Andrew.

"For Henderson, of course, an' I reckon all the women here with votes ought, too."

"And why, pray?" asked grandma, her eyes flashing a challenge, while her faithful guardswomen, Carry and Dawn, suspended work to see how the argument ended.

"For the look of the thing to start with. It don't look well to see the wimmen of the family goin' agen the men."

"No, it don't look like Nature as men make believe it ought to be, for once to see a woman have a opinion of her own, and not the man just telling that his opinion wuz hers too, without knowing anythink about it, an' women having to hold their tongue for peace' sake because they wasn't in a position to help theirselves. An' if it seems so dreadful that way, you better come over to our side, as there's more of us than you, an' majority ought to rule."

"What did you do at *your* meeting last night, uncle?" inquired Dawn.

"Old Hollis is head of the committee, an' he says the first thing for all the committee men to do was to see the women of the men goin' for Henderson was the same way," he replied.

"Oh, an' so you thought you could come the Czar on us, did you? an' the Government, accordin' to Hollis's make out, is a fool to give women a vote; like in your case instead of giving me an' Carry a vote each, it ought to have give you three."

"Oh, Mr Sorrel!" said I, "what a joke! Was he really so ignorant as that; surely he was joking too?"

Uncle Jake had sufficient wit to take this opportunity of changing his tactics.

"No," he said, "some people is terrible narrer; for

my part' I always believe in wimmen holdin' their own opinion."

"So long as they didn't run contrary to yours," said grandma with a sniff. "There's heaps more like you. Women can always think as much as they like, an' they could get up on a platform an' talk till they bust, as long as they didn't want the world to be made no better, an' they wouldn't be thought unwomanly. It's soon as a woman wants any practical good done that she is considered a unwomanly creature."

Uncle Jake was outdone and relapsed into silence.

"An' that's just what I would have expected of old Hollis," continued grandma, who seemed to have a knowledge of people's doings rivalling that necessary to an efficient police officer. "I'll tell you what he is," and the old dame directed her remarks to me. "He is the old chap Mrs Bray was sayin' ain't goin' to vote this time because the women has got one and the monkeys will be havin' one next. Just what the likes of him would say! He's a old crawler whose wife does all the work while he walks around an' tells how he killed the bear, an' that's the sort of man who's always to be heard sayin' woman is a inferior animal that ought to be kep' on a chain as he thinks fit. You'll never hear the kind of man like Bray (who is a man an' keeps his wife like a princess) sayin' that sort of thing—it's only the old Hollises and such. I'll tell you what old Hollis is. He got out of work here a few years back, w'en things was terrible dull, an' so his wife had to keep him, and with a child for every year they had been married. She rared chickens an' plucked 'em and sold 'em around the town, an' went without necessaries w'en she was nursin' to keep him in tobacco. That's the kind of man *he* is, if you want to know. Of course, bein'

a animal twice her superior, he had to go about suckin' a
pipe, and of course he couldn't deny hisself anythink.
What do you think of that?"

"That its pathos lies in its commonness."

"I reckon you didn't hear of him goin' out an' pluckin'
the fowls then an' sayin', 'Wife, a woman's place w'en she
has a young family is in the house.' No fear! She
worked at this poultry business, an' it was surprisin' how
she got on—worked it up to a big poultry farm, till he took
a hand in doin' a little of the work an' takin' *all* the credit.
Now they live by it altogether; an' he was interviewed by
the papers a little while ago, and it was blew about the
reward of enterprise,—how he had started from nothink,
an' it never said a word how she started an' rared his
babies an' done it all, an' does most now, while he walks
about to illustrate what a superior bein' he is. That's
the way with all the poultry industry. Women was the
pioneers in it, an' now it's worked up to be payin', men
has took it over and think they have done a stroke. Not
so far back a man would consider hisself disgraced that
knew one kind of fowls from another, — he would be
thought a old molly-coddle. The women tried to keep a
few hens an' the men always tried to kill them, an' said
they'd ruin the place, an' at the same time they hunt them
was always cryin' out an' gruntin' that there wasn't enough
eggs to eat, an' why didn't the hens lay the same as they
used w'en they was boys. They expected the women to
rare them on nothink, or at odd moments, the same way as
they expect them to do everythink else. Now, even the
swells is gone hen mad, an' the papers are full of poultry
bein' a great industry, but it was women started it."

Upon strolling abroad that morning we found a huge
placard bearing the advice—"Vote for Olliver Henderson,

M.L.A., the Local Candidate," decorating the post of the gateway through which we gained the highroad.

Uncle Jake was credited with this erection, so Andrew made himself absent at a time when there was need of his presence, and thereby caused a deal of friction in the vicinity of grandma, but with the result that by midday Uncle Jake's placard was covered by another, reading: "Vote for Leslie Walker, the Opposition Candidate, and Save the Country !"

At three o'clock this was obscured by a reappearance of Henderson's advertisement, which was the cause of Uncle Jake being too late to catch that evening's train with a load of oranges he had been set to pack. At the risk of leaving the milking late, Andrew was setting out to once more eclipse this by Walker's poster, only that grandma adjudicated regarding the matter.

"Jake, you have one side of the gate, an' Andrew you take the other. Put up your papers side by side and that will be a good advertisement of liberty of opinion; an' Jake, if you haven't got sense to stick to this at your time of life, I'm sorry for you; and if you haven't Andrew at yours, I'll have to knock it into you with a strap,—now *mind!* An' if you don't get your work done you'll go to no more meetin's."

"Right O! I'll vote for me grandma every time," responded Andrew.

This proved an effective threat, for political meetings had become the joy of life to the electors of Noonoon. As a tallow candle if placed near can obscure the light of the moon, so the approaching election lying at the door shut out all other worldly doings. The Russo-Japanese war became a movement of no moment; the season, the price of lemons and oranges, the doings of Mrs Tinker, the inability of the municipal council to make the roads good, and all other happenings, became tame by comparison with politics. They were discussed with unabating interest all day and every day, and by every one upon all occasions. Even the children battled out differences regarding their respective candidates on the way home from school, rival committees worked with unflagging energy, and all buildings and fences were plastered with opposing placards. This pitch of enthusiasm was reached long before the sitting parliament had dissolved or a polling day had been fixed; for this State election was contested with unprecedented energy all over the country, but in no electorate was it more vigorously and, to its credit, more good-humouredly fought than in the fertile old valley of Noonoon.

It was the only chance the unfortunate electors had of bullying the lordly M.P.'s and would-be M.P.'s, who, once elected, would fatten on the parliamentary screw and pickings without showing any return, and right eagerly the electors took their present opportunity.

Zest was added to the contest by both the contestants being wealthy men, and with youth as well as means to carry it out on expensive lines. They were equally independent of parliament as a means of living, and being men of leisure were merely anxious for office to raise them from the rank and file of nonentityism. Independent means are a great advantage to a member of parliament. The penniless man elected on sheer merit, to whom the country could look for good things, becomes dependent upon politics for a living, is often handicapped by a family who are loth to leave the society and comfort to which their bread-winner's official position has raised them, and he, held by his affection, is ready to sacrifice all convictions and principle to remain in power. To this man politics becomes a desperate gamble, and the country's interests can go to the dogs so long as he can ensure re-election.

Another advantage in the Noonoon candidates which should have silenced the pessimists, who averred there were no good clean men to enter parliament, was that these men were both such exemplary citizens, morally, physically, and socially, that it seemed a sheer waste of goodness that only one could be elected.

The newspapers went politically mad, and those not any hysterical country rags, but the big metropolitan dailies, and there was one thing to be noted in regard to their statements that seriously needed rectifying. What is the purpose of the great dailies but to keep the people correctly informed as to the progress of public affairs and events of the community at large? Most of the people are too hard at work to forage information for themselves, or even to be thoroughly cognisant of that collected in the newspapers, and therefore parliamentary candidates, if not correct in their figures and statements, should be publicly arraigned for perjury. The Ministerialists gave one set of figures dealing with national financial statistics and the Oppositionists gave widely different. How was an elector to act when the platform of the former contained nothing but a few false statements and glowing promises, and the policy of the latter was only a few counteracting war-whoops, and there was no honesty, commonsense, or matter-of-fact business in the campaign from end to end?

In this connection that remote rag, 'The Noonoon Advertiser,' shone as a reproach to its great contemporaries. Not by their grandeur and acclamations shall they be judged, but by the quality of their fruits.

No bias or spleen seemed to sway the mind of this journal to one side or the other. It recognised itself as a newspaper, not as a political tout for this party or that, and so kept its head cool and its honour bright and shining.

Three days after Leslie Walker's second speech he sent up a woman advocate to address *the ladies* and start the business of house-to-house canvassing. This plenipotentiary, a person of rather plethoric appearance, made herself extremely popular by assuring every second *vote-lady* she met that she was sure she (the vote-lady) was intended by nature for a public speaker. This worked without a hitch until the votresses began to tell each other what the great speaker had said, when it naturally followed that Mrs Dash, though she thought that Mrs Speaker had been discerning to discover this latent oratorical talent in herself, immediately had the effervescence taken out of her self-complacence on finding that that stupid Mrs Blank had been assured of equal ability.

Then the Ministerialists discovered Mrs Speaker's place of abode in Sydney, and averred her children ran about so untended as to be undistinguishable from aboriginals, and that her housekeeping was sending her husband to perdition; and such is the texture of human nature unearthed at political crises, that some even went so far as to suggest that she was a weakness of Walker's, and sneered at the *ladies'* candidate who had to be " wet-nursed " in his campaign by women speakers. Henderson, they averred, had not to do this, but fought his own battle.

"Yes," said Grandma Clay; "he mightn't be-wet-nursed,

but he is bottled, *brandy*-bottled, by the men." And this could not be denied.

The women rallied round Walker because he was a temperance candidate, whereas the tag-rag rolled up *en masse* for Henderson, who shouted free drinks and carried the publican's flag.

Each candidate, while praising his opponent, wound up with *but*—and after that conjunction spoke most damningly of his policy.

Underneath the ostensible war-whoops many private and personal cross-fires were at work to intensify the contest. The people on the land quite naturally had a grudge against the railway folk, who only had to work eight hours per day for more than a farmer could make in sixteen; further, the perquisites of the railway employés were inconceivable. By an unwritten but nevertheless imperative etiquette, farmers had to render them tribute in the form of a portion of whatever fruit or vegetables were consigned at Noonoon, and the townspeople also had little to say in favour of them, averring they were a floating population who had no interest in the welfare of the town in which they resided, were bad customers—patronising the publicans more than the storekeepers, and by means of their connection with the railway were able to buy their meat and other necessaries where they listed—where it was cheapest, and frequently this was otherwhere than Noonoon, and yet they were in such numbers that they could rule the political market.

Then the men on the Ministerial side were nearly gangrene with disgust, because, as one put it, "nearly all Walker's men were women," and rallied round him thick and strong, and with a thoroughness and energy worthy of their recent emancipation.

Dawn's next day for Sydney fell on another night when Leslie Walker was speaking, but she and I did not attend this meeting, the family being represented on this occasion by Andrew, and we went to bed and discussed the Sydney trip while waiting for his return.

Ernest Breslaw, it appeared, had again had urgent business in Sydney that day.

"Dawn," I said, "this is somewhat suspicious. Are you sure you are not flirting with Ernest? I can't have his wings singed; I think too much of him, and shall have to warn him that you are booked for 'Dora' Eweword." This was said experimentally, for to do Dawn justice, though she had every temptation, she had nothing of the flirt in her composition.

"I can't go and say to him, 'Don't you fall in love with me,'" said Dawn contentiously.

"Are you sure he has never in any way attempted to pay you a lover's attentions?"

"Well, it's this way," she said confidentially—"you won't think me conceited if I tell you everything straight? There have been two or three men in love with me, and I was always able to see it straight away, long before *they* knew; but with Ernest, sometimes he seems to be like they were, and then I'm afraid he's not,— at least not *afraid*—I don't care a hang, only I wonder does he think he can flirt with me, when he is so nice and just waltzes round the subject without coming up to it?"

Ah! ha! In that *afraid*, which she sought to recover, the young lady betrayed that her affections were in danger of leaving her and betaking themselves to a new ruler, and this sudden inability to see through another's state of mind towards her was a further sign that they were not secure.

We are very clear of vision as to the affection tendered us, so long as we remain unmoved, but once our feelings are stirred, their palpitating fears so smear our sight that it becomes unreliable.

"Oh, well, it does not matter to you," I said; "you are not likely to think of him, he's so unattractive, but I must take care that he does not grow fond of you. If I see any danger of it, I'll tell him something about you that will nip his affections in the bud. You won't mind me doing that—just some little thing that won't hurt you, but will save him unnecessary pain?" And to this she replied with seeming indifference—

"I wish you'd tell Dora Eweword something that would shoo him off that he'd never come back, and then I would have seen the last of him, which would be a treat."

After this we were silent, and I thought she had gone to sleep, for there was no sound until Andrew came tumbling up the stairs leading from his room.

"I say!" he called, "have you got any more of that toothache stuff from the dentist?"

"Come along," I answered, "I'll put some in for you."

"I think it's the oranges that's doin' it, I eat nearly eight dozen to-day."

"Enough to give you the pip; you ought to slack off a little," I said, extending him the courtesy of his own vernacular.

"I bet I'd vote for Henderson after all if I could," he continued, in referring to the meeting, "only I'll gammon I wouldn't just to nark Uncle Jake. Henderson is the men's man, that other bloke belongs to wimmen.

You should have heard 'em to-night! The fellers behind
was tip-top, and made such a noise at last that Walker
could only talk to the wimmen in the front. We gave
him slops because he gets wimmen up to speak for him,
an' we can't give *them* gyp. One man asked him was
he in favour of ring-barkin' thistles, and another wanted
to know was he in favour of puttin' a tax on caterpillars.
He thinks no end of himself, because he's one of these
Johnnies the wimmen always runs after," gravely ex-
plained Andrew, aged sixteen.

"We cock-a-doodled and pip-pipped till you couldn't
hear your ears. Half couldn't get in, they was climbed
up an' hangin' in the windows—little girls too along
with the boys. I suppose now that they're as near got
a vote as we have, they'll be poked everywhere just the
same as if they had as good a right as us," said the boy
with the despondence of one to whom all is lost.

"It's a terrible thing they can't be made stay at home
out of all the fun like boys think they ought to be. No
mistake the woman having a vote is a terrible nark to
the men—almost too much for 'em to bear," said Dawn,
whom I had thought asleep.

"I reckon I'm goin' to every meetin', they're all right
fun," continued Andrew. "At the both committee room
they're givin' out tickets with the men's names on, an'
whoever likes can get them an' wear 'em in their hats.
Me an' Jack Bray went to this Johnny Walker's rooms
and gammoned we was for him, an' got a dozen tickets,
an' when we got outside tore 'em to smithereens; that's
what we'll do all the time."

After this Andrew disappeared down the stairs, spill-
ing grease, and being admonished by Dawn as he went
as the clumsiest creature she had ever seen.

Silence reigned between us for some time, and in listening to the trains I had forgotten the girl till her voice came across the room.

"I say, don't tell that Ernest anything not nice about me, will you ?   I'll take care not to flirt with him, and I wouldn't like him to think me not nice.   I wouldn't care about any one else a scrap, but he's such a great friend of yours, and as I hope to be with you a lot, it would be awkward; and you know he has *said* nothing, it might only be my conceit to think he's going the way of other men.   He took me to afternoon tea to-day at such a lovely place,—he said he wanted to be good to your friends, that's why he is nice to me.   I don't suppose he ever thinks of me at all any other way," she said with the despondence of love.

So this had been chasing sleep from Beauty's eyes, as such trifles have a knack of doing!

"Very likely," I said complacently, and smiled to myself.   The only thing to be discovered now was if the young athlete's emotions were at the same ebb, and then what was there against plain sailing to the happy port where honeymoons are spent ?

Fortune favours the persevering, and next afternoon an opportunity occurred for procuring the desired knowledge.

Ernest and Ada Grosvenor came in together, and to the casual observer seemed much engrossed with each other, but I noticed that Dawn could not speak or move, but a pair of quick dark eyes caught every detail.   So far so good, but it was necessary for Dawn to think the prize just a little farther out of reach than it was to make it attractive to her disposition, so I set about attaining this end by a very simple method.

Miss Grosvenor had called to invite us to a meeting she had convened, to listen to a public address by a lady who was going to head a deputation to Walker afterwards, and we had decided to go. Mrs Bray's husband also dropped in, and to my surprise proved not the henpecked nonentity one would expect after hearing his wife's aggressive diatribes, but a stalwart man of six feet, with a comely face bespeaking solid determination in every line. And when one comes to think of it, it is not the big blustering man or woman that rules, but the quiet, apparently inane specimens that look so meek that they are held up as models of propriety and gentleness. Miss Grosvenor immediately nailed him for her meeting, and politics being the only subject discussed, he aired his particular bug. This was his disgust at the top-heaviness of the Labour party's demands, and the railway people's easy times as compared with that of the farmer.

"I believe," said he, "in every man, if he can, working only eight hours a-day—though I have to work sixteen myself for precious little return, but these fellows are running the country to blazes. The rules of supply and demand must sway the labour or any other market all the world over, and they'll have to see that and haul in their sails."

"Who are you going to vote for?" inquired Andrew.

"I'm goin' for Henderson, and the missus for Walker."

"It's a wonder you don't compel Mrs Bray to vote for your man."

"No fear; I'm pleased she's taken the opposite chap, just to illustrate my opinion on what liberty of opinion should be; but I won't deny," he concluded, with a humorous smile, "that I mightn't be so pleased with her going against me if I was set on either of them, but as it is neither are worth a vote, so that I'm pretty well sitting on a rail myself."

"I thought your first announcement almost too liberal to be true," laughed Miss Grosvenor.

"No, I will say that Mr Bray is a man does treat his women proper, and give 'em liberty," said grandma.

"An' a nice way they use it," sniffed Carry *sotto voce*.

As we set out to the meeting Miss Grosvenor mentioned to me that she was endeavouring to find suitable speakers to address her association, and asked did I know of any one. Here was an opening for a thrust in the game of parry I was setting on foot between Dawn and Ernest Breslaw.

"Ask my friend Mr Ernest to deliver an address: 'Women in Politics,'" I said, "that is his particular subject. He is a most fluent speaker, and loves speaking in public, nothing will delight him more."

"I'll ask him at once," said she.

This was as foundationless a fairy-tale as was ever spun, for Ernest could not say two words in public upon any occasion. That he was usually tendered a dinner and was called upon to make a speech, he considered the drawback of wresting any athletic honours. Whether women were in politics or the wash-house was a sociological abstrusity beyond his line of thought, and not though it cost him all his fortune to refuse could he have decently addressed any association even on beloved sporting matters. Hence his consternation when Miss Grosvenor approached him. At first he was nonplussed, and next thing, taking it as a joke on my part, was highly amused. Miss Grosvenor, on her side, thought he was joking, with the result that there was the liveliest and most laughable conversation between them.

Dawn did not know the reason of it. She could only see that Ernest and Miss Grosvenor were engrossed, and at first curious, a little later she was annoyed with the former.

"I think," she whispered to me, "it's Mr Ernest you'll have to see doesn't flirt with every girl he comes across."

"Perhaps he isn't flirting," I coolly replied.

"Not *now*, perhaps," she said pointedly; "perhaps he's in earnest with one and practises with others."

Arrived at the hall, we found the women swarming around Walker like bees.

"Good Lord! Look what Les. has let himself in for," laughed Ernest; "I wouldn't stand in his shoes for a tenner."

"Go on! Surely you too are partial to ladies?"

"Yes; but——"

"But there must be reason in everythink," I quoted. He laughed.

"Yes; and reason in this sort of thing to suit my taste would be a small medium. But what a fine old sport the old dame Clay would have made—no danger of her not standing up to a mauling or baulking at any of her fences, eh?"

Dawn would not look at Ernest after the meeting and deputation came to an end, but walked home with "Dora" Eweword, laughing and talking in ostentatious enjoyment; while Ernest and the Grosvenor girl were none the less entertained.

"'Pon my soul, I couldn't make a speech to save my life," he reiterated. "My friend only laid you on for a lark, did you not?" he said, turning to me, whom he gallantly insisted upon supporting on his arm — that splendid arm in which the muscles could expand till they were like iron bands.

"Don't you believe him, Miss Grosvenor," I replied; "he's a born orator, but is unaccountably lazy and vain, and only wants to be pressed; insist upon his speaking, he's longing to do so." And then his merry protesting laugh, and the girl's equally happy, rang out on the crisp starlight air, as they went over and over the same ground.

As we neared Clay's I suggested that he should see Miss Grosvenor home, while I attached myself to Dawn and "Dora"; and I invited him to come and sing some songs with us afterwards, for the night was yet young.

To this he agreed, and supposed to be with the other young couple, I slipped behind, and could hear their conversation as they progressed.

"You're not struck on that red-headed mug, are you?" said Eweword, for general though political talk had become, there was still another branch of politics more vitally interesting to some of the electors.

"I'm not the style to be struck on a fellow that doesn't care for me."

"But he does!"

"Looks like it, doesn't it?" she said sarcastically.

"Yes, it does, or what would he be hanging around here so long for?"

"Perhaps to see Ada Grosvenor; I suppose she'd have him, red hair and all."

"Pooh! he never goes there; but he comes to your place though, too deuced often for my pleasure."

"He comes to see the boarder—he's a great friend of hers."

"Humph! that's all in my eye. He'd be a long time

coming to see her if you weren't there, if she was twice
as great a friend. What sort of an old party is she?
Must have some means."

"Oh, lovely!"

"I suppose the red-headed mug thinks so too, as she
is touting for him."

"For him and Ada Grosvenor."

"Have it that way if you like it, but you know what
I mean all right."

"I don't."

"Oh, don't you! I say, Dawn, just stop out here a
moment will you? I want to tell you something else,
I mean."

"Oh, tell it to me some other time," said she, "it's
too beastly cold to stay out another minute. Come and
tell it to me while we are having supper round the
fire."

"I'd have a pretty show of telling it there. I don't
want it put in the 'Noonoon Advertiser,' but that's what
I'll have to do if you won't give me a chance. If you
keep pretending you don't get my letters, I'll write all
that I put in them to your grandma, and tell her to
tell you," he said jokingly; but the girl took him up
shortly.

"If you dare do that," said she, aroused from her
indifference, "I'd never speak to you again the longest
day I live, so you needn't think you'll get over me that
way. You'd better tell Uncle Jake and Andrew too
while you're about it, and Dora Cowper might be vexed
if you don't tell her."

"Well, I bet you'd listen to what the red-headed mug
said quick enough," replied "Dora" Eweword in an
injured tone.

"The red-headed mug, as you call him—and his hair isn't much redder than yours, and is twice as nice," she retaliated, "he would be a gentleman anyhow, and not a bear with a scalded head."

By this time they had reached the gate, and Dawn was carelessly inviting him to enter, but he declined in rather a crestfallen tone.

"Better invite red-head, not me, if you won't listen to what I say, and pretend you never received my letters."

"Thank you for the good advice. I hope he'll accept my invitation, because he is always pleasant and agreeable," she retorted.

NINETEEN.

AN OPPORTUNELY INOPPORTUNE DOUCHE.

IT was just as well that "Dora" Eweword had been too chopfallen to come in, for we found the place in what grandma termed "a uproar."

As we had gone out Mrs Bray had arrived to relate her speculations in regard to Mrs Rooney - Molyneux. Mrs Bray did not live a great distance from the latter's cottage, and as she had not seen her about during the day, wondered had she come to her travail.

Andrew decided the matter when he came home by relating what he had heard when passing the cottage; and he supplemented the statement by the deplorable information that "the old bloke is up at Jimmeny's tryin' if he can get a free drink."

"I must go to her," said grandma, rising in haste.

"I wouldn't if I was you," said Mrs Bray. "You don't never get no thanks for nothing like that, and might get yourself into a mess; I believe in leaving people to manage their own affairs."

Carry sniffed in the background.

"I'll risk all that," said grandma. "For shame's sake an' the sake of me daughters, an' every other woman, I couldn't leave one of me sex in that predicament."

"Oh, well, some people is wonderful strong in the nerve that way," said Mrs Bray, and Carry interjected in an aside—

"And others are mighty strong in the nerve of self-ishness."

"Of course nothing would give me greater pleasure than to go," continued Mrs Bray, "but I would be of no use. I'm so pitiful, sensitive, and nervous that way."

"It's a grand thing, then, that some are hard and not so sensitive, or people could die and no one would help 'em," said Carry, no longer able to contain her measure of Mrs Bray.

Uncle Jake had the sulky in readiness, and grandma with a collection of requisites appeared with a great old shawl about her, Irish fashion.

"Come you, Dawn, I might want your help, I'm not as strong as I was once; and Andrew, you come too, you'll do to send for the doctor; an' who'll take care of the pony?"

I volunteered, and though a rotten stick to depend on, was accepted, and we three women rode in the sulky while Andrew ran behind. Having arrived at the little cottage half-way between Clay's and town, we found it was too sadly true that the poor little woman was alone in her trouble, and worse, she had not had the means to prepare for it, while most ghastly of all, there was no trace of her having had any nourishment that day.

These are the sad cases of poverty, when the helpless victim is not of the calibre which can beg, and suffers an empty larder in silence and behind an appearance of respectability.

The capable old grandmother had prepared herself for this possibility, and from under her capacious shawl produced a bottle of broth which she set about warming. She may not have been at first-hand acquainted with the few silk-wrapped lives run according to the methods scheduled in first-class etiquette books, but she had a very resourceful and far-seeing grip of that style of existence into which, regardless of inclination or capability, the great majority are forced by domineering circumstance; and being competent to grapple with its emergencies, she took hold of this case without humbug and with the fortitude and skill of a Japanese general.

As though the main trouble were not enough, the poor little wife was further smitten with the two-edged mental anguish which is the experience of sensitive women whose husbands neglect them at this crisis of the maternal gethsemane. Doctor Smalley, who soon appeared after receiving Andrew's message, was not sufficiently finely strung to fully estimate the evil effect of Rooney-Molyneux's behaviour at this juncture; but not so the fine old woman of the ranks, with her quick perceptions and high and sensitive sentiment regarding the bed-rock relations of life. Calling the doctor out during an interval she discussed the matter within my hearing.

"Poor little thing, she's just heart-broke with the way her husband's carryin' on. I wish I could deliver him up to Mrs Bray to scald; he's one of 'em deserves it, pure an' simple! If Jim Clay had forsook me an' demeaned me like this I would have died, but he was always tenderer than a mother. Somethink will have to be done. I'll send Andrew to Jimmeny's with the sulky to get him; he can get Danby to help him if he can't manage him hisself, and take the old varmint down to my place and keep him there secure. Tell Jake there it's got to be done, an' I'll make up a yarn to pacify the poor thing;" and returning to her patient, to the old dame's credit, truthful though she was, I heard her say—

"Your husband's been fidgeting me, an' I never can stand any one but the doctor about at these times, so I bundled him off down to stay with Jake, and gave him strict instructions not to poke his nose back here till he's sent for."

What diplomat could have made it more kindly tactful than that ?

"Quite right too," said the doctor, upholding her. "When I see it's going to be a good case like this, I always banish the man too."

"But I could have seen him, and the poor fellow I'm sure is overwhelmed with anxiety," said the hapless little martyr in the brave make-believe that is a compulsory science with most women.

"Well, *we* ain't so anxious about him as we are about you," said the valiant old woman. "You're the chief person now. He ain't no consideration at all, an' can go an' bag his head for all we care, while we get you out of this fix."

I sat upon the verandah until Andrew passed, taking home with him the noble Rooney-Molyneux, lordly scion of an ancient and doubtless effete house, and then the doctor banished Dawn from the house, giving her into my charge, with instructions to take her home and calm her down.

Had she been the heroine of a romance she would have been a born nurse. Without any training or experience she could have surpassed Florence Nightingale, but, alas ! she was merely an everyday girl in real life, and this being her first actual experience of the tragedy of birth, and the terror of it being intensified and aggravated by the pitiable surrounding circumstances, she was beside herself. She clung to me, choked with a flood of tears, and palpitating in an unbearable tumult of emotion.

This case, so pathetically ordinary that most of us are debased by acquaintance with similar, to this girl was fresh, and striking her in all its inexcusable barbarity without any extenuating gloze, made her furious with pained and righteous indignation.

I led her about by devious ways that her heart might cool ere we reached Clay's.

The cloudless, breezeless night, though not yet severely cold, was crisp with the purity of frost and sweet with the exquisite scent of flowering loquats. The only sounds breaking its stillness were the trains passing across the long viaduct approaching the bridge, and the rumble of the vehicles as they ground their homeward way along the stony road, their lights flashing as they passed, and snatches of the occupants' conversation reaching us where we walked on a path beside the main thoroughfare. The heavens were a spangled glory, and the dark sleeping lands gave forth a fresh, pleasant odour. Man provided the only discordant note; but for the jarring of his misdoings there would have been perfect peace.

Oh, the hot young heart that raged by my side! I too had forded the cruel torrent of facts that was torturing her mind; I knew; I understood. By-and-by she would arrive at my phase and have somewhat of my calmness, but to tell her so would merely have been the preaching so deservedly and naturally abhorred by the young, and except for holding her hand in a tight clasp, I was apparently unresponsive.

As she grew quieter I steered for home, and eventually we arrived at the door of the kitchen and found there Jake, Andrew, and the Rooney-Molyneux—a small man with a large beard and the type of aristocratic face furnished with a long protruding nose and a narrow retreating forehead. Carry, up aloft like the angels, could be heard practising on my piano, and the soiled utensils scattered on the table illustrated that the gentlemen had had refreshments.

It being Dawn's week in the kitchen, she set about collecting the cups in the wash-up dish, and presently some maudlin expression of sentiment on the part of the Rooney - Molyneux reopened the vials of her indignation.

" I'm naturally anxious that it may be a son," he drivelled, " as there are so few male representatives of the old name now."

" And the sooner there's none the better. There is no excuse for the likes of you being alive. I'd like to assist in the extermination of your family by putting you in the boiling copper on washing day. That would give you a taste of your deserts," raged the girl.

She was speaking without restraint in the light of the high demands of crude, impetuous, merciless youth. I had once felt as she did, but now I could see the cruel train of conditions behind certain characters forcing them into different positions, and in place of Dawn's wholesome, justifiable, hot - headed rage against the likes of Rooney-hyphen, I felt for him a contempt so immeasurable that it almost toppled over and became pity.

Seeing the little sense of responsibility that is inculcated regarding the laws of being, instead of being shocked at the familiarity of the Rooney-Molyneux type of husband and father, I gave myself up to agreeable surprise owing to the large number of noble and worthy parents I had discovered.

"The world does soil our minds and we soil it—
Time brings the tolerance that hides the truth,"

but Dawn had not yet sunk to the apathy engendered by
experience and familiarity. She adjudged the case on its
merits, as it would be handled by an administrator of the
law—the common law we all must keep. She did not
imagine a network of exculpatory conditions or go squint-
ing round corners to draw it into line as an act for which
circumstances rather than the culprit were responsible ;
she gazed straight and honestly and saw a crime.

"Dawn, you shameless hussy, you ought to be ashamed
of yourself," said her uncle.

"Oh yes, I'm well aware that any girl who says the
straight truth about the things that concern them most in
life, *ought* to be ashamed of herself. They should hold
their tongues except to flatter the men who trample them
in the dust,—that's the proper and *womanly* attitude for a
girl, I know," she said desperately.

"I'm sure this is uncalled for," simpered the hero of the
act, rising and showing signs of looking for his hat.

"You'd better run and tell your wife you've been
insulted, poor little dear !" said Dawn.

"Look !" said Andrew to me uneasily, "tell Dawn to
dry up, will you ; she'll take no notice of me, an' if that
feller goes home actin' the goat I'll get the blame, an'
he ain't drunk enough to be shut up. Blow him, I
say !"

"I'm sure," said Mr Rooney-Molyneux, who apparently
had various things mixed with politics, "that some men,
though the women have taken the votes and their man-
hood, still have some rights ; bless me, it *must* be acknow-
ledged they have some rights in creation !"

Here he made an ineffectual grab for his hat and a

sprawling plunge in the direction of the door, saying,
"I've never been so insulted!"

"Blow you! Sit down, Mr Mooney-Rollyno, or what-
ever you are," said Andrew, "you've got to stay here; and
Dawn, hold your mag! You'd give any one the pip with
your infernal gab."

"I'm sure it must be conceded that men have some
rights?" Mr Rooney-Molyneux appealed to me. I was
the most responsible person present, Uncle Jake did not
count, the other three were children, and so it behoved me
to take a grip of the situation.

"Rights in creation! I should rather think so! In
creation men have the rights, or perhaps duties, of gods
—to protect, to nurture, to guard and to love, and when
as a majority men rise to them we shall be a great
people, but for the present the only rights many of
them wrest and assert by mere superior brute force
are those of bullies and selfish cowards. Sit down
immediately!"

He sat without delay.

"All that Dawn says of you is deserved. The least
you can do now to repair matters is to swallow your
pill noiselessly and give no further trouble until you are
called upon to obstruct the way again in semblance of
discharging responsibilities of which a cat would be twice
as capable."

"Yes," said Dawn, "if you dare to talk of going home
to worry your wife I'll throw this dish of water right on
you, and when I come to think of things, I feel like
throwing a hot one on every man."

As she said this she swirled her dishcloth to clean the
bowl, and turning to toss the water into the drain outside
the door, confronted Ernest Breslaw.

Quite two hours had elapsed since he had parted from us to conduct Miss Grosvenor to her home, where he had been long delayed in argument concerning whether he could or could not address a public meeting. I discovered later that an opportunity to gracefully take his leave from Grosvenor's had not occurred earlier, and that he had quite relinquished hope of calling at Clay's that night, but to his surprise, seeing the place lighted as he was passing, he came towards the kitchen door.

Dawn was doubtless piqued that he should have spent so much time with Miss Grosvenor, which, considering his previous attentions to her, and the rules of the game as observed in this stratum of society, gave him the semblance of flirting — perfidious action, worthy of the miscreant man in the beginning of a career which at a maturer stage should cover cruelty and cowardice equalling that of Rooney-Molyneux! Dawn lacked restraint in her emotional outbursts; the poor girl's state of nervousness bordered on hysteria; the water was nearly out of her hand in any case, and with a smack of that irritated divergence from lawful and decorous conduct of which the sanest of us are at times the victim, she pitched the dish of greasy, warm water fairly on the immaculate young athlete, accompanying the action with the ejaculation—

"That's what you deserve, too!"

"I demand——" he exclaimed, but further utterance was drowned by a hearty guffaw from Andrew which fully confirmed the outrageous insult.

"Just what I should expect of you," sneered Uncle Jake, while Mr Rooney-Molyneux, his attention thus diverted from his own affairs, gazed in watery-eyed surprise at a second victim of the retributive Dawn.

"Well, that's about what you'd expect from *a thing earning her living,* but never of a young lady in a *good* home of her own and living with *the mother of a family,*" said Carry, appearing in time to witness the accident.

I said nothing to the white-faced girl, for there was more urgent work to be done in repairing the damage. Hurrying through the house, and reefing my skirts on the naked rose-bushes under Miss Flipp's window, where the dead girl's skirts had caught as she went out to die, I gained a point intercepting Ernest as he strode along the path leading to the bridge.

"Ernest!"

"You must excuse me to-night," he said, showing that my intervention was most unwelcome.

"Ernest, if you have any friendship for me, stop. I must speak to you, and I'm not feeling able for much more to-night."

Thus did I make a lever of my invalidism, and in the gentleness of his strength he submitted to be detained.

Some men would have covered their annoyance with humorous satire, but Ernest was not furnished with this weapon. He only had physical strength, and that could not avail him in such an instance. I placed my hand on his arm, ostensibly for support, but in reality to be sure of his detention, and found that he was saturated. Not a pleasant experience on a frosty night, but there was no danger of it proving deleterious to one in his present state of excitement. Being one of those natures whose emotions, though not subtle, make up for this deficiency in wholesome thoroughness, he was furious with the rage of heated youth not given to spending itself on every adventitious excuse for annoyance, and debarred by conditions from any sort of retaliation. In addition to being bitterly wounded, his sporting instinct was bruised, and he chafed under the unfairness of the blow.

The beauty of the cloudless, breezeless night had been supplemented by a lop-sided moon, risen sufficiently to show the exquisite mists hanging like great swathes of white gossamer in the hollows, and to cast the shadows of the buildings and trees in the silent river, at this time of the year looking so cold and treacherous in its ripple-less flow. The wet grass was stiffening with frost, and the only sounds disturbing the chillier purity of advancing night were the erratic bell at the bridge and the far-off rumble of a train on the mountain-side. Man still afforded the discordant note, and the only heat in the surroundings was that in the burning young heart that raged by my side.

Oh, youth! youth! You must each look back and see for yourselves, in the aft-light cast by later experience, the mountains and fiery ordeals you made for yourselves out of mole-hills in the matter of heartbreak. We, whose hair is white, cannot help you, though we have gone before and know so well the cruel stretches on the road you travel.

Ernest waited for me to take the initiative, and as everything that rose to my lips seemed banal, we stood awkwardly silent till he was forced into saying—

"I'm afraid you are overdoing yourself. Can I not help you to your room? You will be ill."

"The only thing that would overdo me is that you should be upset about this. It must not make any difference."

"Difference between you and me?—nothing short of an earthquake could do that," he replied.

"I mean with Dawn. It must not make any difference with her. It was only a freak."

"Certainly; I would be a long time retaliating upon a *lady*, no matter what she did to me; but when—when ——" (he could not bring himself to name it, it struck him as so disgraceful)—"she intimates to me, as plainly as was done to-night, that she disapproves of my presence in her house, well, a fellow would want pole-axing if he hadn't pride to take a hint like that."

"She did not mean anything. She will be more hurt than you are."

"Mean anything! Had it been a joke I could have managed to endure it, or an accident about which she would have worried, I would have been amused, but it was deliberate; and if it had been *clean* water—but ugh! it was greasy slop-water, to make it as bad as it could be; and if a man had done it——"

The muscles of his arm expanded under my interested touch as he made a fist of the strong brown hand.

"But being a girl I can only put up with it," he said with the helplessness of the athlete in dealing with such a delinquent.

"Did you hear what she said too? Great Scott! it is not as though I had done her any harm! I merely came here to see a friend, and made myself agreeable because you said she was good to you; and, dear me!" His voice broke with the fervour of his perturbation. He had been wounded to the core of his manly *amour propre;* and to state that he was not more than twenty-five, gives a better idea of his state of mind than could any amount of laborious diagnosis.

"What can I have done?" he further ejaculated. "Can some one have told her falsely that I'm a cad

in any way? She might have waited until she proved
it. *I* would not have believed had any one spoken
badly of *her*." (Here an inadvertent confession of the
growing affection he felt for her.) "Even if I were de-
serving of such ignominy, it was none of her business.
I only came to see you,—she had nothing to do with
me."

Then I took hold of this splendidly muscular young
creature wounded to the quick. I determinedly usurped
a mother's privilege in regard to the situation, and
glancing back over my barren life I would that I had
been mother of just such a son. What a kingdom
'twould have been; and, in the order of things, being
forced to surrender him to another's keeping, I could
not have chosen a better or more suitable than Dawn.
Entering his principality to reign as queen, while his
manhood was yet an unsacked stronghold, she was of
the character and determination to steer him in the
way of uprightness to the end.

Wistfulness upsprung as I reviewed my empty life,
but rude reality suddenly uprose and obliterated ideality.
It put on the scroll a picture of motherhood, and mother-
love wantonly squandered, trodden in the mire, and,
instead of being recognised as a kingdom, treated only
as a weakness, and traded upon to enslave women. I
turned with a sigh, and we walked round a corner of
the garden where, in one recent instance, appallingly
common, a poor frail woman had crept out in the dead
of night to pay alone the penalty of a crime incurred
by two—one foolish and weak, the other murderously
selfishly a coward.

I addressed Ernest Breslaw regarding the painful effect
this tragedy had produced on the mind of Dawn, and

how it had been further overstrung by the later one, and concluded—

"Had I expressed my inward feelings in outward actions at Dawn's age, and being armed with a dish of water, to have thrown it on the nearest individual would have been a very mild ebullition; but I set my teeth against outward expression and let it fester in my heart, while the beauty of Dawn's disposition is that her feelings all come out. She has disgraced herself by making outward demonstration of what many inwardly feel; but understanding what I have put before you, you must not hold the girl responsible for her action."

With masculine simplicity he was unable to comprehend the complexity of feminine emotions engendered by the exigencies of the more artificial and suppressed conditions of life as forced upon women.

"I understand about old Rooney; I feel as disgusted with him as any one does, but *I* am not going to emulate him. I'd jolly well cut my throat first; and if I could lay my hand on the snake at the root of the drowning case, I'd make one to roast him alive! What made Miss Dawn confound me with that sort?"

"She doesn't for an instant do so. On the contrary, she would be the first to repudiate such a suggestion."

"Good Lord! then why did she throw that stuff on me? It was only fit for a criminal."

"Can you not grasp that she was irritated beyond endurance with the unwholesomeness of the whole system of life in relation to women, and that for the moment you appeared as one of the army of oppressors?"

"But that isn't fair! *I* know enough of women—some women—to make one shudder with repulsion; but there would be no sense or justice in venting my disgust on you or the other good ones," he contended.

"Quite so; but our moral laws are such that some issues are more repulsive to a woman than a man, and you must admit there are heavy arguments could be brought in extenuation of Dawn's attitude of mind when the water slipped out of her hand."

"There's no doubt women do have to swallow a lot," he said.

"You don't feel so angry on account of the impetuous Dawn's act now, do you?"

"It doesn't look so bad in the teeth of your argument, and if she would only say something to explain, I won't mind; but otherwise I'll have sense to make myself scarce in this neighbourhood."

"I'm afraid her vanity will be too wounded for her to give in."

"I'll make it as easy for her as I can; but, good Lord! I can't go to her and apologise because she threw dirty water on me."

"Well, I'll bid you good-night. I must run in to Dawn. I expect she is sobbing her heart out by this, and biting her pretty curled lips to relieve her feelings,—her lips that were meant for kisses, not cruel usage."

"Good heavens! Do you really think she'll feel like that?" he asked in astonishment.

"I'm certain."

"But I can't see why—she might have had reason had I been the aggressor."

"If you had hurt her she would not feel half so bad. You would be a hopeless booby if you could not understand that."

" Really, now, if I thought she would take it that way, it would make all the difference in the world. But had she desired to despatch me, half that energy of insult would do," he said, drawing up, while hardness crept into his voice, but it softened again as he concluded—

" I wouldn't like her to be upset about it, though, if she didn't quite mean it."

" Well, you can be sure that in regard to you she was very far from meaning it, and that she will be dreadfully upset about it; so think of what I've said, and come and see me in the morning."

Now that he had grown calm, he was shivering with the cold, so I bade him run home.

On returning to the house I found Andrew the solitary watcher of his charge, who, covered by an old cloak, was snoring on the kitchen sofa.

" Dear me, where are they all ? "

" In bed ; and look at his nibbs there. I reckon I took a wrinkle from Dawn as how to manage him. Soon as every one's back was turned he began actin' the goat again an' makin' for home, an' I thought here goes, I don't care a hang if all the others roused on me like blazes, so long as grandma don't, — she's the only one makes me sit up,—so I flung water on him, not warm water but real cold. It took seven years' growth out of him, an' then I gave him a drink of hot coffee, an' undressed him, an' he was jolly glad to lay down there."

" Why, you'll give the man a cold ! "

" No jolly fear. I took his clothes off. I've got 'em dryin' here. I couldn't find any of my gear, an' wasn't game to ask Uncle Jake, so I clapped him into a night-dress of grandma's. Look ! he's got his hand out. I reckon the frill looks all so gay, don't you? I bet grandma will rouse, but I'll have a little peace with him now an' chance the ducks," said the resourceful warder, whose charge really looked so absurd that I was provoked to laughter.

"How did you manage him? Was he tractable?"

"He soon dropped that there was no good in bein' nothing else. He spluttered something about me disgracin' him, because something on his crest said he was brave or something; but I told him I didn't care a hang if he had a crest the size of a cockatoo or was as bald as Uncle Jake, that I was full of him actin' the goat, an' that finished him."

"Enough too," I laughed, as I bade the Australian lad, with the very Australian estimate of the unimportance of some things sacred to English minds, the Australian parting salute—

"So long!"

TWENTY.

"ALAS! HOW EASILY THINGS GO WRONG!"

ON ascending to my room I did not, as expected, find Dawn sobbing, but she had her face so determinedly turned away that I refrained from remark. I was none the worse for the diverting incidents of the evening, because the excitement of them had come from without instead of within. The rush of the trains soon became a far-away sound, and the light that flashed from their engine-doors as they climbed the first zig of the moun tain, and which could be seen from my bed, had been shut from my sight by the fogs of approaching sleep, when I was aroused by heart-broken sobbing from the bed by the opposite wall.

After a while I got out of bed, bent on an attempt to comfort.

"Dawn, what is it?"

"I'm sorry I waked you, I thought you were sound asleep," she said, pulling in with a violent effort but speedily breaking into renewed sobs.

"I was thinking of poor little Mrs Rooney-Molyneux, and how my mother died," said the girl, rolling over and burying her lovely head in her tear-drenched pillow. "I can't help thinking about the sadness and cruelty of life to women."

I felt certain that a matter less deep and lying farther from the core of being was perturbing her more, but as she chose to ignore it, I did likewise.

"Well, we must not dwell too sadly on that for which we are not responsible, and women are privileged in being able to repay the cost of their being."

"Yes, I always remember that, and often shudder to think I might have been a man, with their greater possibilities of cowardliness and selfish cruelty, as illustrated by old Rooney and Miss Flipp's destroyer."

Not a word concerning her action to Ernest. Thought of it stung too much for mention, so there was nothing to do but comfort her till she fell asleep and await from Ernest the next turn of events bearing on the situation.

The next turn of events in the Clay household bore down upon us next morning after breakfast when grandma came home, having left the first-born of Rooney-Molyneux comfortably asleep in the swaddling clothes which had contained Dawn at the date when she had been "a little winjin' thing," with whom everything had disagreed, and which garments were lent to the new-born babe until grandma could provide him with others. The hale old dame was not too fatigued to be in a state of lively ire, and opened fire upon her circle with—

"I met old Hollis on the way home, an' do you believe, he says to me, 'Well, Mrs Clay, so I believe you've took to rabbit ketchin' in your old days.' It was like his cheek, the same as w'en he said the monkeys would be havin' a vote next. *Rabbit ketchin'* indeed! No wonder women has got sense at last to make the birth-rate decline, when you see cases like that, and even the people that go to help them out of the fix—an' that out of kindness, not for no reward nor pleasure—is demeaned to their face an' called

rabbit ketchers, if you please! I reckon all women ought
to be compelled to be *rabbit ketchers* for a time, an' it
would be such a eye-opener to them that if there wasn't
some alterations made in the tone of the whole business
they would all strike so there'd be no need of *rabbit
ketchin'*, as some call it, to make things more disagreeabler;
and that's what has been goin' on lately in a underhand
way, but *some people*," concluded the intelligent old lady
with her customary choler, coming to a full stop ere
recapitulating the misdoings of these unmentionable
members of society.

"Rabbit ketching," as midwifery is contemptuously
termed in the vernacular, does require a status, and those
who have need of it merit some consideration. Civilisa-
tion, stretching up to recognise that every child is a
portion of State wealth, may presently make some move-
ment to recognise maternity as a business or office need-
ing time and strength, not as a mere passing detail thrown
in among mountains of other slavery.

During the whole forenoon I busied myself with the
construction of garments for the new arrival in this vale
of woe, and at the same time was on the alert for the
commanded appearance of Ernest Breslaw. Instead of
himself he sent as messenger a well-spoken lad, who
presented Mr Ernest's compliments, and hoped that I was
not feeling any ill effects from my unusual exertion during
the previous evening.

I sent a request, per return, that he should call upon
me during the afternoon, but he did not regard it. The
next being Dawn's day for Sydney, I waited for this event
to hatch some progress in the case, but upon her return
she had no favours to share with me or merry tale to tell
of being taken to afternoon tea by Ernest.

Eweword figured in this account, and so prominently as to suggest that her talk of the fun she had had with him was a little forced, so on the following morning I took it upon myself to call upon the backward knight in his own castle. Unmooring one of the boats, I rowed with great caution obliquely across the stream till, reaching the desired pier, I tethered my craft and ascended among an orange-grove laden with its golden fruit, and between the rattling canes of the vineyard dismantled by winter, till I reached the house where at present my young friend sojourned, and I was thankful that bleached as well as unfaded locks having their own peculiar privileges, I was able to make this call with propriety.

The young gentleman was in, and without delay appeared to the beautiful lady's self-directed and appointed ambassadress.

" I suppose I may pay you a visit," I said with a smile as he seated me in the drawing-room which we had to ourselves. " As you didn't seem to care whether I were dead or alive I have come over to practically illustrate that I'm still above ground. Why did you not come to see me ? "

Ernest reddened and fidgeted, and said haltingly—

" You know if you had been ill I would have been the first to go to you, but I knew you were quite well, and I've been so busy," he finished lamely.

" Now, you know that I know that you have been idle— quite unendurably idle," I retorted, a remark he received in embarrassed silence, which endured till I broke it with—

" Well, I suppose you are waiting for me to divulge the real object of my pilgrimage, and that is to know why you haven't kept your agreement about making that little mistake as easy as you could for Miss Dawn. She's fretting herself pale about it."

Ernest stood up, his colour flaming into his tanned cheeks till they were as bright as his locks, while he made as though to speak once or twice, but hesitated, and at length exclaimed—

"This is not fair—you must, you have no reason to bother — you," and there he foundered. Ernest could neither lie, snub, nor evade. He was totally devoid of all the attributes of a smart politician.

"Have you not sufficient faith in my regard for you to trust my motive in thus apparently seeking to pry into your private life?" I asked.

"You know I think more of you than any one, and I'll tell you the whole thing," he replied, taking a seat beside me.

"You have made a mistake in assuming that Miss Clay, or whatever her real name might be (his indifference was well assumed), did not fully mean her action, and I was a fool to believe you when I had more than sufficient proof to the contrary. Yesterday morning I happened to go to Sydney in the same train as she did, and as I happened— entirely by chance and quite unexpectedly—to meet her on the platform, I lifted my hat as usual to make it easy for her, and a nice fool I made of myself. She didn't merely pretend not to see me, but hurried by me in contempt and came back with that Eweword, who glared at me as though I were a tramp who had attempted to molest her. I am sure you could not expect me to go any farther than that, and I only did that because you call her a friend of yours. Perhaps Eweword doesn't do things that necessitate the throwing of dirty water on him. It was rather an uncalled-for thing to do to any one. Perhaps the old dame doesn't allow her boarders to have visitors, and that is the polite way they have of informing one to the contrary."

The sky looked rather murky. I said nothing, having nothing ready to say.

"Oh, by the way, I'm leaving here to-morrow for Adelaide, where I am to play in some inter - colonial football matches against the New Zealanders. Is there anything I could do for you over there?" he said, as though having dismissed the other unworthy trifle from his mind.

"Going to run away because a girl, half accidentally and half out of nervous irritation, threw a little water on you!"

There I had said what I really thought, and half expected the snub which, according to the rules of tact, I deserved for my divergence therefrom, but it did not come; he was a man of the field, and in this type of encounter had not a chance against one of my perceptions.

He laughed forcedly. "That would be something to turn tail for, wouldn't it?"

"But are you not doing so? If a beautiful girl did such a thing to me it would only make me the more set to woo her to graciousness," I said.

"Perhaps so, if she were some girl you specially considered, but in the case of a passing stranger that I may never meet again, it would not be worth wasting time, especially as her action was so uncalled for and unwomanly."

"But you are sure to meet her again if you continue our friendship, as I hope to have her with me, and that is why I'm taking the trouble to thus interfere in what does not apparently concern either you or me very much. *I* don't consider Dawn as a passing stranger. I think her especially honest and especially beautiful, and it worries me to think she has thus erred. Her action was *unwomanly*, if you like, but peculiarly feminine, with the unavoidable hysterical femininity engendered in women by their subjected environment. Are you quite sure you consider Dawn merely a passing stranger not worth consideration?" I asked, looking him fair in the eyes; and the quick lowering of them and the tightening of his mouth satisfied me that he could not truthfully answer in the affirmative.

"It is a matter of what she considers me," he said.

"Oh, well," I said indifferently, now that I had gained my point, "it doesn't matter to me, but I'll be sorry to lose your company, and I thought you were taking an interest in Leslie's candidature, and we could have enjoyed it together."

"So I do."

"Well, come back as soon as you get these matches played, and we'll have some good times together again, and I'll keep the reprehensible Dawn out of the way; and anyhow, remember she didn't throw *cold* water on you, and that's something."

"Very well, I'll be back in about three weeks' time to see how Les. gets on. Polling-day hasn't been fixed yet. I'd like to see it through now I've started."

"Of course," said I, considering it a good move that he should disappear for a short time, and after this he rowed me on the Noonoon till Clay's dinner-bell sounded and I went up to eat.

That evening "Dora" Eweword came in to tea and

remained afterwards. He informed us that the red-
headed chap who had been loafing around Kelman's had
gone to Europe.

"Has he? Did he tell you?" interestedly inquired
Andrew.

"He mentioned that he would leave for South Aus-
tralia by the express this evening," I replied, but did not
add that his going to Europe was a little stretched.

Dawn was quiet. Her merry impudence did not en-
liven the company that night, and after tea, when
Eweword caught her alone for a few moments as I was
leaving the room, he said—

"So you cleared the red-headed mug out after all.
Andrew says it was alright. You won't listen to me,
but you haven't chucked the wash-up water on me yet,
that's one thing." His complacence was very pronounced.
To his surprise Dawn made no reply, but biting her lip
to keep back her tears, walked out of the room, and in
the dark of the passage smote her dimpled palms together,
exclaiming—

"Would to heaven I had thrown the water over this
galoot instead of *him*," and the thermometer of "Dora's"
self-satisfaction fell considerably when she did not appear
again that evening.

That night, when the waning moon got far enough on
her westward way to surmount the old house on the
knoll beside the Noonoon and cast its shadow in the
deep clear water, the silver beams strayed through a little
window facing the great ranges, and found the features
of a beautiful sleeper disfigured by weeping; but youth's
rest was sound despite the tear-stains, and the old moon
smiled at such ephemeral sorrow. The night wind coming
down the gorges with the river sighed along the valley

as the moon remembered all the faces which, though tear-less under her nocturnal inspection, yet were pale from the inward sobs, only giving outward evidence in bleach-ing locks and shadowy eyes. Even within sound of the engines roaring down the spur, many of the little night-wrapped houses, hard set upon the plain, had inmates kept from sleep by deeper sorrows than Dawn had ever known.

The first fortnight of Ernest's absence, believed by his doubting young lady to be final, was a stirring time in Noonoon, and particularly full at Clay's. Jam-making was the star item on the latter's domestic bill. Baskets and baskets of golden oranges and paler lemons and shaddocks were converted into jam and marmalade, and ranged on the shelves of the already replete storehouse, in readiness to tempt the summer palate of the week-end boarders which should appear when the days stretched out again. We were occupied in this business to such an extent that the sight of oranges became a weariness, and Andrew averred that the very name of marmalade gave him the pip.

At night we enjoyed the diversion of the meetings, and talk and gossip of them made conversation for the days. The previously mentioned political addresses were but mild fanfares by comparison with the flamboyance of the gasconading now in progress, and in its reports of these bursts of oratory the 'Noonoon Advertiser' gave further evidence of its broad-minded liberality.

"Mrs Gas Ranter," it reported, "addressed a packed meeting in the Citizens' Hall last night, and proved her-self the best public speaker who has been heard in Noonoon during the present campaign," &c. It recog-nised worth, and gamely gave the palm to the deserving, irrespective of party or sex,—did not so much as insert the narrow quibble that she was the best for a woman.

Among other incidents, the lady canvassers called at Clay's and received a piece of grandma's mind.

"Thanks; I don't want no one to tell me how to vote. I've rared two or three families and gave a hand with more, and have intelligence the same as others, and at my time of my life don't want no one to tell me my business. I reckon I could tell a good many others how to vote."

The pity of it was that it was immaterial how any electors cast their vote. Neither party had a sensible grip of affairs, and besides, love of country in a patriotic way is not a trait engendered in Australians. In politics, as in private life, all is selfishness. The city people thought only of building a greater Sydney, the residents of Noonoon and other little towns had mind for nothing but their own small centre,—all seeing no farther than their noses, or that what directly benefited their little want might not be good for the country at large, and that legislature must, to be successful, better the living conditions of the masses, not merely of one class or section. Then city men, unacquainted with the practical working of the land, could not possibly handle the land question effectively, and, moreover, a man might understand how to manage the coastal district and remain at sea regarding the great areas west of the watershed.

Another big mistake lay in over representation of the city and the under representation of the man on the land. The producer should be the first care, and while he is woefully disregarded and ill-considered a country cannot thrive. The reason of this state of affairs was the division of electorates on a population basis. This meant that a

city electorate covered a very small area, and that prac-
tically all its wants were attended by the municipality,
so that the city member had leisure to ply the trade of
merchant, doctor, or barrister within a few minutes of
the house of parliament; whereas the country member,
to become acquainted with the vast area he represented
and the requirements of its inhabitants and attend par-
liamentary sittings, had no time left to be anything but
a member of parliament, precariously depending upon
re-election for a livelihood.

Dawn threw herself into the contest with great en-
thusiasm, and also industriously pursued her vocal studies,
but for her was exceptionally subdued and inclined to be
cross on the smallest provocation. She had become so
engrossed in political meetings that "Dora" Eweword,
who was continually at Clay's since the retreat of Ernest,
one day remonstrated with her. She had made a political
meeting the excuse for declining to go rowing with him,
whereupon he remarked—

"Oh, leave 'em to the old maids, Dawn. "You'll grow
into a scarecrow that would frighten any man away if
you hang on to politics much more."

"Well, if it would frighten *some* men away, I'd go in
for them twice as much," snapped the girl. "I suppose
you admire the style of girls who are going around now
saying, after some straightforward women have said
what we all feel and got the vote, 'Oh, I don't care for
the vote. Let men rule; they are the stronger vessel.
Politics don't belong to women,' and so on. You'd think
me a sweet little womanly dear if I croaked like that;
but you keep your brightest eye on that sort of a
squarker, and for all her noise about being content with
her rights, you'll see that she takes more than her share

of the good of the reforms that other women have
worked for."

"Oh Lord!" good - temperedly giggled "Dora," for
home truths that would be considered sheer spleen from
a plain girl are taken as fine fun when uttered by a
girl as physically attractive as Dawn.

During the second week of the footballer's absence, who
should appear to lend a hand on the side of Leslie Walker
but Mr Pornsch, *uncle* of the late Miss Flipp.   He arrived
with the callousness worthy of a certain department of
man's character, and addressed a meeting with as much
pomp and self-confidence and talk of bettering the morals
of the people, as though he had been an Ellice Hopkins.
He had the further effrontery to visit Clay's and feign
crocodile grief for the deplorable fate of his niece.   He
protested his shame and horror, together with a desire
for revenge, so loudly that I resolved that he should
not be disappointed, that the dead girl should be in a
slight measure avenged, and he should not only know
but feel it.

"I ain't got me voting paper.   Me an' Carry will go up
for 'em to-morrer," said grandma one evening from her
arm-chair near the fireplace.

There had been the usual meeting, and Ada Grosvenor
and others had called in to discuss it.

"Why, didn't the police deliver yours?" inquired Miss
Grosvenor.

"No, we was missed somehow."

"Easy to see Danby wasn't on the racket of deliverin'
electors' rights, or you would have had two or three
apiece," Andrew chipped in.

"I'm going for Walker straight," announced grandma.
"He's temperance at all events, and that is some-

think w'en there ain't any common-sense in any of them."

"If I had twenty votes I wouldn't give one to that Walker," said Andrew. "All the women are after him because they think he's good-lookin', an' he's got bandy legs. They clap him like fury, and look round like as they'd eat any one that goes to ask him a question. They seem to reckon he's an angel that oughtn't to be asked nothink he can't answer. I believe they'd all kiss him an' marry him if they could. I hate him. Vote for Henderson, he wouldn't give the women a vote, and only men are workin' on his committee."

"Oh my, what's this!" exclaimed Dawn.

"Well, you know, the women *are* making fools of themselves about this Walker," said Ada Grosvenor, with her intelligently humorous laugh. "I don't think much of him myself. In spite of his choice phrasing of the usual hustings' bellowing, if women had not already the franchise he would be slow to admit them on a footing of equality with men as regards being. There are two extremes of men, you know. One thinks that woman's position in life is to act squaw to her lord and master. The other regards her as a toy—an article to be handed in and out of carriages like choice china—a drawing-room ornament, to be decked in wonderful gowns, and whose whole philosophy of existence should be to add to the material delight of men. Walker is a representative of the latter type, and old Hollis, who thinks that monkeys have as good a right to vote as women, belongs to the other. At a surface glance their views regarding women seem to be diametrically opposed, but to me it has always appeared that they equally serve the purpose of degrading the position of women. You should have seen how cruel

Walker looked to-night when an old man asked if he approved of women entering the senate.   He said *no* like a clap of thunder."

It was probably this perspicacity on the part of Ada Grosvenor, coupled with a sense of humour, that earned for her the reputation of " trying to ape the swells."

" Well, good-night everybody, and, Mrs Clay, don't forget to apply for your right in time, or you won't be able to vote," she said in parting.

" No fear," responded grandma.   " I've not been counted among mad people an' criminals, an' done out of me simple rights till this time of life without appreciatin' 'em w'en I've got 'em at last."

Next day, true to intention, the old dame and Carry went up town for their " voting papers," and to repeat the former's words, " was downright insulted, so to speak."

The civil servant whose duty it was to give rights to those electors who were not already in possession of such, was carrying affairs with a high hand, and had the brazen effrontery to tell Grandma Clay that it was a disgrace to see a woman of her years " running after a vote," as he elegantly expressed it ; and he also suggested to Carry that it would suit her better to be at home doing her housework, and to put the cap on his gross misconduct, he persuaded them that they had left it too late to obtain the coveted document, the first outward and visible proof that men considered their women complete rational beings.

Carry had retorted that it would suit him better to do the work he was paid for than to exhibit his ignorance in meddling with the private affairs of others, and that if she could discharge his duties as well as she did her house-work, he wouldn't make an ass of himself by showing his fangs about women having the vote in the way he did.

The two electresses thus bluffed came down the street and told their grievance to Mr Oscar Lawyer, for the nonce head of the Opposition League, and at ordinary seasons a father of his people, to whom all the town made in times of necessity,—whether it was an old beldame requiring assistance from the Benevolent Society or a lad seeking a situation and requiring a testimonial of character.

With Mr Oscar Lawyer they also ran upon Mr Pornsch; and it was discovered that the churlish clerk's statement was utterly false, and made because he was on the side of Henderson and these two women were not. There was more talk than there is space for here, but the upshot of it was the clerk was routed, and grandma and Carry came home triumphantly, each in possession of one of the magic sheets of blue paper, which they spread out on the table for us all to see.

"Well, well!" said grandma, "I seen the convicts flogged in days w'en this was nothink but a colony to ship them to, and I drove coaches w'en the line was only as far out of Sydney as here; and to think I should have lived to see the last of the convicts gone, coaches nearly become a novelty of the past, us callin' ourselves a nation, an' here a paper in me hand to show I can vote a man into this parliament and the other that the king's son hisself come out to open. I'm glad to see us lived that we can have our say in the laws now same as the men, and not have to swaller anythink they liked to put upon us to soot theirselves," and the old dame, with a splendid light in her eye, rubbed the creases out of the paper and spread it out again.

"Pooh, it's the same as we've had all along. You didn't think a elector's right was anythink to be grinnin' at w'en the men had it. I never seen you gapin' at mine; you'd think it was somethink wonderful now when you've got one of your own," said Uncle Jake, coming in.

"Well, I never! Jake Sorrel! Of course we don't think much of other people's things! What is the good of another woman's baby or husband or *frying-pan*, that is, if it was equally a thing you couldn't borrer? And if you was blind, what pleasure would you get out of some one else seein' the blue sky, or warnin' that there was a snake there to be trod on, an' that's what it's been like with the elector's rights."

"Well, but what difference does that bit of paper make to you now? You won't live no longer nor find your appetite no better, an' it won't pay the taxes for you," contended uncle.

"Then if it is of so little account, why does it gruel you so much to see me with it? An' little as it is, there ain't that paper's reason why we shouldn't have always voted; and little though it is, that's all the difference has stood all these years between men voting and women not; and little as you think it is for a woman to have done without, it's what men would shed their blood for if *they* was done out of it. It ain't what things actually are, it's all they stand for," and grandma gathered up her *right* and went to take off her bonnet and change the bristling black dress which she donned for public appearance.

I sat musing while she was away. "It ain't what things actually are, it's all they stand for," as the old dame had said; and her delight in being a freed citizen, no longer ranked with criminals and lunatics, had touched my higher self more profoundly than anything had had power to do for years.

Though taking a vivid interest in the electioneering, owing to the large distillation of the essence of human nature it afforded, as neither of the candidates had a practical grip of public business, I cared not which should poll highest; but now I resolved to procure my right and go to the ballot, and, if nothing more, make an informal vote *for the sake of all that it stood for.*

At back of the simple paper were arrayed the spirits of countless noble and fearless men and women who had so loved justice and their fellows that they had spent their lives in working for this betterment of the conditions of living, and the little paper further stood for an improvement in the position of women, and consequently of all humanity, inconceivable to cursory observation.

As for a woman going to the poll and voting for Jones or Smith, that was harmless in either case, and would not help her live or die or pay her debts, as Uncle Jake expressed it; but excepting the female vote for the House of Keys in the Isle of Man, the enfranchisement of women, spreading from one to the other of the Australian States, represented the first time that woman, even in our vauntedly great and highly civilised British Empire, was constitutionally, statutably recognised as a human being, —equal with her brothers. That women shall compete equally with men in the utilitarian industrialism of every walk of life is not the ultimate ideal of universal adult franchise. Such emancipation is sought as the most condensed and direct method of abolishing the female sex disability which in time shall bring the human intelligence, regardless of sex, to an understanding of the superiority of the mother sex as it concerns the race—as it is the race, the whole race, and consequently worthy of a status in life where it shall neither have to battle at the polls for its rights nor be sold in the market-place for bread.

The empty-headed cannot be expected to perceive the magnitude of this upward step in the evolution of man, and its machinery may not run smoothly for a span; we nor our children's children may not know much benefit from what it symbolises, but shall we who are comfortable in rights wrested from ignorance and prejudice but never enjoyed by past generations, be too selfish and small to rejoice in the possibility of bettered conditions those ahead may live under as the fruits of the self-sacrificing labour of those now fighting for their ideals?

NO!

TWENTY-ONE.

THINGS GO MORE WRONG.

GRANDMA could think of nothing but the clerk's insult when she had gone for her electoral right.

"Him! that thing! What's he employed for but to do this work, and if he ain't prepared to do it decent, why don't he give up an' let a better man in his place? They're easy to be got. 'Runnin' after a vote,' indeed! But that's where I made me big mistake. I should have stayed at home and writ to him, an' he'd have been compelled to send the police with it. That's what I ought to have done, an' let me servants that I'm taxed to keep do the work they're dying for want of, instead of doin' it meself; but at any rate I got me right safe an' sure," she said with satisfaction. "A long time we'd be getting them if all men was like him, which, thank God, they ain't. But that's the way with all these fellers in a Government job; they think they're Lord Muck, and too good to speak to the folk that's keeping them there, and only for which they wouldn't be there at all. Only for Oscar Lawyer and Mr Pornsch—and Dawn, where are you? Mr Pornsch was very nice to me, an' I asked him to tea, an' to come down for some of them little things belongin' to his niece. He's very cut up about her."

"Yes, about as cut up about her as Uncle Jake would be over me."

"Now, Dawn, how do you know?" severely inquired the old dame.

"I know very well that old men with his delightful slenderness of figure, and men who have drunk all the champagne and other poison it must have taken to colour his nose that way, haven't got much true feeling left, except for a bottle of wine, and a feed of something high and well seasoned."

However, Mr Pornsch presently arrived, and illustrated by his smickering at Dawn that notwithstanding his grief for a dead girl he yet retained an eye for the charms of a living one. It also transpired that he would not have waited for an invitation to call upon us.

This sweet bachelor champion of Women's Protection Bills, who had so long deprived some woman of the felicity of being his wife, had apparently determined to hastily repair the omission, and it soon became evident that he meant to honour no less a person than Dawn in this connection—Dawn! a princess in her own right, by reason of her health, her beauty, her youth, and her honest maidenhood!

He took Ernest's place in going to Sydney with her, thrust costly trifles upon her; he was fifty-five if he were a day, and a repulsive debauchee at that. Dawn, so healthy and wholesome, loathed him. She sat on her bed at night with her dainty toes on the floor, and raved while she combed her fine-spun brown hair. I let her rave, believing this a good antidote for the worry of that dish of water that was rarely out of her thoughts. I knew that she never omitted to scan the football news in hopes of seeing the doings of a certain red-headed

player recorded there, and I also knew that she was
doomed to disappointment, unless she could connect
R. E. Breslaw with R. Ernest of the wash-up water
incident.

A man of Pornsch's calibre is hard to abash, or Dawn
would have abashed him, but failing to do so, at last she
came to me requesting that I should assist her to get
rid of him.

"I don't want to complain to grandma," said she. "It
might get abroad if she took it in hand, so I'd like to
choke him off myself if I could. I have enough to suffer
already;" and I knew she was again thinking of that fatal
dish of water, and how "Dora" Eweword twitted her
concerning it.

Then I took Dawn on my knee as it were, and told
her a story. It was such a painful story that I first
extracted from her a solemn promise that she would
not make a fuss of any sort, for this young woman lacked
restraint—that command over her emotions which, if
carefully adjusted and gauged, will make the work of
a talented artist pass for genius, and that of a genius
pass for the work of a god.

When his connection with the ill-fated young girl, who
had slipped out in the dead of night to throw herself in
the gently gliding Noonoon, became known to Dawn, I
was afraid her horror would so betray her that any
subsequent plans for the punishment of the miscreant
might fall through.

"I'll knock him down with the poker next time he
comes. I'll throw a kettle of boiling water on him as
sure as eggs are eggs. Fancy the reptile leering around
me: I felt nearly poisoned as it was, but I didn't
know he was a murderer as well! Oh, the hide of

him to come here! I really will throw boiling water on him!"

Dawn continued in this strain for some time, but as she quieted down became possessed of a notion to tar and feather him in the manner mentioned by her grandmother in one of her anecdotes. Carry and I were to be called upon to assist in this ceremony, which was to take place upon the return of Mr Pornsch. For the present he had disappeared to attend to some business.

In the interim, the meetings continued without a break, and Dawn unremittingly looked for the football news, now with the war crowded into a far corner, by the special complexion that each daily chose to put on political affairs.

"Just look up the football news," I said one day, "and see how my friend Ernest is doing."

"He made a lot of goals as 'forward' in the last match. See!" she coolly replied, putting her tapering forefinger on the name of R. E. Breslaw, as she handed me the paper.

"Did he tell you he wanted to disguise his identity while here?"

"Yes; he told me all about it one day when we went to Sydney," she replied, leaving me wondering what else they might have confided during these jaunts.

Now that we required his presence Mr Pornsch was not in evidence, and neither was anything to be heard of the red-headed footballer's reappearance, though he had been absent four weeks, and this brought us towards the end of June. At this date there appeared a paragraph stating that Breslaw and several other amateur sportsmen were contemplating a tour of America, to include the St Louis Exposition.

That night some one besides myself heard the roar of the passing locomotives, but she did not confess the cause of her sleeplessness. It was one of those irritations one cannot tell, so she let off her irritation in other channels.

Matters did not brighten as the days went on. Two nights after Ernest's reported departure for the States, "Dora" Eweword brought Dawn home from Walker's committee meeting, and remained talking to her in the otherwise deserted dining-room till a late hour. As soon as he left Dawn came upstairs, and throwing herself face downwards on her bed burst into violent weeping.

"What has come to you lately, Dawn?" I inquired. "Tell me what sort of a twist you have put in your affairs so that I may be able to help you."

"No one can help me," she crossly replied.

"Don't you think that I was once young, and have suffered all these worries too? It is not so long since I was your age that I have forgotten what may torment a girl's heart."

Thus abjured she presently made me her father-confessor.

Eweword it appeared had grown very pressing, and her grandma had urged her to accept him as the best of her admirers. The old dame had not observed the trend of matters with Ernest. In a house where week-end boarders came and went, and the landlady had a pretty granddaughter, there were strings of ardent admirers who came and went like the weeks, and in all probability transferred their week-end affections as frequently and with as great pleasure as they did their person, and the old lady was too sensible to place any reliance in their earnestness, while Dawn too was very level-headed in the matter. Thus Ernest, if considered anything more than my friend, would have merely been placed in the week-end category. The old lady, not feeling so vigorous as usual, was anxious to have Dawn settled, and had tried to put a spoke in "Dora" Eweword's wheel by threatening Dawn with deprivation of her coveted singing lessons did she not receive him favourably. Dawn in a fit of the blues, probably brought on by seeing the announcement of Ernest's departure, had accepted Eweword conditionally. The conditions were that he should wait two years and keep the engagement entirely secret, and she had promised her grandma that she would think of marriage with him at the end of that time, provided her vocal studies should be continued till then.

"That's the way I'll keep grandma agreeable to pay for the lessons, and in that time, do you think, I'll be able to go on the stage and do what I like and be somebody?" asked the girl from out the depths of her inexperience.

"And what of 'Dora'?"

"He can go back to Dora Cowper then. I'll tell him I was only 'pulling his leg,' like he said about her. It will do him good."

"You might break his heart," I said with mock compassion.

"Break his heart! His heart! He's got the sort of heart to be compensated by a good plate of roast-beef and plum-pudding—like a good many more!"

"Will he consent to this?"

"He'll have to or do the other thing; he can please himself which. I don't care a hang. He said that if I would marry him soon he would let me continue the singing lessons and get me a lovely piano,—all the soft-

soap men always give a girl beforehand. I wonder did
he think me one of the folks who would swallow it?
Couldn't I see as soon as I was married all the privi-
leges I would get would be to settle down and drudge
all the time till I was broken down and telling the same
hair-lifting tales against marriage as aired by every other
married woman one meets;" and Dawn, her cheeks flushed
and her white teeth gleaming between her pretty lips,
looked the personification of furious irritation.

"All I care for now is to get the singing lessons, as
long as I don't have to do anything too bad to get
them."

I suddenly turned on her and asked—

"Honestly, why did you throw that dish of water
on Ernest Breslaw?" Thus unexpectedly attacked, her
answer slipped out before she had time to prevaricate.

"Because I was a mad-headed silly fool—the biggest
idiot that ever walked. That's why I did it!"

"Do you know that it hurt him very, very keenly?"
No answer.

"Do you know that he cared more for you than he
understood himself?"
No answer.

"Dawn, do *you* care?"

"Not in that way; but oh, I care terribly that I
made such a fool of myself. Had it been any one
else it wouldn't have mattered, but he will think I did
it because I was an ignorant commoner who knew no
better. That's what stings; but I'm not going to think
any more of it. I'm going to give my life up to sing-
ing, and it doesn't matter. I suppose I'll never see him
again, and he'll never know but that I did it out of
ignorance."

I smiled at the despondence in her tone as I extinguished the kerosene lamp-light.

There is a stage in the course of most love affairs when the knight is despised and rejected by the lady, when the sun and the salt of life depart, and he finds no more pleasure in it; when he is seized with an irresistible desire to go forth in the world and by his prowess dazzle all mankind for the purpose of attracting one pair of eyes. The same occurs to the lady, and she determines to make all men fall at her feet by way of illustrating to one adamantine heart that he was a dullard to have passed over her charms. And this young lady of the rose and lily complexion, and knight of the bright-hued locks and herculean muscles, being young —sufficiently young to be downcast by imaginary stumbling-blocks—had reached it. Goosey-gander knight! Gander-goosey lady!

I smiled again, for in my pocket was a letter that morning received from the former himself, stating that he had been booked for a trip to the St Louis Exposition, but had flung it up at the last moment in favour of seeing how Les. got on at the election, and that he would be back in Noonoon before polling-day. Considering he could have seen how the election progressed equally as well in Sydney as Noonoon, and that to see how his step-brother polled, when he took little interest in politics, had grown preferable to a trip to America, quite contented me regarding the probable termination of affairs.

However, I did not show this letter, as in match-making, like in good cooking, things have to be done to the turn, and this was not the opportune turn.

"Oh, well," I said, "so long as you don't let your

little arrangement get abroad, I don't expect it will harm
Eweword."

"No fear of it getting abroad. I've threatened him if
it does that a contradiction that will be true will also
get abroad by being put in the 'Noonoon Advertiser.'

Next night, however, I found Dawn stamping on
something glittering that spread about the floor, and
by inquiry elicited—

"That infernal 'Dora' Eweword has had the cheek
to give me a ring, and that's what I've done with it,
and that's all the hope he has of ever marrying me,"
she exclaimed, bringing the heel of her high-arched foot
another thump on the fragments.

"He's a bit too quick with his signs and badges of
slavery. He's so complacent with himself, and thinks
he's ousted the 'red-headed mug' as he calls him, that
I hate him."

"He has a right to be complacent. You have given
him reason to be. He has won you, so you have told
him, and he believes you."

"Yes, I know, and it makes me all the madder to
think of it."

I suppressed a chuckle; even before attaining my teens
I had never been so splendidly, autocratically *young* as
this beautiful high-spirited creature !

"Let things settle awhile, and then we'll pour them
off the dregs," I advised.

TWENTY-TWO.

"O Spirit, and the Nine Angels who watch us,
And Thy Son, and Mary Virgin,
Heal us of the wrong of man."

OUTSIDE politics the next item of interest on the Clay programme was the reappearance of Mr Pornsch, who came for afternoon tea, during which he invited himself to evening tea later on, and before it took Dawn's time in the drawing - room trying some late songs. Dawn averred that it was with difficulty she had restrained from setting fire to him or attacking him with the piano-stool.

He got so far with his "love-making" on this occasion that he had asked Dawn to take a little walk with him, which she had readily consented to do, as it would enable her to entrap him for the tarring-and-feathering upon which she had determined.

"He is going to meet me over among the grapes in the shade of the osage breakwind. Do you think we will be able to manage him? Let us be sure to have everything well arranged," whispered Dawn to me as we came to evening tea.

Near the appointed time of tryst, when the first division of the Western mail was roaring by—the warm red lights from its windows shedding a glow by the viaduct—she and I betook ourselves to the far end of Grandma Clay's vineyard, where we were securely screened by the osage orange hedge on one side and the grape-canes and their stakes on the other. Dawn carried a two-pound treacle-tin filled with tar, and which had been sitting on the end of the stove during the afternoon to melt into working order. Carry, who had entered into the affair with vim, had her share of the arrangements in readiness, and was secreted nearer the house to act as sentinel, and to run to our assistance if summoned by a prearranged whistle.

Dawn placed me and the superannuated hair broom, with which she had armed me, behind a grape-vine, and herself took up a position before it and beside a hole about eighteen inches deep and two feet square which she had excavated.

Mr Pornsch was soon to be heard tripping and blundering along, while the starlight, to which our eyes had grown accustomed, showed the river where the dead girl whom we were there to avenge had ended her miserable existence.

"Dawn, my pet, where are you? Curse the grape-vines," he gasped.

"I'm here, *uncle darling*," she responded, the two last words under her breath.

Directed by her voice, he neared till we could discern his bulk.

"My little queen," he exclaimed, the tone of his voice betraying that which defiled the crisp glory of the night for as far as it carried.

"Just wait a minute till I see where we are," said

Dawn, " or we will be getting all tangled up in these canes."

With this she started back, causing him to do likewise, and drawing a swab on a stick from the pot in her hand, she brought a consignment of the black sticky tar a resounding smack on his face, and following it with others thick and fast, exclaimed—

"There! There! That's all for you!"

Mr Pornsch naturally stepped backwards into the excavation, as designed, and sat down as completely and largely helplessly as one of his figure could be counted upon to do, and coming to Dawn's assistance I planted the broom on his chest, and bore with my feeble strength upon him. It was quite sufficient to detain him, seeing he was now stretched on the broad of his back with his amidship departments foundered in two feet of indentation.

Dawn thoroughly plastered his face and head, and in spitting to keep his mouth clear he lost his false teeth. He attempted to bellow, but jabbing his mouth full Dawn soon cowed him into quietude.

"Shut up, you old fool; if you make a noise we have six more girls waiting in a boat to fling you in the river and drag you up and down for a while tied on to a rope like a porpoise.   Do you think you'll float?"

This had the desired effect, though he spluttered a little.

"What is the meaning of this? Have you all gone mad? I met you here at your own request to speak about helping you with your singing, and you've evidently put a wicked construction on my action.   I demand a full explanation and an abject apology."

"Well," said Dawn, punctuating her remarks with little

dabs of the tar, "the explanation is that we're doing
this to show what we think of a murderer. Even if
Miss Flipp had not drowned herself, but had lived to
be an outcast, you would be still a murderer of her
soul."

"What's this ?" he blustered.

"We have several witnesses ready to give evidence
regarding all that passed between you and the un-
fortunate girl supposed to be your niece during your
midnight calls upon her," I interposed, speaking for the
first time, "so bluff or pretence of any kind on your part
is unavailing. Remain silent and hear what we intend
to say."

"We're dealing with this case privately," continued
Dawn, "because the laws are not fixed up yet to deal
with it publicly. Old alligators—one couldn't call you
men, and it's enough to make decent men squirm that you
should be at large and be called by the same name—can
act like you and yet be considered respectable, but this is
to show you what *decent* women think of your likes, and
their spirits are with us in armies to-night in what we are
doing. They'd all like to be giving your sort a wipe from
the tar-pot, and then if you were set alight it would not be
half sufficient punishment for your crimes. We haven't
a law to squash you yet, but soon as we can we'll make
one that the likes of you shall be publicly tarred and
feathered by those made outcasts by the system of
morality you patronise," vehemently said this ardent and
practical young social reformer, who was more rabid than
a veteran temperance advocate in fighting for her ideal of
social purity.

There was silence a moment while we listened to ascer-
tain was there any likelihood of our being disturbed, but

the only man-made sounds breaking the noisy crickets'
chorus were the rumble of vehicles along the highroad
and the shunting of the engines at the station, so I chimed
in with promised support.

"Yes, good women have to continually suffer the
degradation of your type in all life's most sacred rela-
tions. They have to endure you at their board and in
their homes, and leering at their sweet young daughters;
and, alack! many in shame and humiliation own your
stamp as their father or the father of their sons and
daughters. They have had to endure it with a smile and
hear it bolstered up as right, but those whose moral
illumination has taken place would be with us in armies
to-night if they could."

"I'm dying to give him a piece of my mind," said Carry,
coming up.

"How do you like our little illustration of what we
think of you? We've done it out of a long smouldering
resentment against your reign, and this is a species of
jubilation to find that the majority of Australian men are
with us, because in the vote they have furnished us with
a means of redress," and Carry finished her previously
prepared speech by throwing a clod of dirt on him.

"My grey hairs should have protected me," he
muttered.

"You mean they should have protected Miss Flipp," said
Dawn, "and when a man with grey hairs carries on like
this the crime is twice as deadly. There was nothing
about grey hairs when you used a lead comb and got
yourself up to kill. I thought you didn't want to make
an especial feature of them, and that's why I'm dyeing
them this beautiful treacley black. They'll look bosker
when I'm done."

"Get up out of that, lest I'm tempted to do you a per-
manent injury," I said, taking the broom off him.

"You can go to the stable," said Dawn, "and I hope
you won't contaminate it.   Carry has a lantern and some
grease and hot water, so you can clean yourself there and
put on your overcoat.   Never let us hear of you on a
platform spouting about moral bills again unless you say
it is on account of the practical experience you've had of
the need of them to save weak and foolish young women
from the clutches of such as you."

Mr Pornsch arose with difficulty while Dawn struck
matches to see what he was like, and a more deplorably
ludicrous spectacle never could be seen in a pantomime.
The only pity of it was that it was not a punishment
more frequently meted out to the sinners of his degree.
He raved and stuttered how he would move in the
matter, but Dawn, who had a commendable fearlessness
in carrying out her undertakings, only laughed merry
little peals, and told him the best way for him to move in
the tar was towards the stable, and the best way to move
out of it was by the aid of grease, soap, hot water, and
soda.   The expression of his eyes rolling and glaring
amid the black was quite eerie, but eventually we
reached the stable, where Carry instructed him how to
clean himself, while Dawn jeered at him during the
operation.

Having cleaned his face somewhat, he hid his neck and
clothes in his overcoat which Carry handed, put on his
hat, muffled his face in his handkerchief, and went away,
Dawn administering a parting shot.

"Now, Uncle Pornsch, dear, next time you go ogling
and leering round a *decent* girl, remember, though she may
be so situated that she has to endure you, yet she feels

just as we do, that is, if she is a decent girl, whose eyes have been opened to the facts of life."

"I feel better than I have done for a long time," she concluded, as bearing the implements used in the adventure we three, who had agreed upon secrecy, made towards the house.

"So do I," said Carry.   "If we could only do it to all who deserve the like, it would be grand!"

TWENTY-THREE.

UNIVERSAL ADULT SUFFRAGE.

I.

ELECTIONEERING matters ripened, and so did Carry's love affair with Larry Witcom. In fact it got so far that she gave grandma notice, and announced her intention of going to a married sister's home for that process known as "getting her things ready," while Larry, in keeping up his end of the stick, bought a neat cottage and began furnishing it in the style approved by his circle, with bright linoleum on the floors, plush chairs in the "parler," and china ornaments on the overmantels.

Mrs Bray, one of those very everyday folk whose god was mammon, and who naturally hung on every word issuing from a person of means while she would ignore the most inimitable witticism from an impecunious individual, began to regard the lady-help from a new point of view.

"She mightn't have done so bad for herself after all. Some of these girls knockin' about the world not havin' nothink to their name, don't baulk at things the same as you an' me would who's been used to plenty and like to pick our goods, so to speak. The way things is, Larry is as likely as most to be in a good position yet," was a sample of the modified sentiments falling from her full red lips.

Carry was to remain at Clay's until after the election day, so that she could cast her vote for Leslie Walker.

The political candidate thus favoured scarcely allowed three days to pass without personally or by proxy stumping the Noonoon end of the electorate. His last meeting in the Citizens' Hall was jam-pack an hour before the advertised time of speaking.

The candidate on this occasion made no fresh utterances to entertain, he merely repeated the catch cries of his party; but the air was heavily charged with human electricity, and the questions and "barracking" of the crowd were supremely diverting.

"Are you in favour of the Chows going to South Africa?" bawled one elector.

"My dear fellow, we are going to govern New South Wales—not South Africa."

"Yes; but when we sent contingents out to fight for the Empire in the Transvaal, do you think it fair that white men should be passed over in favour of Chows in the South African labour market?"

This question being ignored another was interjected.

"Are you in favour of the newspapers running New South Wales?"

"Certainly not!"

This being a satisfactory answer, the old favourite question, "Are you in favour of black gins wearing white stockings?" was put; and the candidate having assured us that, provided they could manage the laundry bill, he certainly was in favour of these ladies wearing any hosiery they preferred; and the loud guffaw which greeted this information having subsided, he continued—

"Now, don't vote for *me* or for *Henderson*,—vote for the best measures for the country. (Henderson was driving the personal ticket of having lived among them,—hence this warning.) I think it an unparalleled impertinence for a man to ask an intelligent body of electors to vote for *him*——"

"When there's a swell bloke like you in the field."

"Pip! pip! Hooray! Cock-a-doodle-do!" came the chorus. The "Pip! pip!" was a new sound to them, having been introduced to represent the noise made by the propulsion of a motor-car, in which set the candidate shone.

"Are you in favour of gas and water running up the one pipe?" inquired another, when the din had once more fallen to comparative silence.

"Don't you think that ladies ought to wear big boots now that they've got the vote?"

All such important questions having been put, the chairman called for three cheers for Mr Walker.

"Three cheers for Henderson," yelled the rabble at the back, which were given deafeningly, and the candidate, with the lively tact which bade fair to develop into his most prominent characteristic, joined in the cheers for his opponent, till some one had the grace to call "Three cheers for Mr Walker now"; and in the most delightfully uproarious, holiday-spirited clamour thus ended the last meeting but one before the election.

This was fixed for the 6th of August, and, notwithstanding there being several other towns in the electorate equally as important as Noonoon, on polling eve both candidates were to make their final speech there at the same hour.

During the week intervening, Leslie Walker's "Ladies' Committee" were very busy in the construction of dainty rosettes of pink and blue ribbon to be worn by his followers; and not to be outdone, Henderson's committee of "mere men" armed themselves with little squares of hatband ribbon of red, white, and blue—the Ministerial colours.

These were not such dainty badges as the rosettes, but they served the purpose equally well; and the sterner sex, in our present stage of evolution ever to be trusted to make up in downright usefulness what they lack in mere prettiness, had attached a safety-pin to each piece of ribbon for its masculinely substantial affixing.

II.

Polling eve arrived, and the Ministerialists having secured the hall, the Oppositionists had perforce to hold an open - air meeting. We attended the hall first, intending to move on to the street entertainment later, and Dawn was attacked by an old dame in the opposing camp because she was displaying Walker's colours.

"If I liked him I'd go an' stand in the street an' listen to him, not take up the room of them as has a hall hired for 'em by the *best* man, who has lived among us, and not some city lah-de-dah married to a hussy off the stage, an' who had women who might be any character goin' round speakin' for him," she tiraded, and turning to me aggressively demanded—

"Where are *your* colours?"

"Could you supply me with some?" I replied; and only too pleased, she squalled to an urchin who was distributing the squares plus a safety-pin. I was such a well-poised "rail-sitter" that I was entitled to wear both colours; and as this one was being ostentatiously fastened to the lapel of my over-jacket, I remembered the injunction to live at peace with all.

A brass band played the people in, and a trio of youngsters unfurled red, white, and blue parachutes,— alias gamps, alias ginghams, alias umberellers,—which were a popular feature of the "turn."

The committee appeared on the platform one by one, each received with noisy approval, and one facetiously wearing a rosette the size of a large cabbage was tendered a particularly deafening ovation.

After these crept Henderson, who, though not a particularly inspiring individual, was wildly and vociferously cheered for everything and nothing, and after listening awhile to his catch cries,—which differed from those of Walker only in the irritatingly halting and unimpressive way they were delivered,—we rose and scrambled our way out, jeered by the old dame as we went, and our departure was further commented upon from the platform by the speaker himself, in the words—

"Getting too hot for some of the ladies," which, if correct, could not by any means have been attributed to the winter air or the dull and weakly maudlin speech he was trying to deliver.

Walker spoke from a balcony crowded by devotees— mostly women—to an audience in the street, which was further enlivened by the fighting of the numerous dogs I have previously mentioned as addicted to holding municipal meetings. Their loud differences of opinion occasionally drowned the speakers, and the main street being also the public thoroughfare,—in fact, no less a place than the great Western Road,—there was no by-law or political etiquette to prevent the Ministerial band from strolling that way at intervals; so, much to the delight of all who were out for fun and the annoyance of those who were sensibly interested in the practical welfare of their country, and who imagined that the policy of this party would materially better matters, the cut-and-dried denouncement of the Ministry was at times drowned by the strains of "Molly Riley," "He's a Jolly Good Fellow," and "See the Conquering Hero Comes!"

The followers of Walker contended that Henderson was the worst of scorpions to thus come to Noonoon on the last night; but considering that he had only addressed Noonoon once to Walker's thrice, as an impartial wiggle-waggle I could not help seeing that the Ministerialists had most cause for complaint.

Dawn pinned the badge I had acquired to the coat-tail of a local bank manager who, though on her side, had lately distinguished himself by a public denouncement of "Women's Rights," so savagely virulent and idiotically tyrannous in principle as to suggest that his household contained representatives of the "shrieking sisterhood," who had been one too many for him. The boys who saw the joke enjoyed it very much indeed, as he strolled along with the self-importance befitting so prominent a citizen.

The beautiful voice of the candidate rose and fell, occasionally halting till the usual cheers or guffaws died away, and the meeting ended in the customary way. What good to the country was likely to accrue from it? On the other hand—what harm?

To be abroad in the open air with comfort at that time of the year, and at that hour of the night, illustrated the beautiful climate of that latitude if nothing more, and every one was harmlessly entertained, for good-humour characterised the whole affair.

Tea, coffee, and cheese abounded for all comers at the committee rooms of Leslie Walker—the candidate supported by the temperance societies; and on behalf of Olliver Henderson there was an "open night" at Jimmeny's "pub.," with the result—as published by the Oppositionists—that boys of fourteen and sixteen were lying drunk in the gutters.

The next day, however, was the culmination of the whole thing.

Dawn almost wept that she was not of age to vote, and as I was so comfortably indifferent as to which man won, I offered to cast my vote for the one she favoured, but she declined.

"That would only be the same as men having the vote and thinking they know how to represent us," she said.

But though she couldn't vote she worked hard for her side, and with a big rosette of pink and blue decorating her dimpling bosom, and streamers of the same flying from her whip and her pony's headstall, she was out all day driving voters to the booth, where for the first time in that town women produced an electoral right. The Federal election had been conducted without them.

In the forenoon Larry Witcom drove Carry to vote in state—otherwise a brand-new sulky he had recently

purchased ; and such is human nature that we were all
sufficiently malicious to be secretly pleased that poor old
Uncle Jake could not vote at all, because he had only an
obsolete red elector's right, and he should have procured
an up-to-date blue one.

It was a genial sunshiny day, and the lucerne and rape
fields and the Chinese gardens on either hand were beauti-
fully green, as grandma noticed when during the afternoon
she and I drove in the old sulky to cast our vote.

"Poor Jake! I'm sorry he can't vote, though he ain't
goin' for my man," she remarked. "But don't it seem
like a judgment on him for bein' so narked about the
women bein' set free ? That's always the way in life. If
you are spiteful about anythink it always comes back on
yourself."

The street opposite the court-house—for the time con-
verted into a polling-booth—was thronged like a show-
day with an orderly crowd of citizens of both sexes. The
voting had become so congested that vehicle loads of
voters were being conveyed over to Kangaroo, and each
contingent set out amid the cheers of small boys, who
were most ardent politicians.

Laughing and banter were exchanged between people
of all ages and classes, one as important as the other for
the time being.

As we crowded round the door, a jovial-looking man
with a twinkle in his eyes, as he was unceremoniously
shoved against a pillar, announced that women should
not have been allowed the vote, for its disastrous results
were already evident in this crush ; while the equally
pleasant-faced policeman, who, as soon as intimation came
from within that there was a vacancy, wheeled us in like
so many bales of wool, replied—

"Women jolly well have as much right to vote as men,
and more, because they can do it without getting drunk or
breaking their heads."

Many displayed colours and some did not. There was
the truculent woman who voted as she thought fit, and
who loudly advertised this fact; the man who voted for
Henderson because he lived in the district; and the
woman who supported Leslie Walker because he was
rich and would be able to subscribe liberally to all local
institutions. A shallow - pated Miss favoured Walker
because his colours were the prettier; and an addle-pated
old man balanced this by voting for Henderson because
he "shouted,"[1] and Walker was temperance. There
was a silly little flaxen - haired woman who also sup-
ported the Opposition to spite her husband,—a Hender-
son man, and the prototype of Mr Pornsch,—because,
being over - grogful, he had made tracks for the
polling-booth alone, leaving his wife to go as best she
could. Alas! there was a poor little woman at home who
could not vote at all because she had succumbed to the
gentlemanliness of Leslie Walker, and her husband being
against him had tyrannously taken her right from her;
and there was also the woman who *would* not vote at all,
because she considered men were superior to women, and
boisterously proclaimed this to all who would listen, in
hopes of currying favour with the men; but fortunately
this, in the case of the best men, is becoming an obsolete
bid for popularity. There was the woman who voted for
the man her father named, and those electors of each sex
who voted to the best of their discernment great or small.
Quite a crop of Uncle Jakes were disfranchised through
their rights being back numbers, and the nobodies who

---

[1] To treat to free drinks.

imagined themselves something altogether too lofty to consider anything so mundane as law-making at all, were also rather numerous.   Ada Grosvenor's bright happy face shone like a star amid her companions, and she discharged this duty honestly and thoughtfully as she did all others, recognising it as the practical way of working for the brave, bright ideals guiding her life.

Among the electresses were all the same types of vote as cast by men, except that those sold for a glass of beer were not so frequent; and as civilisation climbs higher, universal suffrage, and the better methods of administration to which it will give birth, will be exercised for the adjustment of the great human question now so trivially divided into squabbles of sex and class.

The bright Australian sun shone with genial approval on all, and in the air was a hint of the scent of the jonquils and violets, so early in that temperate region.   Grandma Clay must not be forgotten, for in her immaculate silk-cloth dress and cape, her bonnet of the best material, and her "lastings," with her spectacles in one hand and her properly - prized electoral right in the other, and her irreproachable respectability oozing from her every action, she could not be overlooked.   As she neared the door the gentlemen and younger ladies crowding there politely stood back and cancelled their turn in her favour ; and Mrs Martha Clay, a flush on her cheeks, a flash in her eyes, and with her splendidly active, upright figure carried valiantly, at the age of seventy-five, disappeared within the polling - booth to cast her first vote for the State Parliament.

What a girl she must have been in those far-off teens when she had handled a team of five in Cobb & Co.'s lumbering coaches, when her curls, blowing in the rain and wind, had been bronze, when with a feather-weight bound she could spring from the high box-seat to the ground! Lucky Jim Clay, to have held such vigorous love and splendid personality all his own. All his own to this late day, for the old dame returning said to me, "This is a great day to me, and I only wish that Jim Clay had lived to see me vote;" and there was a pathetic quiver in the old voice inexpressibly sweet to the ear of one believing in true love.

After Grandma Clay there was myself—a widely different type of voter. In one way it did not matter whether I voted or not. Neither candidate had a clear-cut policy to rescue public affairs from their chaotic state. The electors themselves had no definite idea what they required, but this was in no way alarming—all the materials for national prosperity were at hand, presently matters would evolve, and the demand for able statesmen would be filled when the demand grew clearly defined.

Which man would do most for women and children was also immaterial; the mere fact of women no longer being redressless creatures, but invested with rights of full citizenship, was even at that early stage having its effect. Politicians were trimming their sails to catch the great female vote by announcing their readiness to make issues of questions relative to the peculiar welfare of the big bulk of the human race represented by women and children. Inspired by women's newly-granted power of electing a real representative of their demands, would-be M.P.'s were hastening in one session to insert in their platform planks which much - vaunted "womanly influence" had been unable to get there during generations of masculine chivalry and feminine disenfranchisement.

Let the women vote!

As Grandma Clay expressed it, "It ain't what things actually are, it's all they stand for." For this reason I meant to exercise my right.

A sovereign in itself may not be much, but to a starving man within reach of shops see what it means in twenty shillings' worth of food. Similarly the right to vote in a self-governed country meant many a mile in the upward evolution of mankind.

Countless brave women and good men had sacrificed all that for which the human heart hankers, that women should be raised to this estate, and what a coward and insolent ignoramus would I be to lightly consider what had been so dearly bought and hard fought! And so thinking I presented my right, received my ballot-paper, and though not bothering to meddle with either candidate's name, I folded it correctly, and for the sake of all that stood behind and ahead of the right to perform this simple action, dropped it in the ballot-box.

It closed at six o'clock, and then came a lull till the first returns should have time to come in. The candidates were not in Noonoon but Townend, where the head polling-booth was situated, though nothing could have exceeded the excitement in Noonoon.

Grandma said she would wait quietly at home till next day to hear the result, but at nine o'clock the strains of a band, the glow of the town-lights like a red jewel through the night, and the sound of distant cheering proved too enticing to us two left alone in the house, so we locked it up, put the pony in the sulky, and sallied forth into the winter night, which in this genial climate was pleasant in an over-jacket added to one's ordinary indoor attire.

We had the road to ourselves, for the strings of vehicles from which it was seldom free were all ahead of us.

The candidates had tiny globes of electric light representing their colours hung across the street from their respective committee rooms, and the proprietor of 'The Noonoon Advertiser' had a splendid placard erected on his office balcony and well lighted by electricity, on which the names of members were pasted as they were elected, and in view of this had gathered one of the most good-humoured crowds imaginable. Irrespective of party, the hoisting of each name was wildly cheered by the embryo electors who, being at that time of life when to yell is a joy, took the opportunity of doing so in full.

Leaving grandma in charge of the vehicle I got out to reconnoitre, and slipped in among the crowd desiring to be unobserved, but that was impossible; a good-tempered man invariably discovered me behind him, and insisted upon putting me forward where there was a better view of the numbers and names.

"Let the women have a show. This is their first election and it ought to be their night," and similarly good-natured remarks in conjunction with a little "chyacking" from either party as the numbers fluctuated, were to be heard on all sides.

Where were all the insults and ignominy that opponents of women franchise had been fearfully anticipating for women if they should consent to lower themselves by going to the polling - booth ? If one excepted the discomfort that non-smokers have to suffer in any crowd owing to the indulgence of this selfish, disgusting, and absolutely idiotic vice, it was one of the best-mannered crowds I have been among.

I espied Larry and Carry carefully among the shades of the trees on the outskirts of the gathering, and even in the teeth of a political crisis not so thoroughly " up-to-date " that they could forego a revival of the old, old story that will outlive voting and many other customs of many other times.

Among the crowd of mercurial and lustily cheering boys was my friend Andrew, and a little farther on, lo! the knight himself. A motor cap was jammed on his warm curls, and a football guernsey displayed the proportions of his broad chest as his Chesterfield fell open, while with a gaiety and freedom he lacked when addressing girls he exchanged comments with some other young fellows, evidently fellow-motorists.

My feeble pulse quickened out of sympathy with Dawn as I caught sight of him. It was easy to understand the hastened throb of her heart upon first becoming aware of his presence. Who has not known what it is to unexpectedly recognise the turn of a certain profile or the characteristic carriage of a pair of shoulders, meaning more to the inner heart than had a meteor flashed across the sky? Most of us have known some one whose smile could make heaven or whose indifference could spell hell to us, and those who by some fortuitous circumstances have spent their life without encountering either one or both these experiences, are still sufficiently human to regret having missed them, and to understand how much it could have meant.

Had Dawn's blue eyes yet discovered the goodly sight?

When I presently found her the light in them betrayed that they had.

Her face shone with the inward gladness of a princess when she has come into view of a desired kingdom—whether it shall endure or be destroyed and replaced by the greyness of disappointment, depends upon the prince reciprocating and making her queen of his heart.

"Dora" Eweword was in attendance, so I despatched him to ascertain if grandma were all right, and took advantage of his absence to say—

"I see Ernest has returned to see the result of Leslie Walker's candidature."

"Then it's a wonder he didn't stay in Townend. They'll know the results there sooner," she replied with studied indifference.

Our pony fell sound asleep where she stood and in spite of the cheering, as though she were well acquainted with women taking a live interest in an election. We let her sleep till twelve, when to grandma's disappointment Leslie Walker was more than a hundred votes behind. There were yet other returns to come in, but these were not large enough to alter present results.

When we left the street was still crowded and the cheering unabatedly vigorous.

On our way home grandma remarked with satisfaction that Dawn seemed to be regarding Eweword sensibly at last, and I seized the opening to inquire if she were really anxious that the girl should marry him.

"I am if she couldn't get no one better," replied the old lady, and I considered that this condition saved the situation.

III.

The poll had been taken on a Saturday, and on Monday both the elected and defeated candidates appeared in Noonoon to return thanks.

The former came into town at the head of a long cortége of vehicles, and with the red, white, and blue parasols very prominently in evidence. The streets were

hung with bunting, and at night the newly elected M.P.
was lifted into a buggy in which he was drawn through
the streets by youths, at the head of a glorified procession
led by a brass band; and there were not only little boys
covered with electioneering tickets from top to toe
and yelling as they marched and waved flags, but also
little girls, now equally with their brothers, electors to be.
More power to them and their emancipation!

It came on to rain, so black umbrellas, big and business-
like, went up by dozens around the three special ones,
and became an amusing feature of the train of miscel-
laneous people who came to a halt within earshot of
a balcony in the main street.   Henderson was carried
upstairs on some enthusiasts' shoulders, and when landed
there followed the usual "gassating" and flattery—the
re-elected member being presented with a gorgeous
bouquet of red, white, and blue flowers.

A little farther up the street the Walkerites also held
a "corroboree," where graceful thanks were returned by
the Opposition candidate, who was overloaded with offer-
ings of blue and white violets and narcissi, and amid great
enthusiasm dragged in a buggy to the railway station.

As they came down the street, though they had the
intention of giving three cheers for the victors as they
passed, the rabble could not be expected to anticipate
such nicety of feeling, and some young irresponsibles
attempted to form a barricade across the route.

"Charge!" was then called out by some braw young
Walkerites in the lead, and mild confusion followed.

I was knocked on to the wheel of Leslie Walker's
buggy, from whence I was rescued by an old gentleman,
himself minus his pipe and cap, but good-humouredly
laughing—

" My word ! aren't the other side dying hard ? "

" Take care you and I do not also die hard," I replied, stepping out of the way of an idiot lad, who, dressed as a jester in Walker's colours, was sitting on a horse whose progress was blocked by the crowd, which began jibing at the rider.

Dawn, indignant at this, dashed forward like a beauteous and infuriated Queen Boadicea, her cheeks red from excitement and the winter air, and with her grandmother's flash in her eyes, exclaimed as she took the bridle rein—

" Cowards, to torment a poor fellow ! "

She attempted to lead the animal through, but the torches of the band were put before it and the indispensable red, white, and blue parasols swirled in its face, till it reared and plunged frantically, catching the excited girl a blow on the shoulder with its chest. She must inevitably have been knocked down in the street and been trampled upon but for the intervention of a hand so timely that it seemed it must have been on guard.

Noonoon was by no means an architectural town, and the ugliness of its always dirty, uneven streets was now accentuated by the mud and rain, but the picture under the dripping flags shown up by the torches of the band was very pretty.

The sturdy young athlete thus triumphantly in the right place at a necessitous moment, held his precious burden with ease and delight, and though she was not in any way hurt she did not seem in a hurry to relinquish the arm so willingly and proudly protecting her. The expression on the young man's face as he bent over the beautiful girl was a revelation to some interested observers but not to me.

Oh, lucky young lady ! to be thus opportunely and

romantically saved from a painful and humiliating if not serious accident !

Oh, happy knight! to be thus at hand at the psychologic moment !

And where was "Dora" Eweword then ?

And where was *my* rescuer ?   Apparently he had forgotten that he had rescued me, or that to have done so was of moment.

Ah, neither of us were in the heyday of youth, and 'tis only during that roseate period that we extract the full enchantment of being alive, and only by looking back from paler days that we understand how intense were the ioys gone by.

TWENTY-FOUR.

LITTLE ODDS AND ENDS OF LIFE.

THE electioneering over, the town fell to a dulness inconceivable, and from which it seemed nothing short of an earthquake could resuscitate it. So great was the lack of entertainment that the doings of the famous Mrs Dr Tinker regained prominence, and the old complaints against the inability of the council to better the roads awoke and cried again.

Two days following Dawn's rescue from the accident, Ernest called upon me, and occupying one of the stiff chairs before the fireplace under the Gorgonean representations of Jim Clay, looked hopelessly self-conscious and inclined to blush like a schoolboy every time the door opened, but Dawn did not make her appearance. I knew he had come hoping that in averting the accident he had been able to illustrate his friendliness towards her, and that she would now meet him as of old, so that the little incident of the wash-up water could be explained and buried. At last, taking pity on the very natural young hope that was being deferred, I excused myself and went in quest of Dawn, and found her in her room sewing with ostentatious industry.

"Dawn, won't you come down and speak to Ernest, he

has called to see how you are after your adventure," I
said with perfect truth, though as a matter of fact he had
studiously refrained from mentioning her.

"Oh, please don't ask me to go down," she implored
excitedly; "you seem to have forgotten!"

"Forgotten what?"

"That dish of water," she faltered with changing colour,
"and then he saved me so cleverly from being trampled
on! If he had ridden over me I wouldn't have cared, as
it would have made things square; but as it is, can't you
understand that I'd rather *die* than see him?" said she
in the exaggerated language of the day, and burying her
face in her hands.

"I can better understand that you are *dying* to see
him," I returned, pulling her head on to my shoulder;
"but never mind, you'll see him some other day, and it
will all come straight in time."

I forbore to press her farther, but that Ernest might
not be too discouraged I gave him some splendid oranges
Andrew had picked for me, and said—

"Miss Dawn kept these for you, but as she is not
visible this afternoon I am going to make the presenta-
tion."

His face perceptibly brightened, and also noticeable
was the brisk way he terminated his call upon learning
that there was no prospect of seeing Dawn that day. I
watched him bounding along the path to the bridge carry-
ing the oranges in his handkerchief, and watched also by
another pair of eyes from an upstairs window.

Carry left us during that week, and as she had now
fixed her wedding-day the tax of wedding presents had to
be met. Grandma, in bidding her good-bye, presented her
with a generous cheque, and paid her a fine compliment.

" I wish you well wherever you go, for I never saw another young woman—unless it was meself when I was young—who could lick you at anythink."

Carry's departure put the cap on our quietude at Clay's, but soon a movement transpired to stir the stagnation.

The out-voted electors of Noonoon were so galled by their defeat that they ignored the British law under which it was their boast to live, and refused to acknowledge that the man who had been voted in by the majority was constitutionally their representative in parliament. They also failed to see that he would serve the purpose quite as well as the other man, and to publish their sentiments more fully, determined to tender Leslie Walker a complimentary entertainment of some kind, and present him with a piece of plate, not as the other side had it, in token of his defeat, but owing to the fact that he was actually the representative of Noonoon town, having in that place polled higher than his opponent. The presentation took the shape of a silver epergne. This to a man who probably did not know what to do with those he already possessed, a wealthy stranger who had contested the electorate for his own glory! Had he been a struggling townsman, who, at a loss to his business, had put up in hopes of benefiting his country, to have paid his expenses might have shown a commendable spirit, but this was such a pure and simple example of greasing the fatted sow, that even those who had supported him openly rebelled, Grandma Clay among them.

" Well, that's the way women crawl to a man because he's got a smooth tongue and a little polish," sneered Uncle Jake.

" And some of the men hadn't gumption to get the proper right to vote for their man, who flew the publican's flag and truckled to the tag-rag," chuckled grandma, who was delighted to prove that this illustration of crawl had originated with the men.

Nevertheless it was decided to present the epergne at a select concert or musical evening, with Mr and Mrs Leslie Walker sitting on the platform, where the audience could gloat upon them. Dawn was asked to contribute to the programme, and relieved her feelings to me forthwith.

"The silly, crawling, ignorant fools!" she exclaimed. "The first item on the programme is a solo by Miss Clay!!!" says the chairman, "and I'll come forward and squark. 'Next item, a recitation by Mrs Thing-amebob.' Can't you just imagine it?" she said in inimitable and exasperated caricature from the folds of her silk kimono. "Good heavens! to give a man like that an amateur concert like ours! Do you know, they say he is the best amateur tenor in Australia, and his wife was a comic opera singer before she married—so a girl was telling me where I get my singing lessons. You'd think even the galoots of Noonoon wouldn't be so leather-headed but they'd know their length well enough not to make fools of themselves in this way! *I* know; why can't they know too? They like these things themselves, and think others ought to like them too. What do they want to be licking Walker's boots at all for? We all voted and worked for him; that was enough! It will just show you the way people will crawl to a bit of money! Oh dear, how Walker must be grinning in his sleeve! I *won't* sing for them!"

But she was not to escape so easily. A member of the committee asked grandma "Would she allow her grand-daughter to contribute a solo?"

"Of course!" said the old lady. "Ain't I getting her

singing lessons to that end?" and down went the girl's
name on the programme, and there was war in the Clay
household on that account.

"I can't sing yet," protested Dawn. "I can't sing in the
old style, and can't manage the new style yet."

"Rubbish!" said grandma, who could not be got to
grasp the intricacies of voice production. "What am I
payin' good money away for? It's near three months
now, and nothing to show for it yet. If you can't sing
now, you ought to give it best at once; and if you can't
sing a song for Mr Walker, and show him you've got a
better voice than some, I think it common-sense to stop
your lessons at the end of the quarter."

"My teacher wouldn't let me sing."

"And who's the most to do with you, your teacher or
me, pray? Who's *he* to say when you shan't sing or the
other thing?" and thus she decided the point; but Dawn
each night dwelt upon the trouble, while I sought to
comfort her.

"It is best to sing to the people who know all about
singing. They will see you have a good voice and
appreciate it far more than could the ignorant."

A fortnight had to elapse before the date of the concert,
and during that time Carry's successor arrived in the form
of a stout "general," as Dawn averred she had sufficient
companion in me, and that a kitchen woman was preferable
to a lady help.

The pruning of a portion of the vineyard, which had
been delayed by electioneering matters till now, also took
place during this time, and Andrew and Uncle Jake,
when working in the far corner, made the extraordinary
discovery of an odontologic gold plate of the best quality
and in perfect order. The find created quite a sensation.

As grandma said, it bore evidence that some one had been stealing grapes during the season, for any person legitimately in the vineyard would have instituted a search for such a valuable piece of property, and for a person who could afford such a first-class gold plate to steal grapes, showed what *some people* were. It did indeed, for this person had been wont to clandestinely enter her premises to perpetrate a far lower grade of crime than pilfering her grapes or destroying her vineyard. The incident trickled into the columns of 'The Noonoon Advertiser,' in conjunction with the facetious remark that the invader would have had to take a lot of grapes to compensate him for what he had lost; and it was further stated that the article being useless except to him—its size bespoke it a man's—for whom it had been modelled, he could have it upon giving satisfactory proof that he was the owner.

Needless to say, Mr Pornsch did not claim his property, and this souvenir was the last we heard of him. Andrew took it to Mr S. Messre, dentist, the man who had seemed to consider it unprofessional that to fill my teeth should take time, and with him the lad bargained that in return for the plate he was to tinker up those teeth whose aching I had allayed with the carbolic acid prescribed for me by the other dentist.

Dawn and I chuckled in secret, sent a copy of 'The Noonoon Advertiser' to Carry, and remarked that it was an ill wind that blew no one any good.

During the fortnight preceding the concert, Ernest Breslaw called at Clay's several times to see me, and saw me unattended by any extras in the form of a beautiful young girl, for Dawn blushingly avoided him. He had to fall back on such outside skirmishing as rowing me on the river, and though there was no longer an impending election to furnish him with excuse for loitering in Noonoon, he did not speak of deserting it in a hurry. He had reached that degree of amorous collapse when he could manage to shadow the haunts of his desired young lady regardless of circumstances, and grandma began to suspect that his attentions had a little more staying power than those of the week-end admirer.

Seeing that the "red-headed mug" had reappeared, in the hope of permanently extirpating him "Dora" Eweword was anxious to announce his engagement, but with threats of immediate extermination if he should so much as give a hint of it, Dawn kept him in abeyance, and altogether behaved so erratically that Andrew candidly published his belief that she had gone "ratty."

Ernest proffered himself as our escort to the Walker presentation, but Eweword having previously secured Dawn, Breslaw had to be satisfied with my company. I had already presented Andrew with a ticket, and as I could not now discard him, I resolved to ignore the injunctions to be found in etiquette books, and accept attentions from two gentlemen at once. Thus it happened that I, at the despised grey-haired stage, sat in state with a most attentive cavalier on either hand, while handsome young ladies sat all alone.

We had entered September, and the early flowers had lifted their heads on every hand in this valley, where they grew in profusion, and that evening were in evidence at women's throats, in men's coats, and in young girls' hair. The stage was a bower of heavenly scented bloom, and many among the audience held bouquets the size of a broccoli in readiness for presentation to the guests of the evening.

Ernest was holding the pony, which was restive, while Andrew buckled her to the sulky, when Dawn came upon the scene after the concert and presented me with a huge bunch of flowers, and Eweword also got his nag ready for home-going. Dawn had not met Ernest since the night in the street, and even now affected not to notice him, so thinking it time to take the situation by the horns, I said—

"Here is Mr Ernest; you didn't see him because he was standing in the shade."

Thus encouraged, he came forward and sturdily put out his hand, and Dawn could not very well fail to observe that, as it was of substantial build and held where the light shone full on it, so she was constrained to meet it with her own, and received, as she afterwards confessed, a lingering and affectionate pressure.

It was not of Ernest, however, but of Mrs Walker that she talked that night as we prepared for rest, with our washhand basins full of violets that had been crowded out of the quantity given to the defeated candidate's wife.

"Fancy being lovely like she is! After looking at her I've given up all hope. I suppose all I'm fit for is Mrs Eweword—Mrs 'Dora' Eweword; do my housework in the morning and take one of these sulkies full of youngsters for a drive in the afternoon like all the other humdrum, tame-hen, *respectable* married women! It's a sweet prospect, isn't it?" she said vexedly, throwing herself on the bed.

"Don't be absolutely absurd! Look in the glass and you will see a far more beautiful face, and one possessed of other qualities that make for success."

"Oh, nonsense, you only say that to put me in a good

humour. But how do women find such good matches as Leslie Walker?—that's what I want to know," she continued.

"Either by being beautiful or using strategic ability in the great lottery. Mrs Walker probably used both these accomplishments. You can achieve similar results by means of the first without the necessity of developing the second. Silly girl, marry Leslie Walker's step-brother, Ernest Breslaw, and if you do not live happily ever after it will not be because you have not been furnished with a better opportunity than most people."

She did not remark the relationship I thus divulged, showing that Ernest's confidences must have included it.

"A girl can't *make* a man marry her," was all she said. "I don't know how to use strategy, and wouldn't crawl to do such a thing if I could."

"Neither would I, but if I loved a man and saw that he loved me, I'd secretly hoist a little flag of encouragement in some place where he could see it," I made reply.

TWENTY-FIVE.

"LOVE'S YOUNG DREAM."

NEXT morning was gloriously spring-like; the violets raised their heads in thick mats of blue and white in every available cranny of the garden and other enclosures where they were allowed to assert themselves, while other plants were opening their garlands to replace them, and the air breathed such a note of balminess that Ernest came to invite me to a boat-ride.

To the practised eye there were certain indications that he hoped for Dawn's company too, but this was out of the question, as under ordinary circumstances it is rarely that girls in Dawn's walk of life can go pleasuring in the forenoon without previous warning, or what would become of the half-cooked midday dinner? So we set out by ourselves, and as the boat shot out to the middle of the stream between the peach orchards, just giving a hint of their coming glory, and past the erstwhile naked grape-canes, not cut away and replaced by a vivid green, the rower made a studiedly casual remark, "Your friend Miss Dawn spoke to me again at last. I wonder why on earth she threw that dish of water on me; did she ever say that she had anything against me?"

"No. If you could be a girl for half an hour you'd

know that the man to whom she shows most favour is frequently the one she most despises, while he whom she ignores or ill - treats is the one she most warmly regards."

"How on earth is that?"

"Oh, a species of shyness like your own, which makes you talk freely of Dawn and Ada Grosvenor, because you have no particular interest in them, whereas there is some name you guard jealously from me," I cunningly replied.

"Is it true that Miss Dawn is engaged to Eweword? If she is let me know in time to send her a wedding present. I'd like to, because she's your friend," he said with such elaborate unconcern that I had difficulty in suppressing a smile. His step-brother, the dilettante, would never have been so clumsily transparent in a similar case.

"Nonsense; she's as much engaged to you as to him," I said reassuringly, and that was all that passed between us on that subject. He energetically confined our con- versation to the lovely odour from the lucerne fields we were passing on the river-bank, but I was not surprised that the afternoon's post brought Dawn a letter that smothered her in blushes, and plunged her in a gay abstraction too complete for either Uncle Jake or Andrew to penetrate.

When we were once more in our big room, command- ing a view of the Western mail with its cosy lights twinkling across the valley, she extended me the privi- lege of perusing one of the simplest and most straight- forward avowals of love from a young man to a maiden it has been my delight to encounter.

"DEAR MISS DAWN,—You will be very surprised at

receiving such a letter from me, but I hope you will not be offended. I have loved you since the first day I saw you, but have kept it so well to myself that no one has suspected it, perhaps not even yourself. Will you be my wife? I love you better than life, and am willing to wait any number of years up to ten, if you can only give me hope of eventually winning you. I do not expect you to care for me at once, but if you can give me hope that you do not dislike me I shall be content to wait. You are so beautiful and good, I am afraid to ask you to marry me, but I would try hard to make you happy, and being in a position to live comfortably, you could continue any studies you like." Here followed a most business-like and lucid statement of his affairs, and the ending—"Please do not keep me waiting long for a reply, and let me know if I am to interview your grandmother. I am sure I can satisfy her in regard to my position and antecedents.—Yours devotedly,

"R. ERNEST BRESLAW."

He was honest. Not fearing that his income might tempt a girl of Dawn's or indeed any other's station, he had in no way attempted to test her affection ere mentioning it. After the manner of his type—one of the best—he would place complete reliance where he loved, and feel sure of the same in return.

"Good heavens! has he really all that money?" she exclaimed.

"So I believe."

"I'd be able to live the life I want, then. Learn to sing, have lovely dresses, and travel about. I'm not thinking only of his money, but don't you think people

who marry on nothing are fools and selfish? A woman
who marries a man who is only able to keep her and
her children in starvation is a fool, and a man who wants
a woman to suffer what wives have to, and drudge in
poverty, is a selfish brute — that's what I've always
thought. As for gassing about love when there's no
comfort to keep it alive, that's about as foundation-
less as we, always being supposed to think men our
superiors, even the ones a blind idiot could see are
inferior."

" Are you going to marry him?"

" I want to, but what on earth am I to do with ' Dora '
Eweword?"

" Break his heart to keep Ernest's together?"

" Break *his* heart! It's the style to break, isn't it?
He can have Dora Cowper or Ada Grosvenor, they both
want him. If grandma got wind of the situation though,
she'd put my pot on properly. She'd carry on like fury,
and let me have neither of them—that would be the end
of it. I can't make out why I fooled with that ' Dora '
at all. I'll write and ask Ernest to give me a week;"
and with her characteristic promptitude she sat down,
and favoured a style as unadorned as that of the knight
himself.

" DEAR MR ERNEST,—Your letter received. I care for
you, but cannot give you a definite answer at once.
There may be obstacles in the way of accepting your
kind offer; if you will give me a week to consider
matters, I will answer you definitely then.—Yours with
love,   DAWN."

As she got into bed she said with a happy giggle, " He

says he loved me from the first day he saw me, and you thought he only came to see you!"

"Well, my dear, you can't expect people whose hearts are broken from overwork, and whose hair is grey from want of love, to be as quick as beautiful young ladies whose affairs have come to a happy head with a splendid young knight;" and what I inwardly thought was, that at all events I had discovered the knight's symptoms long before he had done so.

"Would you like Mr Ernest and me to marry?" she asked.

"Oh, I don't object," I laconically replied.

"Well, I'll marry him as soon as ever he likes if I can get rid of 'Dora.' I'll see 'Dora' and see if I can do it without a rumpus first, but if he hasn't got sense to be quiet, well, I won't give in without a fight. Ernest mightn't like it if he knew, but I bet he will have to keep dark about worse things on his part if I only knew, —he's different to ninety-nine per cent of men if he hasn't," she said as she opened the French lights wider to the crisp breath of scented night and blew out the lamp.

"You don't mind his hair being red now, do you?" I maliciously inquired in the darkness, and though she feigned sleep I knew that owing to a delightful wakefulness another beside myself heard the splendid music of the trains that night. The style of her breathing told that she was still awake some hours later when the old moon climbed high and came shining, shining down the valley, divided in two by its noble river, and laid out in orchard and agricultural squares. The great silver light outlined the glorious hills that walled the west away from the little towns and villages, and here and there a gleaming white cluster of tombstones bespoke the graveyards where slept the early pioneers and the folk who had followed them, and which one by one, as opening buds or withered stalks, were settling their last earthly score. The little homesteads lay royally, peacefully free from danger of molestation amid their wealth of trees and vines. Cottages raised on piles, and vain in the distinction of small protruding gables, pretentiously called bay windows, and with keys rusting for want of use in the cheap patent door-locks, were quickly superseding the earlier dwellings. These squat old cots generally had thresholds higher than the floors; their home-made slab doors knew no fastening but a latch with a string unfailingly on the outside day and night, and with their beetling verandahs and tiny box skillions, were crouchingly hard set upon the genial plain.

TWENTY-SIX.

"OFF WITH THE OLD."

DAWN was not a procrastinator, so she lost no time in sending Eweword a message to meet her next night at eight at the corner of the Gulagong Road for the purpose of a private talk.

She was going to take something to Mrs Rooney-Molyneux and the baby as an excuse to be abroad at that hour of the night, and requested me to accompany her, so that she would not be saddled with Andrew as protector. We set out immediately after tea, and had time for a chat with Mrs Rooney-Molyneux about her son. Both were enjoying good health, thanks to the opportune arrival of a well-to-do sister, and the fact that, in honour of an heir to his name, the father had lately abstained from alcoholic drinks, and made an occasional pound by writing letters for people.

We had some trouble to dissuade him from escorting us home, but emerged at last without him, and within a few minutes of eight o'clock.

The cloudless, breezeless night, though a little chilly, was heavy with the odours of spring and free from the asperity of frost. The only sounds breaking its stillness were the trains passing across the long viaduct approaching the bridge. The vehicles which met from the two roads — the Great Western, leading in from Kangaroo, and the Gulagong, coming from the thickly - populated valley down the river-banks—had gone into town earlier for the Saturday night promenade, and we practically had to ourselves the broad highway, showing white in the soft starlight.

I walked behind Dawn, and she, having found Eweword, who had been first at the tryst, they came back towards the river a few hundred yards and stopped behind some shrubbery, while I took up a place on the other side of it, as directed beforehand by this very business-like young person, to act as witness in case of future trouble.

"Well, Dawn, what has turned up?" said the young man after a pause.

"There's something that might explain the situation better than a lot of talk."

Claude, alias "Dora" Eweword, struck a match, and upon discovering the fragments of his engagement-ring in the piece of paper she had handed him, was silent for a minute or two, and then said—

"Dawn, so you want it to be all off. I knew that this long while, and have been mustering pluck to say so, but it seems you have got in before me."

"Perhaps you were going to say you were pulling my leg like you did with Dora Cowper?"

"No, I was not," and his tone was exceedingly manly. "I was going to say that, much as I care, I'd rather let you go free than hold you to your agreement when I saw you didn't care for me."

"You were mighty smart!"

"No, I'm only a dunce, but even a dunce can liven up sufficiently when he's in love to see whether his sweetheart cares for him or not, and you didn't take much pains to hide the state of affairs," he said with a rueful laugh. "I know enough about girls to know when they really care."

"Practice, like," said Dawn.

"You can say that if you like," he gravely replied.

"Well, things were rather mixed, but now I know what I want."

"And that you don't want me?" he interposed.

"Well, you can marry Ada Grosvenor or Dora Cowper."

"We can leave that to the future; it doesn't enter into this question at all," he said with a dignity that made the girl ashamed of herself. "There will be no difficulty about my marrying, the main thing is whether you are all right. It's easier for a man than a girl if he does make a hash of it."

"Oh, Claude, don't be so good and generous, or you'll make me mad because I'm not going to have you after all."

"Good and generous! Nonsense! I'm only doing what any decent fellow would do; you'd do as much and more for me if things were reversed," he said, taking her hand. "Great Scott, what sort of a crawler did you take me for? Did you think I'd cut up nasty about it? Surely you knew I'd wish you well even if you were not for me; but won't you tell me who it is that has put my light out?"

"Can't you guess?"

"Well, I suppose it's——"

"The red-headed mug," put in Dawn.

"Yes, I saw it all along, but that night in the street finished matters. I knew my chances were as dead as a door-nail after that. You only took me because something went out of gear between you, and that's why you made me keep it dark."

"Oh, I don't want to say that, Claude."

"No, but I'm saying it; and now, is there anything else I can do for you except wish you luck?"

"Only promise not to let grandma or any one know."

"Did you think it necessary to tell me that. I'd not be likely to howl about my set-back. You needn't fear. I'll act with common-sense, and pull through. I won't drown myself and haunt you, or any of that sort of business," he said cheerfully.

"Oh, thank you more than I can say," she exclaimed enthusiastically; "I hope you'll soon find some one better than I—some one as good as yourself. Good-bye!"

"Well, Dawn, I wish you joy anyhow, and good luck to the fellow who has got the best of me. He seems an alright sort from what I can make out, and will be able to give you everything you want. Good-bye!" He drew her to him, and as she did not resist, kissed her warmly on the cheek, and let her go. He wanted to see her to her gate, but she dismissed him, and he walked away through the spring night whistling a cheery air. When he was safely gone I came out from hiding, and taking Dawn's arm moved homewards.

The girl was weeping, but so softly that I was not aware of it till her warm tears fell on my hand.

Oh, the never-ending fret and fume of being! When it is not discarded love or jealousy that is agitating the human bosom, it is unsatisfied ambition, the worry of parental responsibility, or loneliness and regret that one has never tasted them. The past—what has it been? The future—what will it be? The present—what does it matter? but a thousand curses on its pin-pricks, wounding like sword-thrusts, and which all must endure!

"Oh dear, I wish he hadn't been so nice," sobbed the girl. "He has made me feel so ashamed that I don't think I'm fit to marry Ernest! I wish he had been nasty to me, and then I wouldn't have cared. But you don't think he cares, do you? Listen to him whistling so merrily!"

" It is not those who whine loudest who feel most."

" But men don't really have any feelings in this sort of thing, do they?"

" Feeling is not peculiar to any section or sex of the community, but to a percentage of all humanity. This is my belief, but I cannot attempt to judge which feel and which do not."

" Who would have dreamt of him being so sweet-natured about it?"

" Nobility of character and unselfishness are also traits we cannot find in any set place."

" I wish I hadn't been such a cat. I can't forgive myself."

I smiled happily as Eweword's action bespoke a character more in keeping with his imposing physique than that betrayed when he had vulgarly spoken of pulling a girl's leg. That had been like seeing a beautiful house occupied by nothing but poachers, and I loved humanity, so that it always hurt to see even the meanest individual do less than their best.

"Well, cheer up," I said. " Take care not to similarly transgress again. We all are constantly committing regrettable actions, but so long as we are careful not to repeat them we may hope to make some headway."

So the knight received a favourable reply, and the man supplanted by him went another way.

TWENTY-SEVEN.

'One might think better of marriage if one's married friends would not confide in one so much."—*Reflections of a Bachelor Girl.*

MRS MARTHA CLAY proved a little obstreperous in regard to Ernest Breslaw filling the position of grandson-in-law.

"You always get what you don't want," said she; "an' that's why one of the same class as treated me daughter so shocking is now to be pesterin' me for me grandchild in the same way. A girl of the decent class wants to look a long time before she leaps with one of them swells. They just take to a girl out of their own click out of the contrariness of human nature, and then by-and-by give 'em a dog's life. I know there's bad in all classes, but them upstarts have so much more licence to be up to bad capers,—that's where it comes in. And anyhow I ain't breakin' me neck to have Dawn married. None of my people ever had any trouble to get married, an' she can wait a bit an' look round an' see if this feller can stand the test of waitin'," concluded the old dame, with the light of conflict in her steel-blue eye.

Fortunately I was able to bring forward a seductive statement of the case. Walker—the man who had made the money for Breslaw and his step-brother—had been a grand level-headed old labourer, and though his sons had

been educated in the great English schools, they were
not far removed from honest utilitarian folk, and owing
to this, and in conjunction with Dawn, when her real
name was divulged,—being a daughter of one of the
"old families," to wit, the Mudeheepes of Menangle,
the old dame consented to be reconciled.

Now that the oppression of Carry had been removed,
Mrs Bray came over and beamed upon us in her usual
inspiriting way.

The electioneering gossip having died out, she reopened
the old budget concerning the misdoings of the Noonoon
aristocracy, and once more the name of Mrs Tinker figured
so largely on the bill that I deeply regretted my inability
to encounter this much-discussed individual.

However, when Dawn flung into the quiet pool the
bomb of her approaching wedding with one of the best
"catches" of New South Wales, all other topics faded
into insignificance, and every woman who had the
slightest acquaintance with the bride-elect called on
her to warn her against the horrors to be discovered
after she had irrevocably taken the contemplated step
in the dark.

As Dawn was going to take it speedily, they were very
enthusiastic and unanimous in their evidence against the
married state under present conditions, and the thought-
ful student of life on listening to the testimony of these
women of the respectable useful class, supposed to be
comfortably and happily married, will know that not-
withstanding the great epoch of female enfranchisement
the workers for the cause of women have yet no time
for rest.

Dawn was so visibly worried by the revelations
made to her in the most natural way, that grandma

grew concerned and published her mind on the subject.

"Women ought to hold their tongues and let young girls come to things gradual. To have it thrust upon them sudden is too much of a eye-opener for them. The way women tell how their husbands treat them nowadays is surprisin'. We all know that with the best of men marriage ain't a path of roses, but in my day women kep' it to theirselves. They suffered it in silence and thought it was the right thing, but they're getting too much sense now; and perhaps all this cryin' out against it will be a means to an end, for a grievance can't be remedied till it's aired, that's for certain," said she.

Mrs Bray was in great form during those days, and though her assertions frequently lacked logic, and betrayed in her the very shortcomings which she railed against in men, nevertheless I liked her, for she blurted out that with which the little quiet woman rules by keeping it in the background, well hidden under seeming humility.

"Look here, Dawn," said she on one of these occasions, "when you get a home of your own, take my advice and don't never let no other woman in it. You can't, seein' what men are. There's no trustin' none of them, and if you think you can you'll find yourself sold. And try soon as ever you're married to get something into your own hands, as a married woman is helpless to earn her livin'; and once you have any children you're right at the mercy of a man, and if he ain't pleased with you in every way you're in a pretty fix, because the law upholds men in every way. If you don't feel inclined to be their abject slave they can even take your children from you, and

what do you think of that? It shows we ain't got the
vote none too soon, I reckon! I'm not sayin' that you'll
get that kind of a crawler; some of them is good,—a
jolly sight better than some of the women,—but the most,
when you come to live with them, is as hard as nails.
They don't know how to be nothing else. They never
know what it is to be quite helpless and dependent, so
what do they care. They just glory and triumph over
women bein' under them, because they know there's
nothing to bring them down, and you want to set your
wits to get some hold on a man,—he has plenty on you
by law and everything else,—get some property or some-
thing in your name so that he can't make a dishcloth of
you altogether. Bein' rich you'll have a somewhat easier
time, but it's when you've got mountains of work, when
you ain't feelin' as strong as Sandow for it, an' have one
child at your skirts an' another in your arms, an' your
husband to think women ain't intended for nothink better,
—that this is God's design for 'em, like most men do,—
it's then that married life ain't the heaven some young
girls think it's goin' to be. This ain't a description of
no uncommon case but among them all around you, and
supposed to be the fortunate ones. I think girls want
warnin', so they ain't goin' into it with their eyes
shut."

The picture painted by this lady was duplicated by
sadder pictures of the small worn type, and some weeks
of this brought us to advanced spring and a bride-to-be
so worried and unhappy that she had lost her appe-
tite and the roses from her cheeks, and grew visibly
thinner.

Ernest, who managed to snatch a little time from
worshipping his bride-elect wherein to superintend the

furnishing of his house, was exceedingly sensitive that his affianced should look so perceptibly miserable.

"Do you think she doesn't care for me, and would like to be released? I'd rather die than marry her if she doesn't want me," he would say, sometimes with haughtiness and more often with anger. "Good gracious! I don't know why she thinks I'm going to belong to the criminal class. Goodness knows, if I were to judge her the same way there are plenty wives would scare even a Hottentot from matrimony, and if I were to express to Dawn any fears of her being similar, I bet you'd hear of our engagement coming to a sudden death. You seem to understand her better than I do, so say a good word for me if you can."

My opinion of him being so high, saying a word in his favour gave me delight, and I took the first opportunity of saying a good many. At the end of one day, after Dawn had been subjected to a particularly gruesome account of what she might expect, I found her face downwards on her bed, weeping bitterly, and elicited—

"I'm going to tell Ernest to-morrow that I won't marry him. It's too terrible—they all tell you the same. I'd rather earn my living in some other way while I'm able. I'd rather throw up the thing now when most of my trousseau is ready than go on if one quarter of what they say is true. I'm not one of those fools who think life is going to turn out something special for me. Before these women were married I suppose they thought their husbands were going to be kings, but see how they have panned out, and why should I expect any better?"

Time had arrived to take the subject in both hands, so I gripped it firmly.

"You must be thankful to gain one point at a time," I

said, beginning with the lightest end of my argument.
" A little while since you feared you were fated for the
life of those around—household drudgery, with an occa-
sional sulky drive in the afternoon; now that you have
escaped that prospect you are haunted by worse possi-
bilities.   No doubt you hear some saddening and deplor-
able stories, for some of the laws relating to marriage
are degrading, and the lot of the married woman in the
working class where she is wife, mother, cook, laundress,
needlewoman, charwoman, and often many other things
combined, is the most heartbreakingly cruel and tortured
slavery; but you are escaping the probability of such a
purgatorial existence.   Take comfort in knowing that a
great percentage of men are infinitely superior to the
laws under which they live, because law is determined
by public opinion, and though it restrains and modifies
public behaviour it will not mould private character.
Law is shaped for the masses, but there is a small per-
centage of individuals in either sex who are superior
to any workable law, and I think Ernest Breslaw is one
of these."

"Do you?" she said, sitting up eagerly.   "Would you
marry him without any fear if you were me?"

"I would—right at once.   In spite of all its short-
comings I have a profound belief that not woman, as
the poet has it, but all humanity—

'Holds something sacred, something undefiled,
   Some quenchless gleam of the celestial light.'"

The rain that was temporarily washing the perfume
from the flowers pattered against the window-panes and
accentuated the silence, till I added—

"I will tell you my history some day, so that you

may see that when I have belief in my fellows how
little reason you have to fear. I have been an actress,
you know."

"Yes; Ernest told me."

"Well, I'll tell you about it one day." I did not
mention that I had expressly requested Ernest to keep
my past a secret. However, I was not displeased that
he had been unable to do so. If a man of his inex-
perience, and in the zenith of his first overwhelming
passion, had been able to keep such a secret in the
teeth of his love's wheedling, he would have proved
himself of the stuff to make an ambassadorial diplomat,
but not of the calibre to be the affectionate, domesti-
cated husband, having no interests of which his wife
might not be cognisant—the only character to whom I
could without misgiving entrust the hot-headed Dawn.

TWENTY-EIGHT.

LET THERE BE LOVE.

I so nearly "pegged out" with an attack that fell to my lot a little time after the election, that Dr Smalley considered it advisable to summon Dr Tinker to a consultation, but sad to say I was too comatose to have become acquainted with the husband of the famous Mrs Tinker, whose individuality afforded considerable interest, because it was very conspicuous when surrounded by the neutrality of life in Noonoon. However, with the aid of some "powltices" constructed by Grandma Clay and energetically applied by Mrs Bray, and because my hour had not yet come, against the time when we slid into a splendid October I was tottering about once more.

During my time of confinement the old valley had put on its finishing touches of spring glory. Only a few golden oranges now remained on the trees, and amid the bright green leaves were thick clusters of waxy bloom. The perfume from them was heavenly, and sometimes almost too powerful after the sun had toppled behind the great level-browed range which, viewed from the plain, guarded the west of the valley of Noonoon like a mighty wall. Some of the land had been cultivated for a century without attention to artificial renewal of its fertility, but still it gave forth a wondrous variety and wealth of vegetation. The widespreading cedars hung out their scented bloom like heliotrope flags amid surrounding greenery of pine, plane, poplar, and loquat, and the peach and apricot orchards contributed banks of their delicate flowers, which in the glory of their massed bloom could have out-Japanned Japan. Along the lanes, where their stones had been thrown, they sprang up and bloomed and bore liberally; roses of many kinds and colours clambered up verandah posts and peeped over fences; the garden plots were like compressed bouquets; the brilliant, graceful, and exquisitely perfumed pink oleanders grew wild in the fields; and altogether the vale of melons had graduated to a valley of flowers.

The days had stretched out so that the mail from the far West trundled down the mountains in time to cross the queer old bridge across the Noonoon at daybreak, and the first beams of morning turned its windows to gold as the waking flowers were lifting their dew-drenched heads and the soft white mists were dispersing themselves betimes from the plains dotted with ramshackle little homes and cut into squares by barbed-wire fences. The weather had warmed, so that the fashionables' week-end exit to the cool Blue Mountains had begun; and the youngsters near the railway line sometimes left their play and stood agape in the soft twilight to watch the governor's car, painted in a strikingly different colour to all the others and emblazoned with the British coat of arms, go by.

Uncle Jake, a hired man, and Andrew were very busy on the farm, and we none the less engaged in the house, where every article of furniture was made a receptacle for drapery and haberdashery, and where the wedding was the only subject. It so often gave Andrew the "pip" that his constitution must have been seriously impaired by such frequent attacks of this complaint.

In those days Dawn was too engrossed to take me for drives, and Ernest too occupied to pull me on the historic stretch of water running like the moats of old beside his lady's castle, so that Ada Grosvenor, in her office of doing good to all with whom she came in contact, stepped into the breach, and sought to aid my recovery by taking me for gentle exercise.

It was one day when we had driven east from Noonoon that she remarked—

"It's a wonder that Mr Breslaw would care for Dawn's style when he moves in such a smart set. She is a handsome girl, which covers a multitude of sins in that respect, but still she is very downright, and—and, well, doesn't quite conform to the rules of refinement."

I only smiled, and waited till the pony's head was turned for home, when I covered the necessity for reply by admiring the incomparable panorama before us. From the altitude we had reached on the Sydney road, we could see above the unbroken line of the horizon west from Noonoon town, and the Blue Australian Mountains stretched across the view in an endless succession of round-topped peaks painted in their matchless cerulean tints, which, near the end of day, were royal in their splendour. For a hundred miles they reigned supreme before the fringe of the endless plains was reached—peak after peak, gorge on gorge, tier upon tier of beetling walls of rock, disclosing dim shadowy gullies clothed with greenery and ferns where abounded cascades of water and dewy springs in romantic and unrivalled solitude. The sun, surrounded by a gorgeous pageant of flame and gold, rested his chin on one of the peaks as though well pleased with the glowing snowless scene that his offices had in part created, and lingered a moment ere giving it up to the eager night. She sent her forerunners,—twilight, which paled the wondrous blues, and dusk, that left the mountains shadowy and indistinct, when the lady of darkness herself rubbed them right out of the great canvas, and left it no coloured beauty but the gleam of the far stars overhead and the tiny man-made lights below, which, showing from the windows of the little homesteads creeping up the mountain-sides, twinkled like points between earth and sky.

Miss Grosvenor made no further comment regarding Dawn's probable inability to rise to the demands of smart society. Only inexperience had caused her to make any. Ernest fluttered in the smart set; he and I were familiar with it; Miss Grosvenor was not, therefore we were disillusioned and she was not.

We knew that the acme of refinement and culture might possibly be found in the smart set, but that it was a very small island, surrounded by a very large sea of other styles which spoke nothing so much as squandered opportunities. We knew girls too superior to dress themselves without a maid, yet who rolled tipsy to bed after every champagne orgy; supercilious and much-paragraphed misses educated in England, finished in Paris, and presented at Court, but who used more slang than grooms; while an expensive education did not raise their brothers above ribaldry and other vulgar excesses. Ernest and I knew a beautiful, honest, intelligent girl when we had the good fortune to meet her, and had no fears that she could not hold her own in good sets, let alone in the smarter ones of colonial or any other fashionable society, where the majority were animated by nothing higher than an insane and inane pursuit of something to kill time.

Besides, it was wonderful how Dawn suddenly eschewed slang and conspicuous violation of syntax, as she could easily do, for she had been somewhat educated in a school patronised by the Australian *beau monde.* Had not her grandma told me of the magnitude of her education when I had first arrived? and did she not constantly repeat the story now? For having survived the fear of Ernest being too aristocratic, she took pride in his worldly possessions and position, and characterised him as " more likely than most, if he only turns out true to name, which in the case of husbands is as rare as bought seed potatoes turnin' out what they're supposed to be; but there ain't any good of meeting troubles half-way."

As the wedding preparations made so much bother, grandma got in a woman to clean and another to sew, and determined to admit no summer boarders until after Christmas.

" I can do without 'em, only I like to see money changin' hands quicker than happens with a farm," said she; while also, in consideration of the wedding, the doors, whose opening and shutting had been obstructed by the ravages of the white ants, were at last satisfactorily repaired.

Dawn, after the manner of most youthful brides, was desirous of the full torture of " keeping up " her wedding, while Ernest, as usual with bridegrooms, so shrunk from display that he would have paid half a year's income to escape it; but it was only to me he made this confession, to Dawn he was manfully unselfish, allowing her full rein and agreeably falling in with her requirements.

I did not think much of fussy weddings, but these

were such a splendid pair of young things that I was pleased to endure the preparations with a smile instead of a sigh, and contribute some old silks and laces towards the trousseau ; while a few dainty and expensive trifles, sent to me from a traveller over the sea, found a place in the furnishing of the bride's boudoir.

Like all strictly reared girls, a certain prudishness at first caused Dawn to shrink from her love as something that should be resisted, but as her wedding-day drew near her heart grew more at peace regarding her contemplated change of life, and unfolded to the enchanting influence of youth's master passion. The roseate mists it weaves before the vision of its happy and willing victims, blunted even this girl's exceptional and matter-of-fact perspicacity, and with her ears grown suddenly deaf to those who had at first alarmed her by the recapitulation of their unfortunate practical and disillusioning experiences, looked out towards a future beautified with as many shades of blue as the mountain ramparts beyond the river flowing by her door. There was no hitch to speak of. Grandma, being one of a bygone brigade, enforced the almost obsolete rule of a chaperon, and the two evils in this case being represented by Andrew and me, Dawn considered me the lesser, and installed me in the office known by the irreverent as " gooseberrying."

Mostly it is a thankless and objectionable undertaking, but in this instance it was delightful, and we three spent a kind of antenuptial honeymoon that was an experience to be appreciated with a warm glow by one whom the world has all gone by.

I suddenly developed a latent artistic ambition, and no subject would do for my brush but the exquisite scenes far up the quiet river, where its deep clear pools lay like basins under the overhanging cliffs, and numerous species of beautiful flowering creepers clambered over the cool brown rocks shaded by the turpentine- and gum-trees, ti-tree, wild cotton-bush, native hibiscus, and an endless variety of trees and shrubs getting a foothold in the crevices.   These nooks, owing to the rugged and precipitous country, could only be reached by water, so Ernest rowed me up by boat and Dawn went with me for company, for thus do we live the best of our lives under pretence of trivial outside actions.   The river was dotted with other boaters on these summer afternoons, and Grandma Clay's " Best Boats on the River" were seldom idle, while Uncle Jake was also occupied in collecting the tariff from those who hired them, and in seeing that the boats themselves were safely moored again after their jaunts.

I fear that I may have been a better chaperon from Dawn's point of view than from grandma's, but even chaperons, however great their diplomacy, cannot well serve two mistresses.   While I sketched, the young couple made horticultural expeditions up the river-banks where the cliffs were not too precipitous, and though they went beyond my sight and hearing, and after a couple of hours' absence returned with no better specimens of ferns and flowers than were to be plucked within a stone's-throw of the boat, I failed to remark it.   They were equally lenient in the matter of my feeble sketches, which never progressed beyond a certain stage, and which could have been equally well perpetrated at home from memory, for all the justice they did the exquisite little gems of the picturesque river scenery.   Grandma Clay, however, thought them fine, and as the demand for them was not likely to be greater than the supply, I generously presented her with one, unfinished and all though it was, and which she "hung on the line" with Jim Clay; and no doubt it was not so great a caricature of the beauty of the Noonoon as the "enlargements" were of the comeliness of their dead original in the days when he had told life's sweetest story to the dashing damsel who could handle her coaching team of five with as much complacence as her granddaughter drove her small fat pony in the little yellow sulky about the execrably rough but level roads of Noonoon municipality.

This month of real orange blossoms was a time of moonlight, and regardless of the fact that the river scenes were at their best for reproduction on canvas, when the sun was high enough above the gorges to send great quivering shafts of sunlight between the tree-trunks deep into the heart of the pools, and to cast the shadow of the gum leaves in lace-like patterns on their surface, we sometimes delayed our setting out till close upon sundown, and took a billy[1] and provisions, intent upon having our tea on the rocks under the trees by Noonoon's banks.

Ah! glorious summer hours on the happy Noonoon, amid-stream, bright in the hot afternoon sun, cool by the edges where the lilies and reeds abounded, and the beetling cliffs and the limitless eucalypti flung their shade.

There was a joy in going abroad when the sun was nearly on the blue wall of mountain, and its oblique beams poured a golden mist over the blossoming orangeries, the milk-white spiræa in Clay's drive, and intensified the gorgeous red of the regal pomegranate blooms showing against the heliotrope on the lower limbs of the umbrageous cedars. Coming down the little pathway gained

[1] A tin pail.

by the creaking garden gate, we shot out from among the
drooping willows, the steerswoman turning her face up-
stream where, in a southerly direction, the ranges were
cut in a great V-shaped rift that let the waters through.
Anxious to escape from the company and critical observa-
tion of the garden species of the local boater, we went a
long way up-stream. Seven or eight miles were but a
bagatelle to the amateur sculling champion of the State
that held the world's championship, and he pulled his
freight past the evidence of husbandmen, past the straight
historic stretch where the Canadian champion had lost
his laurels to New South Wales; on, on the strong arms
took the craft till a wall of mountain loomed straight
across our way, and the river had every appearance of
coming to a sudden end, but round a sudden surprising
elbow we went till a similar prospect confronted the
navigator, and the river came round another of its many
angles. On, on we steered till the warm rich scent from
the flowering vineyards was left behind and the sound of
the trains could not be heard. Far up the ravines beyond
the pasture lands and men's habitations, we found the
desired privacy, and the solitude was broken only by the
dip of the oars, the flash of an occasional water-fowl, the
cry of some night-bird, or the "plopping" of the fishes
that Andrew could never catch as they fell back after
rising to snatch some unwary insect. The gentle breezes
sighing down the gullies, dim and lone in the eerie moon-
light, were laden with the scent of wattle and other native
flowers, and otherwise fresh and sweet with the inex-
pressible purity of summer night on the great unbroken
bush-land. In such dryad-like resorts we were tempted
to dawdle so long that the big hours of the evening
frequently found us still on the breast of the river. I

was wont to recline on an impromptu couch of rugs in the bottom of the well-built craft identified with our excursions, where I could feign to be asleep. At first Dawn suspected me of only pretending, but I was so emphatic in declaring that the fresh air and motion of the boat induced the sleep I could not woo in bed, that they grew to believe me, and carefully covering me from mosquitoes, it became invariable that at a certain distance on our homeward way the rower relinquished rowing, the steerer stopped steering, and the boat drifted down-stream with the gentle flow, while two-thirds of its occupants tasted of the elixir—

> "That burns beneath the beauty of the rose,
>   And in the hearts of youth and maiden glows,
>   And fills and thrills the world with life and light,
>   And is the soul of all that breathes and grows."

And what did the old moon see in that peaceful valley ere she sank behind the great primeval gum-tree forests on the mountain crests, across which zigzagged the noisy trains? There were heavy crops above ground, vineyards abloom, orchards forming fruit, hundreds of comfortable homes, and no doubt many pairs of lovers abroad, for lovers love their friend the gentle moon; but none were more fitted for love's consummation than the two drifting on the old river whose limpid waters never again "shall blacken below, spear and the shadow of spear, bow and the shadow of bow," and which, after rushing a tortuous way between its wild gorges, steadies by the old settlement on the plain, and saunters smooth and straight and deep a space between fertile banks gardened with lucerne fields, orchards of peach and apricot, and delightful orange groves. The air was intoxicatingly heavy with the ex-

quisite perfume of these bridal blooms, and the soft-
scented breezes laughed as they too kissed the close-
pressed lips of the fair young pair who—

> " Gathered the blossom that rebloom'd, and drank
> The magic cup that filled itself anew."

Ah! Love's idyllic hours on the breast of a grandly
gliding river, when the dews were on the flowers, and all
was enchantingly sweet and fair under the sleep-time
silver of a southern summer moon!

TWENTY-NINE.

"The savage sells or exchanges his daughter, but in civilisation the man gives his away, and is thankful for the opportunity."—*Reflections of a Bachelor Girl.*

DAWN took a great deal of her own way, Ernest and I were privileged to make suggestions so long as we were careful to remember our insignificance, and grandma saw to it that her lawful rights were not altogether usurped.

Occasionally it fell to my lot to act in a slightly mediatorial capacity, owing to the divergence of the swell wishes of the bridegroom-elect, and the plebeian determination of his grandmother-in-law to be, regarding the wedding celebrations, but Ernest was exceptionally unselfish and therefore very long-suffering.

Dawn being under age, her grandmother came forward with a project that her father should be apprised of what was transpiring, requested to give his daughter away, and to bring some of his side of the house to the wedding. Dawn raised vigorous opposition.

"It would be like my father's presumption to interfere in any way, considering his career with my mother. I hate him for a mean coward. He's the very style of man I'd be ashamed to acknowledge as an acquaintance yet alone own as a *father*! I'd like to see him dare to give me away,—he'd have to own me first!"

"Well, Jake, there, will have to give you away then," said grandma.

"I'd give *him* away with pleasure," replied Dawn. "If I *must* be *given* away like a slave or animal, you'll give me away grandma, or I'll stay where I am. 'Who giveth this woman to be married to this man?' the old parson will ask; why won't he also ask, 'Who giveth this man?' as if he too were only a chattel belonging to some one?"

That she would be disposed of by no one but her grandmother rather pleased the old lady than otherwise; so she invested in yet another black silk gown, over which she was to wear a seldom seen cape of point lace worked by Dawn's mother; and she also purchased a wonderful bonnet, and armed herself with a new pair of "lastings." Thus Dawn was to have her way in this particular, but the old dame adhered to her original intention in the matter of the Mudeheepes.

"I've kep' 'em at bay long enough now. I'll just acknowledge 'em this once, or it will seem as if you was a 'illegitimate,'" said she in the plenitude of her worldly wisdom, and thereupon "writ" a stiff though not discourteous letter to Dawn's father, inviting any number of the bride's relatives up to six, to come and spend a week before the wedding in her home, for the purpose of making Dawn's acquaintance.

"There, I have done me duty, and they can suit theirselves whether they come or go to Halifax," she remarked as she despatched the communication.

They came. Dawn's father, his second wife, and his youngest sister, Miss Mudeheepe, arrived three days before the wedding and remained to grace the ceremony.

Dawn, being a mere girl, perhaps it was Ernest's wealth

and position induced them to meet Mrs Martha Clay's overture, for they were thorough snobs, but if they had come prepared to patronise, their intention was killed ere it bore fruit.

The hostess hired the town 'bus to convey them from the station, and despatched Andrew, with many injunctions to "conduct hisself with reason," to meet them there, while she and Dawn waited to receive them on one of the old porches. It was a bower of roses and pot-plants, and further shaded by a graceful pepper - tree, and made a beautiful frame for the grandmother and the maiden,— the old dame so straight and vigorous, the girl as roseate and fresh as her name, but each equally haughty and bent upon maintaining their iron independence of the people who had discarded the girl and her mother ere the former had been born.

Personal appearance was much in their favour, and no practised belle of thirty could have held her own better than the inexperienced girl of nineteen, whose native wit and downright honesty of purpose were more than equal to all the diplomacy of thrust and parry to be gained by living in society. Her stepmother, who was apparently as good-natured as she seemed brainless, was prepared to be gushing, but that was nipped in the bud by the way Dawn extended her pretty, firm hand with the dimpling wrist and knuckles and exquisitely tapering fingers.

Her father and aunt, who were tall and angular, with thin faces of dull expression, met a similar reception, and she presented them to me herself, explaining that I was a very dear friend with her for the wedding.

I had long since risen from a boarder to be a guest and friend of the house, and it had devolved upon me to

exhibit the presents and interview the endless callers at
this time of nine days' wonder.

It being hot, the ladies retired to doff their hats ere
partaking of afternoon tea, and Dawn took her father's
hat while he trumpeted in his handkerchief and attempted
a few commonplace platitudes from the biggest and stiffest
arm-chair in the "parler," into which he had subsided.   I
left the room, but could hear him from where I stood
awaiting the ladies' reappearance, one from the room that
had been Miss Flipp's and the other from the one I had
at first occupied, and Mr George Mudeheepe was to occupy
the third one of these apartments, which had been empty
since the tragedy.

"Dawn, my dear, you are your mother once again," he
said with a sigh; "I have never seen you, and now you
are sufficiently grown to be married."

"Yes," said the girl.

"Will you give me a kiss?"

"I'd rather not.   You see you are only a stranger to me.
I have never heard of you only as the man who was a
monster to my mother.   I never saw her, but I remember
to love her for what she did for me, whereas you, what
did you do for her and me?   I would like you to under-
stand how I feel on this subject, so that there can be no
mistake," said the girl honestly.

"Oh, well, I didn't come here to be told that, but to
give consent to your marriage."

"Oh!" said the girl, rearing the pretty head with its
wealth of bright hair, "as for that, I'm going to marry.
If you like to exercise your authority I'll run away and
you can't unmarry me.   It is at grandma's wish you
are here; she said to let old bitterness sleep for the

time you are here, and so I will now that I have explained that I utterly refuse to recognise that a father is anything but a stranger unless he discharges the responsibilities of the office. For the sake of the race I maintain this ground," she concluded in words that had been put into her mouth by one of the speakers at Ada Grosvenor's election league, and the appearance of the ladies put an end to further contention.

Dawn's judgments were remorseless, as becoming clean-souled, fearless youth as yet unacquainted with the great gulf 'twixt the ideal and real, and untainted by that charity and complaisance which, like senility, come with advancing years.

The aunt was elderly and unprepossessing, and the step-mother of the type bespeaking champagne and too much eating for the exercise taken, for her head was partly sunk in a huge mass of adipose substance that had once been bosom, and the other proportions of her figure were in keeping.

The cups were spread in the dining-room, so thither we repaired to eat and drink while representations of Jim Clay and Jake Sorrel, senior, who had wept for the suffer-ings of the convicts, glowered down upon the gathering of plebeians who were half swells and the swells who were wholly plebeian.

Presently grandma and I excused ourselves and left Dawn with her relations.

"What do you think of 'em? Are they any better than Dawn an' me?" said the old dame as we got out of hearing. "How do I compare with that old sack of charcoal?"

Ay, how did she compare? As a slight, active, handsome woman, still vigorous at seventy-six, with one who, though thirty years her junior, was already almost helpless from obesity and natural clumsiness,—that's how she compared!

"Them's some of the swells for you—one of the 'old families,' who think they're made of different stuff to you an' me. What do you think of Dawn, Jim Clay's granddaughter, who drove the coach, when placed beside her aunt, the granddaughter of an admiral in the army?"

"She looks as though Jim Clay had been a general in the navy and she had done justice to her heredity," I gravely replied.

"Andrew, come here an' tell me how you managed 'em, an' what you think of the great bugs now you've seen 'em," commanded the old lady of that individual, as he emerged from the kitchen with both hands full of cake.

"Did you walk up to 'em 'an say, 'Are you Mr and Mrs Mudeheepe, I'm Mrs Clay's grandson?' like I told you."

"No; I seen it on their luggage without arskin' them, an' one look at 'em was enough for me. I didn't bother tellin' 'em who I was. I didn't care if they had fell down an' broke their necks—the bloomin' long-nosed old goats! I just took hold of their things an' flung 'em in the 'bus, and the old fat one she says, 'Are you Mrs Clay's groom?' an' I says, 'Mrs Clay is my grandma,' an' she says, 'Oh'!"

"Well, you might have introduced yourself a bit better to make things more agreeabler, but they really are the untakin'est people I've seen for a long time. Ain't I delighted that Dawn took after my side! An' now, though she's me own, do you think I'm over conceited to think her fit for the king's son?"

"Certainly not," I replied; for it would have taken a very estimable son of a king to be meet for this Princess of the Break-of-Day, appropriately christened Dawn!

THIRTY.

THAT was a grand wedding celebrated in Noonoon ere the orange blossoms had turned into oranges, but for details it would be better to refer to that most reliable little journal, 'The Noonoon Advertiser.' Only a few particulars remain in my mind, but the paper published a full account, including a minute description of the bride's gown and a careful list of the presents. It was much to the horror of Ernest that the latter was inserted, but it would have been much more horrible to Grandma Clay had the mention of so much as a jam-spoon been omitted, so he consoled himself with the reflection that it was only in 'The Noonoon Advertiser,' and took care to keep the list out of the account which appeared in the Sydney dailies. The curious, by consulting a back number of the little country sheet, may learn that Mrs L. Witcom (*née* Carry, the ex-lady help) gave the bride one of many pairs of shadow-work pillow shams, and that Miss Grosvenor contributed one of the equally numerous drawn-thread table centres. Mrs Bray presented a ribbon-work cushion; Dr Smalley, some of the jam-spoons; Andrew, a bread-fork; and Mr J. Sorrel, great-uncle of the bride, a silver cream-jug; while Mr Claude (alias "Dora") Eweword kept himself in mind by an afternoon tea-set. The complete list took a column, and included dozens of magnificent articles from sporting associations and chums of the bridegroom.

The bride—a glorious vision in Duchesse satin and accessories in keeping, and with real orange blossoms in hair, corsage, and train; the proud shyness of the gentle and stalwart groom standing beside her, and the brave old grandmother drawn up a little in the rear, formed a picture I shall never forget. The old lady performed her office with flashing eyes, a steady voice, and an individuality which none could despise or overlook.

Excepting her grandmother, Dawn was unattended, and as the young couple came down the aisle, by previous request of the bride, I had the honour of accompanying the old lady from the church, and she said, as we drove away over the scattered rose petals to be in readiness to receive the guests—

"I've done it—give me little girl away, an' without misgivin's, for if she's as happy as I was she'll do. When the time was here there was some patches of me life wasn't too soft, but lookin' back, I would marry Jim Clay over again if I could."

The caterpillars that had been eating the grape-vines and giving Andrew exercise as destroyer, had turned into millions of white butterflies that flecked the golden sunlight like a vast flotilla of miniature aerial yachts, and enhanced the splendour of that balmy wedding-day. It was the month of roses, and, intertwined with jasmine and mignonette, they formed the chief decorations in the roomy marquee erected for the breakfast under the big old cedars overlooking the river. All Noonoonites of any importance sat down to the repast, and their names, from that of Mrs Bray to Mrs Dr Tinker, are recorded in 'The Noonoon Advertiser.' The last-mentioned lady did not exhibit any of her famous characteristics at the function further than to use a gorgeous fan she carried in rapping her husband over the knuckles every time his attention wandered from her remarks. The toasts were many and long, and it fell to "Dora" Eweword to respond to that of the "ladies." Since the announcement of Dawn's engagement to Ernest, "Dora" had been frequently seen out driving with Ada Grosvenor, and he paid her marked attention at the wedding; but this was private, not public, information.

After I had helped Dawn into her travelling dress I had a few words apart with Ernest while Grandma Clay bade a private good-bye to his wife.

"Well," he said, with self-contained and pardonable triumph, "I've won her in spite of that dish of water."

"Yes, we three have accomplished our desire."

"What three?"

"Mr and Mrs R. E. Breslaw and myself!"

"Oh, was it your desire too?" he said with a happy laugh.

The bride now appeared, and wringing my hand as he said—

"You'll come to us when we return," he stepped forward to place her in the carriage that took them to the railway.

The paper had better be again consulted for accurate account of the confetti pelting and other customary happenings that took place at the station. These details, and the real greatness of Dawn's match, and her aristocratic relatives, who, as often suspected, had not proved to be only a myth, were the chief theme of conversation for many days.

All the engines in the sheds at the time, and whose music had lulled me to sleep o' nights, blew the bride a royal fanfare as she entered her first, *engaged*, and further cock-a-doodled " good luck " as the train steamed out.

Most keenly of all I remember that it was piteously lonely, and as dreary as though the sun had lost its power, when the panting engine had climbed the hill from the sleepy little town, and dropped out of hearing on the down grade from the old valley of ripening peach and apricot, bearing the girl for ever away from the slow, meandering grooves of life of which her vigorous young soul was weary.

A meeting of the municipal council claimed Uncle Jake that night, Andrew went over to discuss the situation with Jack Bray, and the loneliness of the old dining-room was insupportable to grandma and me. Joy and beauty seemed to have fled from the scented nights beside the river,—even the whistle and rush of the trains breathed a forlorn note to my bereaved fancy, and there was a tear in grandma's eye as she said—

" Well, she's really gone for altogether—she that I helped into the world and rared with my own hand, and named after the Dawn in which she came. That's the order of life. It's always the same—you can't keep any one for always. I couldn't abear it here now—it seems as if everything in life was done, and there's no need for me to stay if Ernest puts Andrew in the way of this electrical engineerin' he's so mad for. Jake can board somewhere. He don't care about things so much. I'll go to Dawn : thank God she wants me, an' I've got plenty to take me away if she gets tired of me, as young folks

often do of the old, and which is only natural after all.
I can let or sell the place, an' w'en I'm gone it will be
enough for Dawn if ever she's threw on the world like
I was.   Everythink seems fair with her now, but this is
a life of ups an' downs, and there's no tellin' what may
happen."

L'ENVOI.

WHAT interest can there be in the play after the knight has settled affairs with the lady, or in the story-book when the heroine and hero have gone on a honeymoon preparatory to living happily ever after?—and that is what befell my tale in Noonoon.

I listen no more to the splendid music of the loco-motives as they roar across the queer old bridge, nor watch the red light flashing from their coaling doors as they climb the Blue Mountain ascent and fire as they go. Their far-carrying rumble has been succeeded by the more thunderous voice of the sea on the rock-walled coast of my native land.

Four months have elapsed since the wedding in Noonoon, yet Ernest is still content to let his athletic ambitions remain in abeyance while he squanders his time in the sweet dalliance of love. Squander, I say; but on review-ing the expired years, how sanely sweet the youthful hours we dallied shine from amid the years we toiled, fumed, cursed, sweated, and strove to step past our brother in the bootless race for pleasure, opulence, or popularity!

Being able to indulge in the insignia of wealth, even without being the good fellow he is, Ernest finds it is of little significance that his hair is "what fond mothers term auburn," while Dawn's triumphs were assured from the outset. As mistress of a fine town mansion, with good looks, with smart ideas of dress, and smarter ability to verbally hold her own in any set, it goes without saying that her grandmother having "kep' a accommodation" is not remembered against her to any harmful extent in everyday life, where a large percentage of folks in all cliques have to survive the knowledge of their progenitors having been worse things than irreproachable proprietors and conductors of most exemplary accommodation houses for those who travel.

As Ada Grosvenor is not a girl in a book but in every-day life, I cannot record that she has married a man worthy of her. Such an one would have to be a leader of men—a prime minister, reformer, or other prominent worker in the cause of humanity—and as these do not abound in the quiet whirlpools of existence, I can only hope that she does not drop in for a too impossible noodle, as is frequently the fate of noble women. "Dora" Eweword would have done very well to discharge the clodhopping work of her earthly journey — could have made her bread-and-butter and carried her parcels, but if I can depend on Andrew's letters, which breathe more heavily of generosity than of grammar and gracefulness, this eligible and strapping young member of Noonoon society has been rejected a second time, so that Mrs Bray's fears that he would be made over conceited by adulation from marriageable girls seems to have been unnecessary.

Noonoon is enshrined in my heart as one of the pleas-antest valleys on earth, so during enforcedly idle hours it has given me delight to paint its beauty, however feebly, and to put some of the doings of some of its folk in a story, that others might possibly enjoy them too. But

I put the MSS. aside till, as the good country doctor so much esteemed in his circle expresses it, I shall have "pegged out," and the heroine and hero of the plot shall then judge whether it is fit or not for publication. It has interested me to write, but

> "My life has crept so long on a broken wing
> . . . .
> That I come to be grateful at last for a little thing,"

and those whose lives are strong, fruitful, and successful may have no patience with the sentimental meanderings of an old woman who has outlived joy and usefulness.

And now, may the Lady of my tale, as her life progresses from dawn to noon, high noon to afternoon, dusk, evening, and night, have the Knight of her choice and peace alway beside her, till new dawns break in other worlds beyond this place of fears and phantoms.

THE END.

VIRAGO MODERN CLASSICS

The first Virago Modern Classic, *Frost in May* by Antonia White, was published in 1978. It launched a list dedicated to the celebration of women writers and to the rediscovery and reprinting of their works. Its aim was, and is, to demonstrate the existence of a female tradition in fiction which is both enriching and enjoyable. The Leavisite notion of the 'Great Tradition', and the narrow, academic definition of a 'classic', has meant the neglect of a large number of interesting secondary works of fiction. In calling the series 'Modern Classics' we do not necessarily mean 'great' — although this is often the case. Published with new critical and biographical introductions, books are chosen for many reasons: sometimes for their importance in literary history; sometimes because they illuminate particular aspects of womens' lives, both personal and public. They may be classics of comedy or storytelling; their interest can be historical, feminist, political or literary.

Initially the Virago Modern Classics concentrated on English novels and short stories published in the early decades of this century. As the series has grown it has broadened to include works of fiction from different centuries, different countries, cultures and literary traditions. In 1984 the Victorian Classics were launched; there are separate lists of Irish, Scottish, European, American, Australian and other English speaking countries; there are books written by Black women, by Catholic and Jewish women, and a few relevant novels by men. There is, too, a companion series of Non-Fiction Classics constituting biography, autobiography, travel, journalism, essays, poetry, letters and diaries.

By the end of 1986 over 250 titles will have been published in these two series, many of which have been suggested by our readers.